THE RUSSIAN-UKRAINIAN WAR
PART 2

THE RUSSIAN-UKRAINIAN WAR

PART 2

EMIL TZOLOV

LitPrime Solutions
East Brunswick Office Evolution
1 Tower Center Boulevard, Ste 1510
East Brunswick, NJ 08816
www.litprime.com
Phone: 1-800-981-9893

© 2026 Emil Tzolov. All rights reserved.

No part of this book may be reproduced, stored in a retrieval system, or transmitted by any means without the written permission of the author.

Published by LitPrime Solutions: 12/18/2025

ISBN: 979-8-88703-496-6(sc)
ISBN: 979-8-88703-497-3(e)

Library of Congress Control Number: 2026900404

Any people depicted in stock imagery provided by iStock are models, and such images are being used for illustrative purposes only.

Certain stock imagery © iStock.

Because of the dynamic nature of the Internet, any web addresses or links contained in this book may have changed since publication and may no longer be valid. The views expressed in this work are solely those of the author and do not necessarily reflect the views of the publisher, and the publisher hereby disclaims any responsibility for them.

"They created a desert and nominated it as "peace""
Tacitus, 347 Before Jesus Christ
24. April 2022 – the start of the "limited military operation of Russia"

EMIL TZOLOV

EMIL TZOLOV *grew up in a family of journalists & moderators of the National television. His Grand parents hid allied prisoners of war with risk for their own lives. He graduated Humboldt University in Berlin, Germany. Speaks fluently German, English,Dutch, Russian & Bulgarian.*

In his second book on Ukraine and its war against Russia the author **Emil Tzolov** displays again his skills as a writer using those foreign languages. So he managed to use his language possession to display the large panorama of events in & behind the happenings using utmost objectivity by the use different channels & sources of information.

Parallel to the military operations of both participants **EMIL TZOLOV** explores the motley panorama of many other countries and politicians helping one way or another to draw conclusions and attitudes without losing neither objectivity nor impartiality nor morality. He describes not only the military sides of the century war but also their actions taken behind the curtains. So he achieves both clarity and reliability leaving sufficient space to the readers to make their own conclusions and convictions in many nuances. The international events are simply the background at which the Ukrainian drama takes place.
The proposal of Western Ukraine to join Poland was barely discussed in Europe; Poland wisely decided to reject it. So **EMIL TZOLOV** mentioned it with ten words only despite the fact that Poland can win the war in ten days. But **EMIL TZOLOV** avoided the temptation to flung in such details which will only make his book clumsy, awkward & boring.

Further on in his book **EMIL TZOLOV** displays a comprehensive list of names- who is who? Not afraid of reprisal or repressions by the both sides of conflict. This list of names – Russian, Ukrainian, German , British or Americans underlines his objectivity in his reports on the events: a motley mosaic of events in which everything and everyone has its place.

Part One of his book "The Russian-Ukrainian war"- part one was published on 5th of May 2024 in the United States of America and now on disposal to find in all big libraries & parliaments all over the world. On line all his 4 books are posted on www. **GOOGLE**.com by typing his name **EMIL TZOLOV** and than clicking on his photos. Because the war will last 7-8 years onwards **EMIL TZOLOV** has sufficient time to transform his book into Hollywood documentary.
THE HAGUE, 20. January 2025.
Kitty Mul

THE RUSSIAN-UKRAINIAN WAR
BY EMIL TZOLOV
PART II

JANUARY 2024

"What is the profit for a man who conquered the World but lost his own soul?!" :
The Gospel, Luke 9:25.

President Putin claimed "the new Russian hypersonic Kindson (King size) missiles are indisputable to USA Patriot-5 anti -rocket defense systems. because of their hypersonic speed- 5 times faster than the ultrasonics- all they are undetectable by any radar installation; even faster in cold weather . President Vl. Putin praised on with thanks Kindson Kindson is their American weapon company
with daughters all over the world.
Later on Euronews chunk off this piece of news off its bulletin which meant "Russia continues to held the initiative of this war". Ukraine proposed "safe return of 460 Russian prisoners in exchange of peace!" No remarks cited both-sided. Last prisoner exchange took place in August 2023. Ukranian President Volodimir Zelenskyy remarked it in his nightly address to the Nation. Every night at 20:00.
Up till now 23,000 Palestinians killed by Israeli air strikes on Gaza incl. a 3-years girl
U.S. President Joe Biden advised Israel to stop the air strikes of genocide.
U.S. State Dpt. Scry. Antony Blinken did the same; both with no result.
Russian air missiles hit badly the Ukranian Military Industry Zone.
Former Polish interior minister Marius Kaminsky (=Kuminsky) arrested in Warsaw by his own party members: multiple charges as a hed of the anti-corruption bureau. The arrest happened despite a Polish presidential decree in his favor; he was chief of the Polish Anti-corruption Bureau.
In his Lithuania visit President Zelensky stressed "...every late EU weapon delivery will only benefit Russian offense.".Russian air raids continued to "exhaust Ukrainian defense strength, also because of "American internal scandals"" , said ZDF.
Louise Rodrigue – Chief of European Central Bank - warned the EU "it can get weak because of the weak euro-currency".
German political turmoil inside - many politicians ask for dismantle the German AfD-party "because of right wing populism!"so ZDF and accused the ruling SPD-party of wrong doing.
New U.S. hypersonic fighter jet tested by the Pentagon. U.S. President Joe Biden put it bluntly "The U.S.A. does not step in for independence of Taiwan ", but advocated independence of Ukraine, so the BBC. Russia increased its hits on Ukraine up to 40 daily so Ukraine was forced to admit humbly "...we cannot resist the Russian invasion anymore", so BBC.
Tripple strikes in Germany

1. The train drivers
2. The tractor drivers: The German tractors farmers threatened "to overwhelm all Europe
   by tractor strikes and "other tractor campaignes!""

3. The medical staff strike- hampers parents to go to work
German Pharmacy Union was Parliament accused for further illegal sale of Corona medicines
usually Germany perscribed on free receipts.
Ukrainian President Volodimir Zelenskyy arrived in Switzerland for the World economic top
in Davos one day in advance:"He was accommodated in a cheap hotel", said his press spokesman.
In Davos the debate between Ukraine and Switzerland on the one side and the EU on the other side.
Little progress vision, China already dismissed the talks as "hopeless".
In Davos Ursula von der Leyen took a smart seat next to President Volodimir Zelenskyy.
Hungary finally agreed to release the $15 billion military help to Ukraine, not clear how.
Because Ukraine lacks munitions; France agreed to supply 6,000 artillery shells monthly.
Ukrainian drone hit the Russian fuel depot Klimsky 60 km East from the border.
Ukrainian President Zelenskyy met Polish PM Donald Tusk on the topic how to disable
Russia in near future; this all on a joint memorial: could happen. Visiting Kyiv he also promised
a defense package for Ukraine: the poor Polish people! The Russian Army started recruiting
Chinese emigrants to fight for Russia; usually their asylum procedures last 2 months. Kiiv
demanded a freeze of all Russian assets abroad – ca. $900 billion- to help rebuilding Ukraine
after the war. No comments were heard yet- at least not by me! German tractorists' strike
spilled over into France, The Netherlands, Poland and Romania.
NATO donated 1.1 billion euro worh of ammunition to Ukraine-in all 424,000 artillery shells
 "If Russia wins this war it will bea tragedy for Ukraine and a danger for all of us!", Jens
 Stoltenberg stated on tv. The Pentagon runs short of ammunition for further support to Ukraine .
Polish prime minister Donald Tusk visited briefly Ukraine and promised money support to its neighbor . Turkey
finally agreed to admit Sweden into the NATO alliance by overwhelming vote
of the Turkish Parliament. Now the vote is favorable for Swedish accession to NATO. Hungary
invited already Swedish experts, specialists and politicians – such as Elf Christiansen - for a
better bilateral coordination. Now Sweden becomes the 31st NATO member state.

Ukraine downed a Russian IL-76 cargo plane transporting 65 Ukrainian prisoners of war for
swap but they all died in the hit; the pilots of the second transport also -also IL-76 - described the
happening from their point of view. According to the Russian general staff the 3 rockets fired
by Ukraine were German made RST missiles. Russia informed duly the UN on the incident.
Only the day after President Zelenskyy asked for international investigation of the 2 black boxes
already in Russian hands; so became clear the planes down by Ukrainian missiles were 2 and not
"only "one. Moscow refused to deliver the 65 dead corpses back to Ukraine. Even more:
For retaliation Moscow fired ca.40 Iranian Shahet drones on Odesa-port wrongfully
repeatedly pronounced multiply as << Shaikh-id= Shake-it>> and not Shahet; could happen in war: judas priest
melodied. The air-to-air Ukrainian missiles rockets were marched as MARSH.
German Court ruled out any entry to Germany by ethnic Austrian fascist Mark Schneller because
of his fascist reputation.
Both countries have a common border esp. for car tourists and common views on fascism.
The German rail way 6 days strike stroke 85% of the traffic so more trains and drivers were needed
to get imported from Switzerland but the German Deutsche Bahn did not give in to the strike. It even
wided wider spilling over to other strikes: of the regional public transportation network, the air ports
staff, teachers and even medical personel-all demanding beter working and living conditions.

Ex U.S. President Donald Trump accused the EU of not doing enough for Ukraine- so for example the U.S. aid to Ukraine was $200 billion while the EU contributed only $20; he claimed "not to dig any further help into the Ukrainian pit if he would elected a President in the fort coming U.S. election in November 2024. The EU entered its $400 billion trade deficit with China.

The formal funeral procedure for Wolfgang Scheuble- former German finance monster- is running right now at ZDF, ARD, WDR and RTL . He died one whole month earlier. French President E. Macron pronounced his condolence speech in good German already yesterday when the funeral was announced. Since than Macron is in Berlin. Temporal quarel in the German Bundestag: Chancellor Scholz criticised sharply his coalition partner Fr. Merz. Chaos in London too-daily anti-Brexit demonstrations, 2,000,000 new work less in Great Britain

Angry French protesters blocked the access to Paris international airport "Charles de Gaul". Many of them protested against cheap Ukrainian grain imports from the EU damned as peasants; Poland denounces this strategy and denounced by the EU "as illegal" "The EU is not there to finance the Ukrainian war on Russia", they stated bluntly and their strike spilled over into neighboring Italy: Only to see what is brothing:

In Northern Ireland Sinn Fein Michel O'Neil got the Belfast Prime Minister chair for first time in history.

A New Zealand member of Parliament was arrested by police for shop lifting. New Zealand has the lowest corruption rate in the world , so Transparency International.

Ukrainian drones hit the Russian Saint Petersburg fuel depot and set it afire. (BBC) Ukraine used American anti-tank missiles BRADLEY to stop the Russian tanks at Avdiivka (BBC). In recent days Kiiv has stepped up its hits on Russian infrastructure objects (Euronews). Ukrainiane marine managed to sank a Russian battle ship in the Black Sea; Russia didn't commented .

The EU was able to deliver only 500,000 artillery shells to Ukraine and not the promised 1 mn. EU-member state Hungary demanded from Ukraine "Hungarian language with a list of the school". 26 EU member states denounced Hungary of "systematical misuse of its veto right". The EU has frozen already 22 billion euro worth of Hungarian assets.

FEBRUARY 2024

Like me Greta Thonberg arrested because of her views on the world. Her trial was in London.
Massive anti-EU demonstrations in Brussels, partly against cheap Ukrainian agriculture imports.
May pak me drusnaha: slaba pamet, slabi coordinacii- 18:00,silen tinitus:
Da si zatwora ustata znachi da si zatvora ochite- njama kak!
Hungary withdrew its veto on EU-bill for 50 billion euro help for Ukraine:
Volodimir Zelenskyy thanked the EU: "A competition EU cannot afford to lose",he bluffed. He thanked however for the EU-delivery of 1,000,000 artillery shells to Ukraine-against Russia- "which came however too late", he minced no words to the EU.
"Such countries have to be withdrawn their veto right!", the mobs chanted.
Ukraine drew no responsibility for the downed Russian airplane;"there was no Russian information of any 65 Ukrainian PoW on board", Kiiv decorated the EU-televisions.
Volodimir Zelenskyy thanked the EU: "A competition EU cannot afford to lose",he bluffed.

The International Court of Justice in The Hague dropped all Ukrainian charges against Russia incl. race discrimination,financing terrorism and all other claim for ostensible Russian violations of international conventions;so Ukraine decided to go to other courts despite its stunting blow.
Russian President Vladimir Putin urged the Russian banks to resume operating in the occupied territories. Ukrainian navy drone sank down a Russian warship in the Black Sea. Correctly "Russian corvette with 40 men crew :Russia didn't manage to rescue any survivor", Kiiv commented maliciously gloat in a video distributed by its omnipotent secrete service. Ukraine supports its officious newspaper Ukrainskaya Pravda- thus not Ukrainskaya gazetta- only in Russian language: than what is the truth and what can we expect from this "service"?! Well, the hit was a hit but how can we trust the Ukrainian video-how they manage to film it:
1. Beforehand ??
2. Afterwards ?! How , how we stupid to believe ?

Massive general strike with 300,000 strikers paralyzed fully Finland, esp. the transport.
The massive French farmers'strikes spillt over also to Spain, Portugal, Italy and Greece,
but EU President Ursula van der Leyen- German CDU- stressed upon "no EU help for them"!
Than from where ?!The farmers'strike in Germany continued and spilled over into France, Spain, Portugal, Italy, Greece and Romania. And here ?
UK-Ukrainian war treaty signed in London.
The U.S. continues frantically building the Mexico-Texas wall against immigrants.
Tough U.S. border security policy. In South Carolina President Joe Biden aged 81 won the election primary. No Donald Trump comments. Dutch police have much more to do because of earlier Mistakes.
Former U.S. President Donald Trump demanded a "mental fitness test for his opponent Joe Biden"- not groundless!He used to dub him "the sleepy man". He has erected the Trump tower

in the heart of New York already long years ago.
A German court acquitted Arabian rap singer Bushido free of most of his charges against him.
Ukrainian President Volodimir Zelenskyy fired his top military advisor General Valerii Zaluzhni.
All Ukrainian men aged between 18 and 60 years are banned from leaving Ukraine to avoid
conscription. Ukrainian (military) courts set up tough prison sentences on all war deserters.
Germany refuted all EU-courts pay penalties on "pay unable German payers".
Russian President Putin granted U.S. Fox tv granted an interview to Russia to explain its war point.
First ever since 2022. His interview was not broad casted in many of languages.
British anti-drugs police brought in many visible victims without any sentence.
Finland was said to be "the world most aging country. All over the world.
Massive anti-war protests in Kiiv where the Government plans to reduce the conscription men age
from 27 to 25 years and to increase duty time to 36 months. Currently Kiiv needs 500,000 new
recruits. Speaking in Brussels NATO Secretary General Yens Stoltenberg promised 1 million artillery
shells to Ukraine:"This is not a charity it is in our own security interest", he stressed"a Russian
victory will weaken us further; this matters both for European security and U.S. security!".
Rather controversial Zelenskyy general mobilization bill brought thousands of Ukrainians to the
streets of Kiiv to protest. (Euronews). Farmer protests rage across Bulgaria and Germany is
paralyzed by Lufthansa personnel strikes all over the country.
With small majority the U.S. Senate rejected U.S. military aid both to Israel and Ukraine.
The Dutch Parliament tests options "how to slash unwanted immigration to the country".
Russian missiles hit the industrial complex in Mykolaev; Russia lost 11 Shahet-drones in the attack .
Above all Zelenskyy fired his top military commander Valery Zaluzhni in exchange for Syrsky-
another top Ukrainian general.
In an televised interview with Fox-news president Tucker Carlson and friend of Ex-President
Donald Trump Russian President Vladimir Putin fixed "...the war in Ukraine will end up as soon
as U.S.A. stops its weapon delivery to Ukraine-something what Donald Trump demands too!".

Acting U.S. President
Biden "rejected all claims of poor memory and mental unfitness despite in an interview he dubbed wrongly "Egyptian
President Asisi" a President of Mexico"as shown by BBC-News. So who is
insane ? In another interview he dubbed – again wrongfully- the dead François Mitterand "a
President of Germany"! Also he predicted "World War Too in the future!" On his 2nd day of
Washington visit German Chancellor Olaf Scholz was not shown shaking hands with Joe Biden.
During his absence Germany and The Netherlands stroke a deal known as "Military Schengen".
Russia and Ukraine exchanged 100 PoW from each side, 3,500 Ukrainians remained in Russian
captivity yet: not very heroic indeed. In a BBC interview Nina Khruschova-grand daughter of the
former Soviet leader Nikitta Khruschov-explained her views.

CNN journalist Samuel Rosenberg praised Joe Biden as "a strong President doing good to his
country and Donald Trump is a weak candidate with 6 court topics against himself"!
"Steal no steal!", CNN Christiane Amanpour. German Chancellor Olaf Scholz ended his U.S.A.
visit crashed by the slogan "American money for America!". His flight back lasted 10 hours.
NATO Secretary General Jens Stoltenberg urged Europe "to increase military production to benefit
more Ukrainians in their war against Russia". In a pre-election speech White House
candidate Donald Trump left ÉU counterparts "down the hell whatsoever". German
Chancellor Olaf Scholz blasted him off without naming him. France accused Russia
of "disinformation" not clearly how.

Russian rockets hit the Ukrainian fuel depot in Harkiv and destroyed it in flames.
German Chancellor Olaf Scholz visited Warsaw to re-assure German support to
Poland amid the White House military scandal; angry Polish farmers spill cheap
Ukrainian wheat on the streets to protest against the Ukrainian aggression. The
German Army (the Bundeswehr) outnumbered 188,000 men, said CNN. The
British foreign minister David Cameron visited Bulgaria and demanded military
production boost for Ukraine; Bulgaria declined it first because Ukraine cannot
pay facing serious shortage of ammunition and manpower. Unnecessarily NATO
seems to impose even a war on the cranky scraggy Bulgarian economy and its
poor scraggy people:Why? Typical Albion ! Only 18 NATO countries aprproved
the NATO $348 billion military program; vagina monologue, CNN.

NATO increased its military expenditures to $680 billion, said NATO Secretary Liar
General Jens Stoltenberg with the minimum of 2% of their GDP pro a member
country; members below will be jilted.(Euronews).
48th mass shooting in U.S.A. for this year of 2024. U.S. lunar investigation despite
current crises. Israel breach of the Geneva Genocide Convention.
After Ivanovets cruise ship Ukraine hit & sank also Russian battle ship Tsezarkin
(Caeser Queen) in the Black Sea. No official confirmation yet.
"The situation in Avdiivka "is a hell"", so Euronews.
Massive Ukrainian front losses forced Ukraine to ask for bilateral war contracts
with both France and Germany (ZDF). Facing massive war losses on the front Ukraine decided
to send in negotiators both to France and Germany to seek war contracts with both countries;
the massive Ukrainian war losses amassed like avalanche.
Euronews dubbed Victor Orban's position on Ukraine "shameful".
Russian front casualties amounted to 300 daily. Finally Avdiivka was given back to Russia.
EU security conference in Munnich, Germany came to nothing (Euronews).
Hungarian Prime Minister Victor Orban delayed Sweden NATO membership by 21 months.
German Cologne festival rose the slogan : "To be or NATO be?!"
Ukraine mourned again "lack of arms". Russia lost 7 soldiers for 1 Ukrainian, Zelenskyy boasted.
U.S. vice-president Camilla Harris stood up with Ukraine and named it "unprovoked aggression".

Ukraine withdrew its important stronghold Avdiivka positions to the Russians;
BBC measured the distance of 800 km between Swedish and Ukrainian border.
BBC war reporter Lies Doucet changed from the Middle East to Europe:
Her voice imitates yet another BBC voice producer:
EU-chief Ursula van der Leyen announced her bid to run for a 2nd EU term.
"Europe must resort frequenter for its own security & defense with 377 billion euro budget".
Russian troops and Russian tanks conquered Avdiivka and flew up Russian flag there.
Ukrainian President Zelenskyy up to tears changed his usual green shirt to a black one.
German Foreign Ministry Afghan war report:"Nothing could worse", the report said.
Ukraine named the Polish farmers'strike "a threat to security".
After the defeat at Avdiivka the Ukrainian soldiers surrendered in thousands upon thousands
to Russian captivity; Kiiv admitted only 6 ! Such a shameful lie ! Frankly spoken Russians are
very bad people but Ukrainians are even worse ! Russian pilot defector Maxim Kuzminov
shot dead in Spain. His defection to Ukraine was well paid by Ukrainian Government plus
protection for his Family and he criticized the Russian war on Ukraine (NPO1).
His bullet-riddled body was found in a LaGalla garage along side his false new name

documents. It took whole year to KGB to trace him down anew. The Russian-
KGB-most wanted black list amounted to 2,000 names abroad:Euronews.

Euronews reporter Galina Polonskaya too went missing from the horizon.
Russia is said to lose 7 soldiers for every Ukrainian killed in combat. Russian President Vladimir
Putin awarded many Russian pilots in Moscow for their Krymsky exploit near Krematorsk.
8,000 Ukrainian soldiers fell in Russian captivity, so ZDF, who confirmed Ukrainian disaster.
The Russian victory cost 15,000 victims, Ukrainian sources gloated.
I loitered deliberately this news for a long time. Amid ripped USA and NATO Russia is the only
force, the only power to rescue the world. Despite the new EU-sanctions Russia experienced
3.55% economic growth,so IMF. German growth-only 0.2% ,so ZDF.

Angry Greek farmers blocked major highway entries out of protest.
Ukrainian oil company bribed U.S. President son Hunter Biden with $5,000,000 corruption bribe.(Euronews). FBI
informant Alexander Smyrnoff arrested in the course of the case.
Ukrainian defense forces divided in 2 : North Ukraine forces and South Ukrainian forces.
British Trident missile firing failed again close to the launch site instead of the 4,000 km planned,
said BBC.
President Vladimir Putin visited aviation factory in Kazan and opened the new TU-160 bomber air
plane. "One third of the Government spending will be on military only", he stressed.
New German growth act adopted in Germany to combat the current crises; building disaster.
137,000 African migrants overwhelmed Italy 2023; not to know what to do: many of them rebuffed
or shunt into neighboring Albania (ZDF). Ukraine exported 737,000 refugees into Germany.
German police massively attacked by help-seekers.(ZDF)
Glücklich einsam sein und unglücklich einsam sein: zwischen Kunst und Mode.
Telefon Zellen polizeilich abgehört. German Bundestag legalized the use,sell & planting cannabis.
German Bundestag approved Marsh-Taurus missile delivery to Ukraine to fight better.
Ukraine marked the second anniversary of the Russian invasion . Amid the dignitaries were the
Belgian Prime minister Alexander Dutreau, Canadian Prime Minister Justin Trudeau, EU-Commission head Ursula
von der Leyen, Italy Prime Minister Meloni and German foreign minister Anneline Baerbok. Ukraine demanded
again more weaponry and ammunition;
Ukrainian pilots started F-16 training in Denmark.In official speech President Zelensky mentioned the losses –
180,000 Russians killed,135,000 Ukrainians; U.S. sources spoke of 70,000 Ukrainians.Direct peace talks are in
sight after whole brigades were dissolved because the lack of weaponry and amunition,said ZDF. At the same time
Ukraine seeks to re-inforce its troops by 500,000 (young)
recruits, so Euronews . Rather contradictive ! It is forced recruitment.

The German Bureaucracy started the struggle against German bureaucracy, so ZDF. In fact the
German Bureaucracy "declared war on the German bureaucracy". Angry Polish farmers attacked
Brussels, erected barricades and set tires to protest against cheap Ukrainian imports; barbed wires and concrete
walls were erected to protect the EU Parliament. Euronews didn't report on the clashes but the BBC reported."After
blocking the streets to the EU-Parliament the protesters could find the way out of the maze of streets and Spanish
farmers followed their pattern in Spanish Capital Madrid": BBC .
Later on the EU-Capital Brussels collapsed in a cold sweat standstill. Nevertheless EU-Commissioner
Ursula von der Leyen decided to run for a second EU-term; her father was a German politician.
The EU-peasants get no money only because they are simply peasants, ZDF broadcasted.
Russia ridiculed the peace talks as "ridiculous" but Ukrainian President Zelenskyy vowed "not to lose the 3rd year
of the Russian war." Hungarian Parliament ratified Swedens NATO

memberships; despite of this Hungary is blamed as "a NATO black sheep "because its close contacts to Russia", BBC said. Sweden has big capacity in air forces and (sub)marine, ZDF said

The news of Russian dissident Alexij Navalny death rumored amid the
process of prisoners' swap. "Meer news gedecleneerd en leuke kinderen op Nederlandse schools!"
Meanwhile the West Bank Palestinian Authority sacked its unpopular President Mahmoud
Abaz (not Hamas), so BBC. British Prime Minister rejected all accusations against him. I would
say his words were correct, but couldn't quell down London Mayorship quarrel in France. French
President Emmanuel Macron "doesn't rule out French ground troops on Ukrainian soil":"We'll do
everything possible to stop Russia of winning this war!". France has already war contracts with Germany and the
UK. France is known for longstanding gangster wars which rip the country, so Euronews. It said also "Russia has
lost 20% of its Black Sea fleet". France possesses 290 nuclear
war heads, so the Ukraine conference in Paris.
Unpopular German Chancellor Olaf Scholz contradicted him saying "no German troops will fight
in Ukraine and "Germany will not deliver Taurus-Marsh missiles to Ukraine". Karlo Makala – professor at the
German Bundeswehr University in Munich said "the current situation in Ukraine is
full kakophony"
Kremlin said "Direct confrontation with Russia will face NATO if it sends in troops to Ukraine. The
new presidential election in Russia is scheduled for mid March.
RAF-terrorist Daniela Klette-65- arrested in Berlin by the German police after civilian tip-off.
In his speech addressing the people Russian President Vladimir Putin bluntly threatened the West
with Russian nuclear weapons. Bulgarian Prime minister Nikolay Denkov refused to sent troops to
fight in Ukraine against the Russians.

MARCH 2024

Russian secrete service tapped down phone calls within the German general staff and published them in "Russia Today"(RT). In the 40 minutes conversation the top commanders discussed the MARSH-missiles delivery to Ukraine and training of Ukrainian soldiers to handle with them. "And this is only the tip of the iceberg", RT said. In the RAF-scandal German police couldn't arrest any one else. And me ? When can they arrest me ?! German police-ZDF polish the British boots of shoes.
Ukraine claimed to have sunk another Russian Black Sea war ship. But the "situation on the ground remains precarious" :CNN. Fashion designer Iris Apfel died at 102 in Germany.
"Any talk on/for Donald Trump will be shameful!", CNN. CNN accused current U.S. President Joe Biden of "being populous", 17:56. Weak U.S. Dollar on all markets.
<< my police officer in charge of me asked me "how old is your Mother?" Reply to it:>>
Another Navalny ! Yogashima – another Tokyo tourist destination; tourists not police!
"Germany has nothing to do with German MARSH-Taurus-missile and we too", said German Defense Minister to the Cameras": and we? What we have to say to ZDF 30 sec bulletin??.
Two further Russian top Commanders indicted by the International War Crimes Tribunal for crimes against humanity. They have little choice but strategize their next move. Ukrainian drone sank another Russian Black Sea war ship. Ukrainian domesticaly produced drones are equipped with camera and GPS and have scope of 1,100 km, carrying up to 1,000 kg explosives with a very low radar profile; to protect the coast line and boost moral, Ukrainian forces said.
In a TV interview Pope Franciscus advised "Ukraine to wave the white flag and negotiate peace with Russia!": Euronews. The Pope will visit Ukraine to witness the hardships of the Ukrainian people. Ukraine protested angrily , saying "There is only one flag-the yellow-blue, which is the Ukrainian flag!", ZDF. Germany emitted "The Constitution 2024-report". The U.S. Embassy in Moscow released a strong warning "against eminent threat of terrorist attacks on the Embassy in few days"(BBC). Sweden was officially admitted into NATO; the officious flag rising admission ceremony took pace in Capital Brussels in which NATO Secretary General Dane Jens Stoltenberg
advised bluntly "German long range Marsh-Taurus missiles deliveries will be helpful to Ukraine even if they don't reach Moscow",BBC. So Russia got locked off the Baltic area. Massive protests because Sweden's NATO membership referendum lack.
This all in the raging controversial Kensington palace
photos (@KensingtonRoyal) and comments about Princes Catherine health after abdominal surgery back in January 2024,BBC. King Charles -aged 75 – did not comment. Kensington Palace refused to release the original source photo and many publishers withdrew it too and the Princes apologized "for her editing experience lack and she was experimenting in editing".
France became NR. 2 in arms exports to the world, mostly to India.
Russia dropped behind to NR. 3 . Ukraine is the 4th biggest world weapon importer.
The German Defense Council demanded from Boris Pistorius clarification over the Russia-tapped

and published phone calls of top German Commanders over Taurus-Marsh missiles delivery. Germany decided "not to deliver them directly to Ukraine but to Britain which will than reexport them to Ukraine", so ZDF. According CNN interview "ex President Donald Trump is accused of "willful leak of U.S.A. sensitive defense information", CNN, not clear to whom"".
Ukraine received its first Oskar.
Russian missile hit the Ukranian metallurgy plant in Krivij Rijh; Ukrainian long range missiles hit the Russian city of Belgorod close to the (than) Ukrainian border.
Japanese state space rocket exploded in fire shortly after its launch into the Space (BBC).
Russia refused to post up its troops along its Finnish border and dubbed the Finnish NATO steps as "senseless". The Russian-Finnish border is 3,000 km long,historic Russian domination at all, ZDF.
Swedish protester activist Greta Thunberg torn, dragged, undressed,pulled by police on the streets as tv shown: International police don't recognize national border as much as Dutch police in The Hague whose victim I really was and am yet again.
Unlike Swedish protester Greta Thunberg I was not disciplined, pulled, undressed nor torn astreet by The Hague Police as you can peruse the News.
Massive German Bundestag debate as to German Taurus-Marsh rockets delivery to Ukraine; Chancellor Olaf Scholz ended this debate categorically "No, no delivery because I am the German Chancellor and I decide clear "NO". This was 3 days before the Russian election in Ukraine…
The German rockets scope is 500 km, the British only 250 km. So Rishi Sunak must decide too!
Scholz fell in into the provocation using "thy" instead "you" for several times…
 In a tv interview President Vladimir Putin said "we are ready for a nuclear war already tomorrow but it doesn't mean we'll start it tomorrow, it all depends on our counterparts":Euronews 20:30 ,
13-03-2024: "We are ready and experienced!" French President Emmanuel Macron stated "all options in the Ukrainian war are possible"speaking on top meeting in Berlin; German foreign minister Anneline Baerbock contradicted openly German Chancellor Olaf Scholz in his refusal to sent German ground troops to Ukraine, saying "If we decrease our support to Ukraine we will bring the war closer to the EU". So united German-French-Polish ground troops are already in sight: "If opposite than the EU
credibility will be reduced to zero", Macron added. 15-03-2024
The British MP salary rose to 91,000 pounds: this is 7,500 pounds
monthly to compensate the inflation. The compensation was 5.5%.
The NATO Secretary General Jens Stoltenber urged the NATO members to
increase their NATO budget contributions far beyond the current 2% (BBC).
 Triangle talks Germany-Françe and Polland in Berlin came to nothing-
they all spoke different languages to reduce (their mutual) conflict. They all
three shook hands not clear for what; German Chancellor Olaf Scholz continued
to oppose sending German ground troops to Ukraine oppose to the German
CDU-Opposition, said ARD. As to the leaked German top Commanders phone calls
to Russia Germany started a court procedure against < www.t-online.de>, so ARD.
A somebody culprit must be found !
Extensive Hungarian President Victor Orban visited ex-U.S. President Donald
Trump in his Florida estate for ample bilateral talks in mutual interest (ZDF).
Germany rages the secrete leak scandal; Chancellor Olaf Scholz continues his
position not to deliver Taurus-Marsh missiles to Ukraine.
The Russian elections are under the slogan "Another Russia , another future".
Russians accused Kremlin of digging in millions in Ukraine war instead putting
them into Russian welfare: BBC. Russian dissident's widow Yulia Navalny is
not sure even from Berlin for the craved Sakharov Price let alone for the Nobel
Price.(BBC) Cockney Rebel Steve Harley died at 73 in London. Ukrainian

missiles British production hit a Russian fuel depot in Russian city of Belgorod and set it afire. In the Russian 'election' 71 men arrested after weapon security check. BBC "Russian economic collapse" while other reports said exactly the opposite. Massive attempts to spoil the ballot papers.
Unpopular German Chancellor Olaf Scholz spoke clumsy English in his Israel visit. Massive pro-Putin support for the Russian President Vladimir Putin at the Red Square in Moscow; the West had to swallow it-Putin reelection was 87% of the popular vote. Putin was reelected as a new Russian President. Euronews lack of news. At a common meeting in Rammstein Germany, France and Poland agreed finally to deliver long range missiles to Ukraine which means escalation of war. Germany started delivering 180,000 shells caliber 155 mm, ZDF said and promised 500 mn euro to Ukraine, not clear where this money will come from. France anchored the right of abortion in its constitution.
SPD-Mützelich demanded from the German Bundestag to freeze down all German help to Ukraine; Chancellor Olaf Scholz refuted him with silly, stupid arguments, so ZDF remained without its usual reports on Ukraine-seemingly lost at sea.
Massive Polish protests and strikes against cheap Ukrainian agriculture imports. The EU decided to use the interest rates of the frozen Russian assets in Europe – 2.4 billion euro lump sum. Moscow announced retaliation. German concern Deutsche Bahn wrote red 2 billion euro never to recover. Germany did not attend the nuclear summit in Brussels because it had switch off its reactors already a year earlie. On a conference in Prague Poland, Hungary, Czechia ans Slovakia disagreed on the topic of weapons to Ukraine. Terrorist attack on Moscow Concert Hall – 143 people dead; than the building was set afire by petrol bombs : Islamic State claimed responsibility, BBC News. The Crocus City Hall building was smoking and fuming even the next day. 11 terrorists arrested, claiming "a warning before the attack"", BBC. I posted a Face Book post already (11:34):
"Ukraine does not sleep at all!", though unposted ! Which
is the next target?! Islamic State public relation service ASTRA/ ARMAK took proud on the "CAUCASUS BRANCH attack" photos.
Russia in shock, U.S. claimed "a warning of eminent attack "beforehand.
"Ukraine denied any involvement in the terrorist attack", a statement I deeply n o t believe. Finger prints collected from the assailors.
As to Russian President Vladimir Putin "Ukraine secured escape road for the terrorists', he stated on State Television. Many Russian sport clubs started donating blood for the injured victims, so BBC. BBC interrogated Sarah Reinsford- its BBC-correspondent in Kiiv, not in Moscow! Escalation of mutual war. Russia accused
"For seeking war escalation excuse".
IS dubbed its Caucasus-Branch if not other branches.
A precious donation to Washington.
President Zelenskyy didn't take a stand up till now – 14:22 GMT the day after.
President Putin announced "The terrorists were arrested trying to flee into Ukraine", BBC, 14:30. Among others U.S. Scry.of State Antony Blinken too- condemned the terrorist attack. President Putin of Russia named it "barbaric" and accused "Ukraine behind the assault".
The U.S. Embassy in Moscow is said "to have issued a warning 16 days earlier". "The Crocus City Hall was burning all night long so the air was thick with smoke." All in all – 133 killed, 180+ wounded. The 4 terrorists were arrested while they tried to slip into neighboring Ukraine over the common border "having a window there".

Ukraine bluntly denied this saying "Russia has killed already 500,000 Ukrainian civilians in an unprovoked war"
On the photo I saw clearly Kalashnikov AK-47 assault sub-machine gun. 2 days later
 all 4 terrorists were apprehended at the Ukrainian eastern border and returned back to
Moskow to face trial in May on terrorism charges which foresee life sentences.
The American warning dated back to 16. March and concerned only the U.S.
Moscow Embassy and only U.S. citizens.

From Baykonur Cosmodrom Russia launched a new Soyuz rocket with a Russian, Belorussian and U.S. American astronauts on board to dock with the Russian ISS
Space Station soon. Peaceful co-existence in action ! Ukraine claimed to "have hit 2
Russian landing ships; so the Russian Black Sea fleet was declined by one third".
Poland accused "Russian forces to have infringed Polish air space for 38 seconds
while bombarding Ukrainian city of Lviv" and demanded explanation.
ISPK-Islamic State Province Kurasan (in Afghanistan)

As expected Katherine Princess of Wales diagnosed and treated for cancer.
She announced "whole health in body and mind"
Many Polish people expressed solidarity with her. Emil ,devoted Christian.
The Princess announced "being healthy in body and mind", which is not my view.
I wish her a speedy recovery just because I am Emil Tzolov.
80% of Ukraine defense production is in private hands, Euronews.
German Lufthansa (LH) ended its strike for 2 years: and than ?
German unemployment rate is 2,700,000. (ZDF)
Ukrainian President Volodimir Zelenskyy visited Ukrainian troops digging
frantically new defense line which means they are on retreat again, Euronews.
This is because Russia increased its attack on Ukraine, esp. on Kiiv and Harkiv.
The "Ukrainians have no air defense systems to defend themselves". Polish
and Ukrainian officials met together to discuss the current agricultural crises due
the cheap Ukrainian imports. Ursula von der Leyen accused of her Nazi
Grand parents backgrounds incl. photos 03-10-1937: "what a handsome man!" she exclaimed…
Russia accused of firing 26 ballistic missiles on Kiiv in a week.

APRIL 2024

Germany legalized the use, possession and sale of cannabis 28 years after The
Netherlands but the pros of the medical cannabis are undisputed.
Bulgaria and Romania jointed the Schengen area.
Russian Government Speaker Dmitry Peskov rejected all claims"Russia used
police brain narcotics to eliminate "political brain functions"" www.Fakenews.de
in Germany. This is not true-ask the Dutch police-experts on this !
Russia started the distribution of 3,000,000 Russian passports among
the population of the occupied territories . British Foreign Minister Lord David
Camerun stated bluntly "NATO will send no troops to fight in Ukraine !".
Russian air strikes on Kharkiv in Easter Ukraine with many victims. Finland closed its Russian
borders 1,300 km long. NATO 75th birth anniversary celebrated in Brussels, NATO SecretaryGeneral
Jens Stoltenburg looked ill, nervous, miserable & nasty brocken, Euronews; born 1959 – one year
before me! Russia seems to win this war but at which cost?? Volodimir Zelenskyy is EU-most
loved figure, so Euronews. Russian killed 8 men in attack the Eastern city of Kharkiv by Iranian-
made drones: how did BBC recognize them as "Iranian made drones"? Sheer discrepancy ! Next:
Iranian drones supply to Russia timetable ? I never ever ever had it.

Russia attacked the city of Kharkiv by drones and missiles; Ukraine paid back with bombardment
of the town of Belgorod close to the common border.
In Germany AfD chief Christoph Berndt won the local election with 184 to 108 votes, ZDF.
26.o Celsius in Munnich: it gets hotter!
U.S. Secretary of State Antony Blinked stated in Brussels "Ukraine will join the NATO very soon"
shortly before his China visit. France started training Ukrainian soldiers in Poland. France has accomplished the
training of 10,000 Ukrainian soldiers up till now.
Germany stationed 2,700 German soldiers in Litauen neighboring Russia.
German defense minister Boris Pistorius gave an ample ZDF-interview shortlly before ample documentary on him
by German TV. ZDF-brand point journal runs on right now.
In a ZDF interview German Defense Minister Boris Pistorius put it bluntly "German troops in
Ukraine is not a business for German Finance Minister." German former Chancellor Gerhardt
Schröder said clear "NO" to German Taurus-rockets delivery to Ukraine. New NATO is further consumption denial,
he said any further. He criticicized German Bundeswehr phone calls security
not to tapped again yet again. France anchored the right on abortion in its Constitution.
The ZDF accused the EU "as major bureaucracy producer".
After Ukraine bombardment of the Zaporizhia atomic power plant, Russia retaliated with bombar
ding Kiiv electricity plant. "Ukraine is short before defeat if the USA doesn't deliver $60 billion weaponry", said
the Ukrainian President Volodimir Zelenskyy, cited by ZDF. "Otherwise-defeat!".
The whole of the Ukrainian electric grid is destroyed by Russian middle-range missiles.(ZDF).

U.S. Ambassador Victor Manuel Rocha sentenced for spying for 40 years for Cuba, (CNN)
Ukraine engaged water-drones with 800 km scope (ZDF). Russia destroyed 92% of the Ukrainian production plants out numbering the Ukrainian forces 5:1 (CNN).
12-04-2024 Police narcotics in my drinks-17.oo

Unpopular German Chancellor Olaf Scholz visited China for 3 days to boost bilateral relations.China posed unprecedented economic growth. German Foreign Minister Anneline Baerbock didn't attend the
visit and stood back in Germany. 2 Russian spies were arrested in Bayreuth, Germany- Alexander
S. and Dieter J. Both will be tried behind closed doors. The indictments read "members of Putin's
espionage and sabotage network aiming to attacks U.S. military bases in Germany", Euronews.
Two others- Thomas & Ina – were arrested in Düsseldorf for spying for China; both have sent to
China a "secret reader", said ZDF and "to sabotage U.S. aid to Ukraine". Massive Hungarian
protests against current Hungarian President Victor Orban who is a close friend to Vladimir Putin.

In an Euronews interview U.S. Vice President Mike Pence put it bluntly "the over running of
Ukraine by the Russans is only matter of time". Ukraine managed to shoot down the
first bombing jet of the type TU-22M3, rich 300 km away of the front line; Russia spoke of
"technical fault". One pilot died the other one was wounded. Germany promised to deliver to Ukraine 3 of its 12
Patriot air missiles systems before it is too late, said ZDF. Ursula von der Leyen was accused to have grandparents with a Nazi past being members of the Nazi Party NSDAP. In an Euronews interview Russian foreign minister
Sergey Lavrov said in good Russian "talks with Volodimir Zelenskyy are senseless; even such talks start there will
be no seize fire on the Ukrainian front".

NATO Secretary General Jens Stoltenberg said to Euronews "Ukraine has the right to hit targets out
side of Ukraine", which is the begin of all-out war on Russia.
Iran repelled recent Israeli air attacks saying "Israeli drones are children toys to us".
Ukrainian drones attacked overnight Russian positions in the Belgorod area leaving any Western
allies unhappy with this development, BBC: they don't want the war continues.

Czech President Petro Pavel promised 1,500,000 artillery shells help for Ukraine (CNN).
Chess marathon in Time Square , New York; victor is a Nigerian after 54 hours chessing.
"The U.S. loitering is a temptation for Putin to hit Ukraine even harder", President Zelensky
said to CNN. The U.S. House of Representatives passed the long waited $61 bn aid package
for Ukraine -57 bn euro -to combat successfully Russia with 311 votes "for" and 112 "against";
it contains ammunition and air defense systems while the Patriot air defense systems remained
rather expensive- $1.2bn each (same exchange rate). Ukraine demanded 7 such systems to
"protect its major cities"but they are useful for all EU-countries to fend up their own airspace.
President Zelensky said "this put the things back on track " and thanked for the billion heavy
aid package:" It will safe Ukrainian lives ;without this aid the war would be lost", he added.

The U.S.A. had already donated $74 billion aid package in the first two years of the war. Russia
reacted angrily to the U.S. aid; a great summer offensive is expected in Ukraine where 30% of
the electricity net work is already destroyed, Ukrainian troops are exhausted and outnumbered
but they are committed to fight to the last soldier. Russia warned Washington "not to get deeper involved into a war
that will end in humiliation". Estonia called the EU-countries to designate
0.25% of their GDP to support Ukraine; this is the so called "Estonian plan" (BBC). The plan
was launched by the Estonian ministry of defense. However Ukraine refused to sit at the

negotiating table in Switzerland to negotiate peace despite the Russian invitation for peace talks in Geneva, (ZDF).
Russia keeps superiority in tanks, munition, airkrafts and missiles. So far only
Germany has donated (only) one Patriot battery to help Ukraine to defend its air space.
EU foreign and defense ministers met in Luxemburg to discuss help for Ukraine.

Israeli secrete service head general Arohan Haliva resigned "for failing to prevent the Arab attack
of 7th October 2023" .Prime Minister Benjamin Netanyahu did not take personal responsibility
amid calls to step down too. London Metropolitan police head came under attack too (ZDF).
Donald Trump money still in his companies assets and they cannot do it without it ; so the so called "Trump trial"
will fail in disaster, end in failure (Euronews). At 15:55 he arrived at Court and said:
"This is a pro-election provocation!". Russia-gate scandal in Italy.
German President Steinmeyer arrived in Istanbul for talks with Turkish opposition leader Amelluloh.
Spice girl Victoria Bekham-married to football legend David Bekham-hit happily her 50th birth day
in London. We live on the money which we don't spend out!(ZDF).
In Dresden German police arrested the Chinese spy-an assistent of Max Krah, candidate for AfD in
the forthcoming election. ZDF blamed Krah of "dancing from one scandal to another". The Chinese
name sounds acoustically as Tsien Ziang. Krah refused to step down "because the election bulletins
are already printed with his name"; massive homelessness in Germany.

U.S. Secretary of Stated Antony Blinken visited China to discuss bilateral
relations. Britain increased its defense expenditure to 2.5% of its GDP. The German defense program
amounted however to 100 billion euro ($107.5 billion) :its defense budget is 250 billion euro annually
111 bn euro for the German defense industry (ZDF). The UN Secretary General Joseph Borell
estimated the Gaza destruction to 90 billion euro comparing it with World War Two. He also urged
the international community to freeze all Russian assets abroad for later rebuild of Ukraine.
In Charkiv Russian missile hit and destroyed the local TV-tower (CNN). In an annual report
Amnesty International accused Russia of "racking civilians and other detainees".

British Prime Minister Rishi Sunak visited Germany to coordinate bilateral measures "which
will curb the aggressor in the Ukrainian war" (BBC). Ukraine donated a shipful of grain to Sudan
despite the running war to Russia because the U.S. grain supply is insufficient (BBC).
U.S. President Joe Biden permitted personally and authorized Ukrainian long range missiles ATACMS-
300 km and more- to use against Russia, "because Russian delivery of such missiles to North Korea", said Biden
.Russia replied by using its outer space satellites in breach of its own 1964 Satellite treaty. Ukraine fired already
2 such missiles while the Spice Girls celebrate the 50th birth day of its Victoria Bekham, former Victoria Adams.
World Space summit is due in June 2024 in Geneva, Switzerland,Russia expected to disrupt it, said Ukraine. In a
Sorbonne speech French President
Emmanuel Macron complained "France is distorted in a rack between China and the U.S.A." In
a televized speech he put it bluntly "the Ukrainian war is a threat to European security". Unpopular
German Chancellor Olaf Scholz congratulated him for his speech. Spanish Prime Minister "Pedro Sanches canceled
all public duties because of a corruption scandal of his wife". France and Germany
agreed to build a common battle tank in near future (Euronews, TV5).

Along with Max Krah another spy – Peter Bystron – was convicted of spying for China in Germany.
Two other Chinese spies were arrested in London- Christopher Cash-32-and Christopher Berry-29.
Quite an age !
Massive Russian attacks on Ukraine yet again:unpopular German Chancellor Olaf Scholz remarked "German-strikes
on Ukraine must be avoided",Euronews . Russia gained control of Cherepeevka-

North-West of Avdeevka in the Donetsk region. President Zelenskyy tried to get control on the situation by introduction of new mobilization law for all Ukrainians.
2,022 Coup-de-Etat terrorists arrested in Germany including a Prince;plus 1,200 guns and rifles, 460,000 rounds ammunition; many GSG soldiers- the German Rapid Reaction Corps.
NATO started procedure for election of new Secretary General.(ZDF, ARD).
95,000 workers of Thyssen-Krupp went on strike in Germany beforehand of 01.May despite 2 bn euro state subsidy & grants. Otherwise many Germans protested and demanded min 80 euro daily. Germany promised more tanks and ammunition to Ukraine but no Patriot missiles. It delivered only 10 tanks, ammunition & Sky Block air missiles but no Patriots (ZDF).
Collectively ZDF,ARD & WDR canceled their work broadcasts because anxiety of 1st of May.
Massive strikes all over Germany :they demand min wage of 80 euro daily. Nicaragua lodged a court demand in Strasbourg "for German weapon deliveries for Israel in the occupied zones".

MAY 2024

1st of May massively celebrated all over Germany.
Not so in The Netherlands – here 1st of May is forbidden to celebrate (Euronews). I live here!
Ukraine applied to the EU already in 2022 and was given candidate status.
Dutch care workers get 16,- euro an hour (NPO).
Massive Nicaraguan strikes and demonstrations against the use of German weapons in Gaza.
02.May - World overcrowding day – Earth Overshoot day.
6 weeks to the World football cup in Germany. Again in Germany 10,000 suicides for 2023.
Massive human rights abuses in both Egypt and Tunis mostly against migrants (ARD).
593,000 Germans left the Protestant church in 2023 (ZDF).
The U.S.A. accused Russia of chemical weapons use in Ukraine- Chloropicrine since February (NPO1). 29. May- New York Court trial. German foreign minister Anneline Baerbock accused
Russian military intelligence of hacking German defense computer and demanded explanation
of the Russian Ambassador in Berlin for the Russian state sponsored cyber attack. British
foreign minister David Cameron visited Ukraine and promised to president Zelenskyy more
funds and more weapons against Russia. Russia changed tactics recently: they send in young
inexperienced soldier first and afterwards-when Ukrainians had run out of ammunition- they
sent in the battle older experienced well trained fresh Russian troops to win battles. In
Ochetinye area the Russian army gained more successes.

German foreign minister Anneline Baerbock visited Australia and New Zealand "to warn up
China" and promised German marine exercises in the Hindu - Pacific area with the same aim.
This is the first visit of German politician in the region in 13 years.
SPD- politician Mattias Ecke badly beaten by extremists in the German city of Dresden;
police dpt.of state protection intervened. He was hospitalized and operated 3 days later.
The German Justice department released free all 4 perpetrators "to be too young for court".
The SPD and the EU Social- Democratic party summoned an extraordinary emergency
congress in Berlin to discuss and to tackle the crisis as the far right attacks continue to increase
not only in Germany but all over Europe. The SPD popularity rating has fallen very much recently;
the entire European Parliament as a whole is expected to shift to the right in the EU election on 06. June 2024, said
Euronews . In a speech to the German CDU congress Friedrich Merz mentioned
with no single word Ukraine and Chancellor Olaf Scholz.

In local election UK Prime Minister Rishi Sunak's Party lost half of the seats: even the mayor of London is labor;
I sent a letter to Rishi already in 2022 and repeated it today.

On the Orthodox Christian Easter Russia attacked by drones Ukrainian cities and towns.
Euronews admitted "Ukraine is losing territories on and on; Russia can attack freely and

at will the backbone of the Ukrainian defenses". The U.S. weapon help is barely enough to resist the Russian attack but not enough to recover back Ukrainian territory already surrendered to Russia.Unpopular German Chancellor Olaf Scholz promised $100 billion to modernize the German Bundeswehr; it is not clear where he's going to take that money from facing sever budget deficit. Chinese
Prezident Xi Jin Ping visited Hungary and Serbia, working actively on establishing an authoritarian ax : both countries are considered as pro-Russian because of their close friendly relations with President Vladimir Putin, called "aggressor" by Hungarian opposition. The EU-trade deficit with China amounted to 396 billion euro. By Xi Jin Ping visit to France China tries to split the EU. Xi Jin Ping named Ukraine "European conflict only and China has nothing to do with it"!
Putin ordered nuclear tactic exercises;
unpopular German Chancellor Olaf Scholz answered with German tank exercises in the Baltic area. France was not included into the German "EU-skies common air defense program because considered too far from Germany, Israel and the U.S.A."
German ZDF and ARD televisions melted together; ZDF"Bares for Rares" Moderator replenished his program with young blood . Italian journalists strike in protest against state supervision on news and comments; In Britain a German sausage hit 10 pounds a piece and in Turkey the inflation rate is over 70% at 700 euro monthly salary; so better live in the EU. In a speech Russian president Vladimir Putin threatened Great Britain with nuclear weapons and nuclear military exercises "free to hit legitimate British targets in Ukraine and beyond!". Xi Jin Ping named Ukraine "European conflict only that China has nothing to do with it: China is not part of the problem", Xi stressed. China doesn't stick to the EU trade embargo imposed on Russia and refused to condemn Russia for its invasion into Ukraine. BBC mirrored no British reaction to both threats.
Chinese hackers hit EU military installations. EU condemned China for "working actively on establishing of authoritarian ax in international relations" said Reinhardt Reng, MEP. French president Emmanuel Macron however thanked China "for not sending Chinese weapons against Ukraine". However Chinese hackers hacked the computer of the UK air forces. Belgian politicians were hacked too.

Unpopular German Chancellor Olaf Scholz was also invited but he preferred to visit the Baltic states afront of the forthcoming Russian atomic exercises close to the mutual frontier with them.

Germany synthesized synthetic diesel fuel-environmentally cleaner than the fossil diesel- and started to sale it on German fuel stations for the same price. Germany will return to nuclear energy production. German interior ministers conference in Thüringen.
Boeing launched new space ship named Star Light to dock with the ISS.

Vladimir Vladimirovich Putin-aged 71- was sworn in again as Russian President for 5th term. He is President of Russia since 1999; he'll reign till 2030.
In his inauguration speech he stressed "we are great nation... nevertheless we don't exclude a dialog with the West!"BBC Russian service dubbed him "a dangerous man... reincarnation of Stalin" while Joe Biden is referred to as "a harmless old man".
After his short speech Putin was greeted with military honesty by his Presidential Regiment . U.S., UK and E.U. boycotted the ceremony which BBC was broadcasting live,
ZDF with 6 hours delay, France, Slovakia and Hungary sent their Ambassadors.
Andrey Ostravsky- BBC Russian service; dubbed Putin "a dangerous man" : the Russian

victims in the Ukrainian war amount to 120,000 deaths; Russia is said to pump 33% of its budget
into its armament industry and its army. Again in Germany-in Berlin- SPD- politician Franziska
Giffey attacked and badly beaten by far right radicals; another attack again in Dresden; 306 in Brandenburg for
2023: this 32 days before the EU-election. Swastikas and Hitler greet are
usual in German schools even for teenagers.
Russia celebrated the 79th anniversary of the victory over Nazi Germany in the Great Patriotic
War 1941-1945. In his speech President Putin said: "We won't allow anyone to threaten us!"
and praised the bravery of the Soviet and Chinese in the World War Two. The military parade
took place on the Red Square in Moscow as usual despite the rainy windy weather. Putin him
self was shattered , with tears in his eyes. However he admitted "Russia faces difficult times".
He stressed "Russia is doing everything to avoid a global conflict, but we will not allow any
form of intimidation: our nuclear weapons are ready day & night . Huraa!".
Katarzina Zysk-professor of Institute of Defense, Norway-sharply critisized him on BBC.

Russian military parade in Moscow:
BBC deliberately interrupted the broad cast not to show the Russian strategic missiles paraded
nor to download them but I used other channels to record them on video (13:00). The Russians
paraded also several regiments of women-soldiers! Such an enthusiasm in the Moscow rain!

There is some difference between Orthodox and Catholic calendar because the Orthodox use
the old-fashioned Julian calendar not the Catholic one.

German defense minister Boris Pistorius visited Washington to buy 60 Boeing transport
helicopters "Chinuk" to cover recent Ukrainian air forces needs. It is not clear where he'll
get the money from. Russia was banned from Eurovision tv already at the begin of the war:
that's why we have no Russian television news. One week after his re-election president
Putin exchanged his prime minister Mishustin with a low profile technocrate ;
further reshuffles are in sight first of all maybe his defense minister Sergey Shoygu;
it is difficult to extract names from the Western propaganda machine here but I try.

U.S.A. granted 392.00 million euro to Ukraine, mostly missiles and air rockets
to beat off Russian attacks.
Mass police evacuations from Harkiiv & Vovchansk where the counter-offensive of the
Ukrainian Army stuck to nothing. Phone 14070. BBC-jamboree.
In the Eurovision Song Competition Swiss contestor Nemo got the price with his very short
neck.
Ukrainian President Volodimir Zelenskyy did not state in his interview how many Ukrainian
towns have fallen to the aggressor yet .
Russian President Vladimir Putin appointed technocrat Andrey Belousov-former deputy Prime
minister - to new Russian defense minister on 12.May 2024 to replace Sergey Shoigu amid
corruption scandal of his deputy Timur Ivanov. In a rare reshuffle of posts Sergey Shoigu
was promoted to a Russian security council secretary as probable Putin's successor.
Estonia increased its military spending to 3.4% of the overall GDP to "avoid Russian assault".
CDU Ursula von der Leyen desired to continue as EU commission president.

Ailing British King Charles appointed his eldest son Williams Prince of Wales to colonel
in chief & supreme commander of the British air force RAF ; he had served already in the RAF
earlier and has proper experience in the sexual women abuse scandals in the British Army.

British prime minister Rishi Sunak Rwanda refugees plan obstructed .
Italian journalists strike in protest against state supervision on news and comments;
in Britain a German sausage hit 10 pounds a piece and in Turkey the inflation rate is
over 70% at 700 euro monthly salary; so better live in the EU?!
Massive police attempts to eliminate my short memory by police narcotics - a wholesome threat
to all Journalists. In my Archive I found deeply embedded Dutch Mind Control Program dated
18. May 1999. George Orwell dated it in 1983 in his notorious book "Animal Farm"!

European Song Festival in Malmö, Sweden winners: 1. Switzerland, 2.Croatia, 3. Ukraine.
German Supreme Court decided against AfD-Alternative for Deutschland: it means the German
constitution protection council can bug,tap & control all phone lines; as German interior
minister Nancy Faeser put it bluntly "we are not afraid"!

The Ukrainian city of Kharkiv is already in the Russian artillery range.
Ukrainian people terrified evacuating even domestic cattle in their exodus.
Ukraine started electricity imports from the West to cope with the Russian destruction of
electricity grid. "In their advance Russian forces lose their soldiers by thousands; even more
in the Kharkiv defense". Ukrainian spokesman did not elaborate on Ukrainian losses.
German Chancellor Olaf Scholz visited Scandinavia to co-ordinate his Ukraine policy.
U.S. secretary of state Anthony Blinken arrived in Kiiv on a sleep train in an unannounced
visit to Ukraine to re- affirm American solidarity with the Ukrainian people in the front of the
Russian aggression ;he played guitar to his Ukrainian fans.
U.S. President Joe Biden stated bluntly "We want for Ukraine to win this war!"

Russia started deploying small assault troops in order to stretch the
Ukrainian defense front and to exhaust the Ukrainian troops there.

Russian President Vladimir Putin is on a state visit to China to boost bilateral relations.
Already 2022 both countries signed a treaty for co-operation, friendship and limitless
relations, incl. military co-operation and common military exercises. China condemned "the
double American moral as to the American weapon deliveries to Ukraine"; condemning the
double U.S. policy and the sanctions against Russia. President Putin visited also Harbin and
laid flowers there on the monument of the Soviet Red Army which liberated China in the
world war two. Both Presidents visited also the Harbin Institute of Technology which the
U.S.A. denounced in 2022 for delivering technologies to the Chines military industry.
In his televised speech President Putin stressed on the importance of the Russian energy
delivery to China both of oil and gas for light and heating; the overall turnover of mutual
trade amounted to $200 billion.

The U.S.A. imposed 100% customs duty on the Chinese electric cars imports.
A new trade war is in vision.
Unpopular German Chancellor Olaf Scholz visited Sweden to beg money for the German budget deficit. His visit is at very strange time:
an attempted coup d'etat of German Prince Heindrich the 13th failed!

Russia has not the number, capacity and patriotism to continue its attack on
Ukraine , parroted futile NATO parrot general Christopher Cavoli .

In his China press conference Russian President Vladimir Putin stated bluntly "Russia has
no intention to capture its Kharkiv city on the Ukrainian border despite the heavy battle there.
It intends 30 km – 20 miles security zone there.
It downed 100 Ukrainian drones over Russian Crimea – where did the Unis get so much drones
from ?? Sheer marionettes ! "Russia has greater aims there, so Jonathan Head, CNN."
Every drone attack is deadly and they are 96-100 daily.
Heavy police electricity black outs in Netherlands, Capital The Hague.

Assassination attempt on Slovakian Prime Minister Fico: he survived the attack. More
details on his attack on his Facebook page; massive police protests against police working
conditions-they should accept opera or ballerina roles!
My new book **"The Russian-Ukrainian war"** was published in the U.S.A.

Massive protests and demonstration in Bucharest against high taxes-42% of the gross
salary compared to the EU average of 38% - imposed by Romanian government which
lavishly sent troops to Afghanistan 2002. Since 1989 5 million people left Romania in search of
a better life abroad while the Romanian work force is 7.7 million of 20 million population.
Massive riots in Amsterdam too – the Mayor and the public prosecutor engaged riot police
forces ; many protesters arrested and hand cuffed after they erected barricades.
The German Bundestag withdrew the Parliamentary immunity of the AfD politician Peter
Bystron.

Ukrainian President Volodimir Zelenskyy complained of "lack of ammunition, troops &
moral"; the air defense covers only 25% of the needs", BBC. The main trouble remains
the lack of moral in the Ukrainian army. A new law is expected to boost conscription.
The Ukrainian army counts now 500,000 soldiers. In the battle for Kharkiv Russia
concentrated 20,000 troops. The new Ukrainian bill aims to boost recruitment even with
active prisoners simply release from jail; they try to make Kharkiv a new Aleppo by
launching over 100 drones. "
After the death of Iran President Ebrahim Raisi in a helicopter crash CNN rushed to
blame him with all vicious talks possible. Among all his "ailing age of 61": what to say
U.S. President Joe Biden aged 74 ?!
2x8 ICC warrants for both of them incl. President Benjamin Netanyahu
"Non-stop advance of Russian forces in Eastern Ukraine", said U.S. defense minister
Lloid Austin to CNN.

Late Alexej Navalny dissident friend Leonid Volkov attacked with a hammer in Lithuania,
where he lives in exile.
A large group of U.S. students decided to turn their backs to Joe Biden as he turned his
back to Palestine.
Former U.S. President Donald Trump demanded "for Joe Biden to take a drug test in
advance of every his speech!"
In Frankfurt am Main began the political trial against Heinrich 13th Prince of Reuss;
he is accused of Coup d'etat against the current German government rule. With him
went on trial 13 German Army officers (Bundeswehr)
German foreign minister Anneline Baerbock visited Kiiv where Ukrainian president
Volodimir Zelenskyy decorated her… with an order! It is her 9th visit to Ukraine.
The EU started electricity supply of Germany by undersea electric cable (ZDF).

$1 billion Ukraine support collected cannot be sent to Ukraine .

President Zelenskyy described the situation in and around Kharkiv as "desperate" and "extremely difficult". Kiiv remained without electricity after a grid black out.

The village of Plevenivka fell to Russian hands "to stop the shelling of the Russian town of Belgorod", just across the border.

British Prime minister Rishi Sunak visited Austria to coordinate the asylum politic of both countries.

France reinforced its police contingents in both Haiti and New Caledonia with new fresh troops.

Poland started investigation of Russian interference in Polish matters for the period 2004-2024.

Ukraine hit two new Russian targets in the occupied Crimea where Russia led military exercises with tactical nuclear weapons.

Russia removed all 24 buoys marking the mutual border with Estonia ahead of expected Russian assault to.

Ukrainian city of Kharkiv is yet again under Ukrainian control despite Russian hit on schools because Ukrainian air defense lack. There is growing concern that Donald Trump re-election in November may hamper Western military help to Ukraine (BBC). Even now the Biden administration is reluctant to deliver medium- and long range missiles to Ukraine because it will escalate the war by hitting targets deep inside Russia as it happens with Belgorod- a Russian city just across the border with Ukraine. As CNN put it Putin plans to protract the war even in 2025.

Ukrainian president Zelenskyy urged the U.S.A. and China to participate in the world peace conference in Switzerland in June 2024. German foreign minister Anneline Baerbock visited Kiiv again and promised military help of 3.8 billion euro. Unpopular German Chancellor Olaf Scholz declared bluntly to the media "no German ground troops in Ukraine". However German defense minister Boris Pistorius inspected the German troops in Litauen to see their combat readiness. A meeting of EU-foreign ministers discussed EU-help to Ukraine to beat off the Russians.

On the 3rd day of his state visit to Germany French President Emanuel Macron urged Germany "for united French-German defense system". Unpopular German Chancellor Olaf Scholz countered "it is naive to build European defense system without the U.S.A."(17:10) Finally he agreed to deliver German medium range missiles to Ukraine which can hit Russian targets across the border. The German missiles have a range of 250 km, the British ones – only 80 km.

Ukrainian President Volodimir Zelenkyy visited Belgium to receive 1 billion euro military aid and 30 F-16 fighter jets. It is not clear where the pilots will be trained. Zelenskyy complained that Ukraine is not allowed to hit targets inside of Russia,a topic Chancellor Scholz fears it could escalate the conflict with nuclear Russia. Short before the EU-elections Russian cyber attacks intensified on European institutions. Russian advance continued in the South-Donetsk region; 2 villiges – Selydove and Oleksejevo-Drushkivka- Russia conquered again. It bombarded also the Beryslavsky district of Cherson, using highly explosive ground bombs; Kramatorsk remained still in Ukrainian hands .

NATO 32 foreign ministers conference started in Prague, Czech republic. The U.S.A. was represented by its foreign secretary Antony Blinken. The EU was also represented. The main issue was permit to Ukraine to hit targets inside of Russia. Antony Blinken expressed again the U.S. reserves to the issue. German Defense minister Boris Pistorius visited the port of Odessa and promised further 500 million euro additional help to Ukraine incl. training of Ukrainian soldiers on the German "Patriot"missiles systems. Antony Blinken left the conference one day earlier before the closing date among full disarray. German foreign minister Anneline Baerbock avoided any comment; it this respect I remembered the American writer Upton Sinclair and his books "King Coal" and "King Oil" both published lavishly in the U.S.A. and in Europe in the 1940ies.

The exchange rate of the Turkish Lira reached 10 for 1 euro because of the inflation (BBC). Turkey too is a NATO member.

On 31. May Germany agreed with the Ukrainian proposal to strike targets inside of Russia; the Czech republic agreed to deliver the much needed ammunition to Ukraine which decided the war out come. Italy disagreed. NATO secretary general Jens Stoltenberg saluted the German decision. Moscow threatened with "asymmetric response", hinting nuclear weapons. Kremlin spokesman Dmitriy Peskov pointed out "the escalation responsibility of the war lays only with the West; Ukrainian soldiers cannot program the German rocket launchers on Russian targets".

German chancellor Olaf Scholz commented only cautiously: "We must avoid the big war between NATO and Russia!" NATO Secretary general Jens Stoltenberg pointed out the Ukrainian right on self defense.

150 prisoners' swap between both countries; the U.A.E. brokered the swap. They exchanged also the dead bodies of soldiers fallen in recent battles.

Donald Trump was found guilty by court in a felony trial; he accused democratic president Joe Biden to stay behind the machination which is rather plausible (Euronews). The presidential elections are scheduled for November 2024.

JUNE 2024

Massive farmers strikes and demonstrations in Vienna, Austria; they demand higher prices for their agricultural products, esp. for dairy products. Once the war is over Ukraine will flood Europe with cheap agricultural products. Already earlier angry Polish farmers spilled cheap Ukrainian wheat on many Polish streets in sign of protest. The demonstrations spilled over into Belgium where the farmers blocked the roads in the capital of Brussels.

Ukrainian President Volodymyr Zelenskyy said "the use of the American weapons delivered is only matter of time". Ukraine experience sharp shortage of munitions to battle the Russian attacks. He said also "Ukraine is ready to apply NATO weapons to hit Russian military targets inside of Russia". Russia however hit 53 power targets with missiles and drones and switched off electricity in many villages. At least 15 Ukrainians were reported killed many other wounded.
Speaking on Singapore Defense Forum president Zelenkyy accused China of "trying to obstruct the peace talks in Switzerland scheduled later this month". He has some proposals on the peace talks
which he'll make public in Geneva. He advocated also for peace security,nuclear security, food security and freedom for the prisoners of war. Zelenskyy accused China bluntly to helping Russia to disrupt the Geneva peace talks. According to Zelenskyy China ostensible pressed other states not to attend the peace talks.
Joint NATO fighter jets exercises in Schleswig-Hohlstein, North Germany with the clear aim to intimidate Russia; 60 allied jets participated in the maneuvers. Russia did not appear bullied.
According to Zelenskyy "Trump could be a loser with bad Ukrainian peace deal".

EU-Council leader Ursula von der Leyen proposed European defense shield of democracy to counter Russian disinformation campaign in Europe and foundation of legal protection of Russian spies. The shield will act in 48 country.
D-DAY celebration in France : on 06-06-1944 on the descent in Normandy on
one day only 12,000 allied soldiers were killed. Russia was not invited to the celebration but Ukraine was, represented by President Volodymyr Zelenskyy among 25 other heads of states.
Unpopular German Chancellor Olaf Scholz was also among the public as shown on television.
British King Charles thanked saying "our gratitude is eternal!". In a commemorating speech
U.S. President Joe Biden praised the U.S. heroes and assured Ukraine of stanch U.S. support against Russia "without which Ukraine will be subjugated, all Europe will be threatened " and "the U.S. has a role to play in the European relations".
Joint forces 1944 were:
55,000 Americans ,
73,000 Brits
22,000 French Canadians.
U.S. democratic President Biden visited also Port York imitating U.S. republican President

Ronald Reagan who delivered a speech there 1984 which rocketed him to 2nd term in WH office. Biden took the same lift: he delivered a long speech speaking by heart not reading anything."The U.S. main task is protecting peace and keep up democracy!" he said among
others and "there is nothing beyond U.S. capacity". He mentioned Ukraine with no single word.
British Prime minister Rishi Sunak left the D-day commemoration earlier than other heads of states but "apologized because of his election itinerary"; in my view he was right ahead of the British election ahead fixed for the 4th of July 2024. The British opposition accused him "of shameful dereliction of duties". The British oppositions stood the day all over the commemoration not allowing the day overshadowed by politics but it is exactly what happened. On the photo Sunak's place was taken by David Cameron.
Currently Sunak lags behind Labor party by 20 points.

Russian President Vladimir Putin criticized sharply the Ukrainian deploy of German missiles against Russian targets and vowed to retaliate with long-range rockets against Germany."It is direct war against Russia: visibly the West is entirely disinterested in Ukraine and cares only of its interests and ambitions against Russia; it creates tension of the international relations".
In the forthcoming EU-elections Germany SPD tries to pose as tough on asylum politic in order to withdraw votes off the German AfD-party.

On the second day of his visit to France President Zelenskyy and his wife Olena Zelensky-how else!- addressed the French National Assembly demanding more weapons to Ukraine:"Europe is not a continent of peace anymore, Russia threatens all of Europe!" Zelenskyy pointed out.
France did not rule out sending French troops to Ukraine; for the time being there are "only" French military trainers and instructors to advise the Ukrainian army on how to fight against Russia which is direct intervention. President Macrone -accused of Macronism- approved the use of French weapons on Russian targets inside of Russia and promised to Ukraine the delivery of French fighter jets Mirage-2000; he promised Ukrainian pilots training. Denmark and The Netherlands promised F-16 fighter jets to Ukraine too and pilot training in Arizona, U.S.A.
The French delivery will occur end of June.
Zelenskyy & wife visited French weapon plant and urged them "to produce more French weaponry for Ukraine, because Russia is a threat to the whole of Europe". He drew a parallel of the European D-day with the current Ukrainian events. Zelenskyy was invited to the Elisay palace to boost Macrone EU-election campaign. Later in the day Zelenskyy gave a press conference.

Later in the day Zelenskyy family met U.S. President Joe Biden who also promised help for Ukraine and Zelenskyy family- $225 million, the sixth U.S. aid package to Ukraine: Russia will not stop at Ukraine, Biden said to the Press. Altogether Biden spent 5 days in France-from Wednesday till Sunday !
The EU-Central Bank reduced the leading interest rate from 4.25% to 4.0%; further rate reductions expected to boost economy and Zelenskyy Family.

President Putin addressed personally the World Economic Forum in St.Petersburg, Russia. Afghanistan was represented by the Taleban. One of the two Putin's daughter addressed the Forum by video link. "The Forum illustrated how successfully Russia can by pass the Western economic sanctions." "Russian economy is growing despite the EU-sanctions", said the IMF (International Monetary Funds) Putin said proudly "Russia trade with its friends is 75% of the Russian turn over." He encouraged the world trade in other currencies and praised current world trade in Russian rubles: pots of gold! "Russia can do it good without Western help". The conflict threatens to escalate into nuclear war!

Volodymyr Zelenskyy held talks in Paris with U.S. President Joe Biden who released other $225 million aid to Ukraine. "How to lose such opportunity", advised his indelible wife Olena! Biden apologized for the $61 billion military aid delay; he encouraged Ukrainian attacks on Russian soil with American weaponry. After the 2-day commemoration of the D-day President Biden flew to Paris for talks with the French President Emanuel Macrone who was accused by the Press of "macronism". Macrone disputed Ukraine, Gaza, China and global economy. Labor crack-down advice on late payments.

Russia delivered 400 ballistic missiles to Iran in return of the Iranian Shahet-drones widely used to destroy Ukrainian infrastructure.
The BBC lost in Greece its correspondent Michael Mosley. How could he disappear in such a small island ?! The rescue operation continued with well-trained police dogs.
Euronews reporter Galina Polonskaya too went missing from the media horizon.
Taylor Swift concert in Edinburgh-900 km north from London.
Heavy Samsung workers strike in South Korea. The stocks fell down and the Dollar rose.
The Netherlands started improving its agriculture politic .
Massive enhance of U.S. brain drain campaign in Europe!
In the EU -elections French President Emanuel Macrone suffered bitter disappointment, dismissed the National Assembly and scheduled new election for it on 30th June and 7th July: because the winner of the EU election was far right nationalist Marine Le Pen.
Unpopular German chancellor Olaf Scholz too had a bitter pill to swallow: he was the
3rd party behind the
CDU-Christian Democratic Union and
AfD-Alternative for Deutschland .
Chancellor Scholz drew no lessons from the EU-elections and refused to step down
unlike his French counter part Emanuel Macron, who was beaten by the far right
Marine Le Pen National Rally with 31% of the vote.
In Bulgaria the main election winner was the GERB-party with 23% of the vote but the right also scored good.

Few days after gaining U.S. and EU permission to strike on Russian targets deep inside of Russia with Western weaponry Ukraine hit a Russian airport 600 miles eastern of the Ukrainian border and destroyed an ultra new Russian strategic bomb jet: it looks like Crimean war 1856 repetition,so Echo of Moscow in Russian which I speak fluently, supervised by **Roskomnadzor:**

The Federal Service for Supervision of Communications, Information Technology and Mass Media,abbreviated as **Roskomnadzor** (RKN) is the Russian federal executive agency responsible
for monitoring, controlling and censoring Russian mass media. Its areas of responsibility include electronic media, mass communications, information technology and telecommunications, supervising compliance with the law, protecting the confidentiality of personal data being processed, and organizing the work of the radio-frequency service.
France drew up conclusions of the President Macrone defeat in the EU-election now the call is stronger for unpopular German Chancellor Olaf Scholz to resign too and did not call new elections in Germany. Belgian Prime Minister Alexander Dutreaux resigned too.
It is not clear what will happen with the 100 independent MEP, possibly they'll joint the far right

block in the EU-Parliament which still misses my books. CDU chief Ursula von der Leyen also
needs the right wing support for her re-election as a President of the European Commission.
French President Emanuel Macron's party earned only 14% of the French vote for the European
Parliament. Far right Marine Le Pen National Rally scored 31% of the vote.

Russia and its ally Belarus started joint military drills with tactical nuclear weapons, tanks and
airplanes: the second of expected 3.
Belarus has no own nuclear weapons on its territory but hoists Russian ones. Russia
has repeatedly threatened the West with nuclear weapons but in vain. Now it demonstrates
superiority in defending its *sovereignty* "if any Russian targets were hit on Russian soil", as
Ukraine repeatedly demanded from the West.
These tactical nuclear weapons are less destructive than conventional nuclear
weapons but can be deployed without danger to friendly troops. "The joint military drills
demonstrates the Russian readiness to defend its *sovereignty* ",stressed Russian new defense
minister. President Vladimir Putin has threatened many times the West with nuclear strikes: this
stage is over!
We don't want nuclear war with Russia, not at all ! Who can win from such a war?!

The Russians will lose nothing: the biggest losers will be Belgium and The Netherlands with their
dense civil populations !

President Zelenskyy arrived in Berlin for talks-and he talked indeed in the German Bundestag
despite the boycott of AfD and BSW-their seats in parliament remained empty. AfD named him
"beggar" and "war president" because his mandate expired already long long months earlier.
The EU was represented by Ursula von der Leyen who promised further 50 billion euro support
to Ukraine till 2027. Her speech to the Bundestag was not broadcasted. Both speakers
looked unimpressed by the joint Russian-Belorussian nuclear military drill. Zelenskyy thanked
for the support and asked again for more German air defense systems against Russia.
According to the IMF Ukraine needs further 560 billion euro for reconstruction which he is likely
to get despite the European crisis. "Half of the Ukrainian electric grid is destroyed",he stressed
unimpressed by the boycott left and right. He is in Berlin already 4 days.

Born 1978 Zelenskyy worked earlier as Ukrainian entertainer, now works as the sixth president of
Ukraine. Corruption is an issue in Ukrainian society going back to the dissolution of the Soviet Union in 1991.
[After declaring independence from the Soviet Union, Ukraine faced a series of politicians from different sides of
the political spectrum, as well as criminal bosses and oligarchs, who used the corruption of police, political parties,
and industry to gain power. Ukrainian corruption remains an obstacle to
joining the EU.

Recently U.S. secretary of state Antony Blinken stated to the Press:"The vote in the security
council happened smoothly with 14 votes "for" which is rare for the security council: only one
voice was "against"and this was us !", said BBC.
German defense minister Boris Pistorius proposed compulsory conscription of youth into the
German Bundeswehr which now counts 180,000 soldiers; 20,000 soldiers still lack .
His proposal was approved by the opposition CDU-party.
A Russian jet bomber SU-34 was downed over North Ossetia.
U.S. President son Hunter Biden was convicted on all 3 charges in his trial.
His Father – Joe Biden – looked unimpressed by the verdict.

NATO Secretary general Jens Stoltenberg will be replaced by November 2024.
Bucharest-9 conference in Romania.
Hungary stopped blocking Ukrainian's membership into NATO after a long delay. However
no Hungarian troops will be sent in on the Ukrainian front and no Hungarian money funds will
be paid to: full escalation of the conflict ! The Hungarian approval came after long systematic
Hungarian veto into NATO troops deploy into Ukraine. He named it "maneuvers' and Jens
Stoltenberg named it "efforts"; no one used the word "war" though it is a sheer war. Full repetition
of the 1856 Crimea war against Russia when Russia was defeated and Turkey deceived.
The Russian attacks switched off 9 gigaWatts of the Ukrainian electric grid; before the war
Ukraine consumed 58 gW daily.
Russia sent nuclear submarine "Kazan" and 3 other battle ships for exercises in the Caribbean as a
reply for the use permission of U.S. weapons by Ukraine against Russian targets deep inside Russia.
Russia had always insisting on diplomatic solution of the Ukrainian war.

The 50th G-7 summit took place in Bari,Italy; the Pope addressed the meeting with a short
speech. It decided to release further 46 billion euro help Ukrainian war efforts;
the money will come from the frozen Russian assets abroad. The BBC dubbed bluntly the
seizure a "theft". Russia can return the move by confiscating Western assets inside of Russia, esp.
U.S. assets. The U.S.A. works on preparing a treaty with Ukraine on friendship and military cooperation. Saudi
Arabian foreign minister said however "Ukraine must find a form of
compromise".

The EU obliged cheap Chinese cars with 38% custom tolls,taxes and tariffs to close the
competition gap. Germany did not agree because it produces its cars Audi, BMV and
Mercedes in China and is afraid of Chinese retaliation amid heavy critic on Germany for
cheap Chinese steel imports. The new toll will be enacted on 5th July 2024. China named it
"wrong decision" and "a trade war".

NATO defense ministers discussed in Brussels a plan of long-term military assistance and
military training of Ukrainian soldiers . NATO secretary general Jens Stoltenberg addressed
the meeting saying "we will grant new long-term support, military assistance,security and
military training for the Ukrainian soldiers;
we also pledge a long-term financial aid to Ukraine.", meaning new 40 billion euro "and
more predictability for Ukraine of the kind and amount of weapons and funds it may get".
All this will be detailed on another NATO meeting scheduled for July on which all members
are expected to agree.
President Joe Biden and president Zelenskyy are expected to sign soon a bilateral security
agreement on military aid ,military assistance and military co-operation.
The U.S.A. declined however direct involvement of U.S. troops in the conflict but agreed to
send one more "Patriot" anti-air craft missile system. Further talks are scheduled for July with
U.S. President Joe Biden. Russia took already advantage of the military U.S. aid lengthy delay
over the 1,000 km long front line. Despite the war Ukraine sent its football team for the European
football championship in Germany which opened with solemnity. Zelensky and Joe Biden signed
a 10-years security treaty and $50 billion agreement (=46 billion euro). Similar deal was signed
with Japan -represented by Fumio Kishida-for 4.6 billion euro-the first deal with a non-NATO
country that's why "historic".
Now the reconstruction payments will be paid from the interests of the frozen Russian assets abroad. The day ended
with a lavish state dinner: Italian prime minister Giorgia Mellony addressed it in

clumsy English.
"Putin's calculation is simple: to protract the war until all
countries abandon Ukraine; the treaties today refuted his calculation!", said German chancellor
Olaf Scholz during the dinner. Volodymyr Zelenskyy thanked the G-7 leaders "for facilitating
the deals" and "Patriot"is an Ukrainian word now". President Joe Biden seemed visibly not aware of what he signs.
Local population protested against the summit under the name "NoG-7"
The Ukrainian football team arrived in Munich for the European championship which will last
till 14. July- exactly one month !
President Vladimir Putin presented the Russian piece plan if:
1. Ukraine pulls out fully its troops from the 4 regions currently occupied by Russia: Donetsk, Lugansk,Zaporizhe
and Cherson.
2. Ukraine abandons its NATO membership plans.
The second however is not realistic because the NATO-membership is anchored in the Ukrainian
constitution."If Ukraine agrees to this I shall stop the fire literally the same minute!", Putin said
proudly. He has little choice-if he stops the war Ukraine will automatically enter NATO.
No single word of reparations and contributions.
German Chancellor Olaf Scholz rejected bluntly Putin's peace plan.

NATO moves its headquarters from Brussels to Wiesbaden, Germany. NATO Secretary General
Jens Stoltenberg accused Russia of sabotage,provocations and other hostile acts "which will find
our respond in ever better coordination and improved information exchange among the members".
Pope Francis criticized sharply the AI because its priority to killing technologies in his speech at
the G-7 summit in Bari , Italy. Quite modernized Pope ! The G-7 concluded its meeting by
adopting 11 resolutions. Saudi Arabian foreign minister however said "Ukraine must find a
form of compromise".
The Russian threat of tactical nuclear weapons resembles to a saber rattle.

The EU-commission fined Hungary 200 million euro for not implementing the EU legislation
towards asylum seekers and emigrants. Hungarian President Victor Orban called the decision
"outrageous": since 2015 1,000,000 emigrants entered the EU illegally, said Euronews.
Hungary is regarded as a "staunch Russian supporter!"
Massive scuffle between deputies in the Italian Parliament,one of them hospitalized as a result.
Italian prime minister Giorgia Melony addressed the G-7 dinner in broken clumsy English.
Climate activists chained themselves at the G-7 Press entry to protest against their current
climate politics.

British King Charles birth day celebration in London though it is actually in November: the
commander of the troops of color parade has to remember 100 words of commands! Amazing !
The Russian 9th of May parade was more impressive though deliberately cut off by
the BBC several times.

An Ukrainian peace summit started its work in Swiss resort Bürgenstock-near Lucern-
at the Vierwaldstädtersee comprising 92 countries incl. Ukraine and India but Russia was not invited,
China declined the invitation- a dreadful escalation on international level!A small radar station was
posed for eventual air raids! German Chancellor Olaf Scholz rejected bluntly Putin's peace plan despite Ukrainian
disadvantage on the current battle ground and named it even "an ultimatum".
"The freezing of the Russian assets abroad should send clear message to President Putin",
said Scholz. President Zelenskyy named the war "criminal unprovoked aggression".

The name of Bürgenstock was carefully cut off in the later reports as well the option of new
Ukrainian peace conference with Russia and China participating too. The timing of the conference
was carefully scheduled too-on the weekend to avoid mass media attention. Another Ukrainian
summit will be scheduled for the end of 2024-Ukraine has nothing against Russia participation
in it; direct bilateral talks will follow later on – but not in Switzerland which is already regarded by Russia from
now on as a non-neutral country any more. The summit discussed also the nuclear
power plant in Zaporizhie. President Zelenskyy demanded short term help to repair the Ukrainian electric grid
ruined by the Russian air attacks. He marked the summit as "success" , "historic" and
"distraction"! Many leaders however-eg.the Kenyan- demanded Russia to be present on the Summit.
On the second day the peace summit demanded:
1.Territorial integrity of Ukraine
2. Prisoners exchange
3. Return of all Ukrainian children
4. Nuclear safety
5. Food security
6. New summit with Russian participation
7. Talking peace is a new territory for Ukraine

8. Humanitarian assistance
9. Long-term investment in the Ukrainian energy grid
10. Respect of international law
11. Human rights
12. Just, comprehensive,lasting peace
13. UN 2023 resolution
14. stable path map to peace
15. It is up to Ukraine to determine the peace conditions.
Rather different from President Putin's peace plan which world leaders slammed at the summit!

British Prime Minister Rishi Sunak spent much time with his new Ukrainian friend Zelenskyy.
Why not-he has as a time lock the UK parliamentary election on 04th July 2024.
The summit stated "This war is a threat to the global economy and global food standards!".
U.S. President Joe Biden returned from funds raising campaign in LA: Logically he didn't attend
the peace summit in Bürgenstock! Simultaneously U.S. Secretary of State Antony Blinken is in
Israel! So which U.S. politician represented the U.S. at the summit ?!
Up till now Biden's election campaign has risen $28 mn.
Some countries-such as India, South Africa, Brasil, Mexico, Saudi Arabia and 18 other countries refused to sign
the joint summit communique after criticizing it. The word "abortion" was not
mentioned which soured the French-Italian relations.

In the town of Pirna German police shot dead a 27 years old Afghan refugee in a scuffle.
In Hamburg German police shot a Dutch man in the dawn of the match Poland-The Netherlands.
In Russian city Rostov-na-Don prison islamists took 6 inmates hostage.
In average 12 young Brits die weekly from cardiac arrest (BBC).
Denmark reduced the passage of Russian oil ships through its aquatoria waters which
increased the bilateral tensions. Massive demonstrations in Brussels to protest against the EU.
The Houthis rebels in Yemen sank an U.S. battle ship.

Massive army dodging of Ukrainian recruits: they merry massively in order to avoid conscription which is

compulsory now; there are forcible drafts esp. in the streets of Odessa. Russian overpowering man power is overwhelming.
Time for peace ! The professional slogan is "together till a victory!"But many men ask themselves "what are we going to die for?" More and more volunteer lack; that's why the conscription age was prolonged between men 25-60 years of age. Later on President Zelenskyy started to recruit Ukrainian prisoners and to send them to fight on the front ! They will gain freedom if they fight to the end of the war against Russia.

After the peace summit German foreign minister Anneline Baerbock worned the West "to support the Ukrainian war otherwise Russia will attack the West": Slowly but surely Europe transforms into a committee to serve President Zelenskyy and his goals. Italian Prime Minister Giorgia Melony scored boost from the Pope support at the G-7 summit. The Council of Europa started its formal procedure of re-election of Ursula von der Leyen for a second term. Other candidates are from Greece, Portugal, Poland, Belgium and Denmark. Last time the selection lasted 3 days but now it could be much faster. ZDF Brussels correspondent Ulf Röller drew attention to the internal discrepancies inside the European Union.
NATO-members agreed to increase their military expenses up to 2% of their GDP. For Germany it means 900 billion euro.

Russian President Vladimir Putin started his visit to North Korea in the "form of friendly state visit" for the fist visit since 24 years. Aim is trade and security co-operation and possible military union of both countries.
Russia will get from North Korean large- caliber artillery shells and ballistic missiles both to be used in its war against Ukraine. 2,000 ballistic missiles were already delivered.
In return Russia will help to the North Korean advanced
nuclear program as it is a long-term ally to Moscow supporting Russian war on Ukraine:
9 months earlier- in 2023 both leaders met in a Russian far East military base. Afterwards -
in May 2023-North Korea launched successfully its own space satellite. It needs Russian food, fuel,foreign currency, nuclear and space technologies. Both countries are united in how to overcome U.N. & U.S. sanctions on them.
North Korea had already delivered 5 million artillery shells to Russia and 2,000 ballistic missiles.
After a red carpet,red roses & military parade a gala concert by military orchestra was given to the Aggressor and he visited the Liberation monument in Pyongyang.
NATO secretary general Jens Stoltenberg-already wearing spectacles- stated "this visit will escalate the war in Europe." White House security advisor John Kirby expressed "U.S. concern of this visit which will prolong the Ukrainian war."

The EU reached no deal on the EU top jobs following the rule "more publicity is a good publicity". Ursula von der Leyen kept her post as president of EU Commission and Antonio Costas became the new EU-Council president. The EU-foreign policy department is headed by a Lithuanian Karel Kalizs. The Socialist goals remained only futile ambitions. For NATO secretary general was appointed the former Dutch prime minister Mark Rutte to replace aging overburdened Jens Stoltenberg. Aged 65 he earned indignation by threatening China with economic blockade for helping Russia economy to warfare against Ukraine. He stated "It is not my job to appoint my successor". Mark Rutte promised "not to force Hungary to send Hungarian troops to fight in Ukraine" and not to spend Hungarian money on Ukrain:earlier Hungary strongly opposed Mark Rutte's appointment as a NATO-secretary general though he enjoys the support of both Germany and the USA-which are the biggest NATO-members. Rutte is expected to support Ukraine without angering Russia too much, more in sorrow than in anger!

On the second day of his visit to North Korea Russian President Vladimir Putin and North Korean President Kim Jon Un signed a treaty for strategic alliance. The other name is "mutual defense pact".
In a clumsy report Euronews didn't even mention the words "strategic alliance treaty" but the BBC did. North Korea leader Kim called "Russia a stanch ally and Putin dearest friend of the Korean people". Ukrainian foreign minister Dmitriy Kuleba said "both countries are highly isolated". South Korea said "Russian shouldn't cross the red line !" and summoned the Russian ambassador to Seoul to protest. It fired warning shots on North Korean troops across the common border.

China has already a strategic alliance treaty with Russia but don't want this to turn into a trilateral treaty. North Korea has already immense amount of ammunition on stock , it has a huge weapon industry nonetheless its weapon factories run on a full scale to help Putin in his war on Ukraine. Kim Jong Un said "the relations to Russia are even bigger than in Soviet times" despite Putin spent less than 24 hours in Pyongyang. Kim vowed "unlimited support of the Russian invasion in Ukraine"; he condemned "the U.S. imperialistic policy ". Putin thanked him and said "the signing of the treaty will boost both countries and will promote mutual aid in case of aggression and deepen military and industrial cooperation".
He badly needs for more ammunition to use against Ukraine and promised to North Korea military-technical support-a bad news for both U.S.A. and Ukraine but "Russia and North Korea showed that they are not world pariah". Putin demonstrated that he still can travel all over the world despite the international arrest warrant against him issued by the International Criminal Court. It is clear the alliance between the both countries will last long.

The strategic alliance treaty was not very much welcomed by China which strives a global dominance and does not like involvement in local wars nor in destruction on the Korean peninsula. The BBC commented that "with this strategic alliance treaty Russia aims not only war in Europe but also in Asia posing a real threat for the global security". Some Western leaders showed already their war fatigue.
Ukrainian foreign minister Dmitriy Kuleba explained the Ukrainian position in a 30 minutes BBC late-night talk show which I skipped though vehemently advertised after BBC-moderator Steven Sakure named Kuleba mistakenly "Prime Minister". South Korea summoned the Russian ambassador in Seoul to explain what it called "a pact of aggression between North Korea and Russia". South Korea fired also warning shots on North Korean troops over the common border "after North Korean soldiers made 3 incursions". It is expected North Korea to deliver 1.6 million artillery shells to Russia, said Washington Post.

After North Korea Russian President Vladimir Putin visited Vietnam to promise more cooperation ,education, science, technology ,trade and military support: he said "Russia assisted largely the Vietnam war against the U.S.A. After Vietnam won that war Russia helped the country rebuilding its economy by sending Russian engineers, doctors and other other qualified specialists to overcome the destruction the U.S. caused in the war".

Putin visited Vietnam last time in 2017. Russia is Vietnam's major supplier of oil and

weapons. It was decided to open a direct fly line between Moscow and Hanoi.
The U.S.A. criticized Vietnam for giving political platform to Putin while his war on Ukraine
still raging . He tries to escape from the isolation achieved by the international arrest warrant
issued by the International Criminal Court in The Hague. He promised liquefied natural gas
(LNG) exports to Vietnam and technical aid and exploration technologies for drilling in search
for domestic oil . Russia is the main provider to Vietnam of military equipment-80% of
Vietnam's arm imports come from Russia. The treaty provides mutual aid in case of war.
Putin seeks to expand Russian ties to Asia although several EU countries still continue to buy
cheap Russian gas- amounting to 8.3 billion euro-but got already banned to re-export it:
France, Belgium, Spain...Re-export over third countries means pass by the sanctions!
Vietnam hopes Russian oil exploration technologies will make the country less dependent on
oil imports by increasing its sovereignty.
Both countries signed multiple treaties for industrial,scientific,constructive,military etc...
cooperation. Nevertheless Vietnam remained neutral on the Russian-Ukrainian war. Putin said
"Russia has to rethink its tactical weapons doctrine" and "neither Korean nor Vietnamese troops
will be sent to fight in Ukraine". However he didn't exclude sending tactical nuclear weapons to
North Korea.
Ukraine by contrast started to recruit prisoners for its army: up till now 3,000 prisoners
were recruited to fight against Russia. "Russia must stop with its imperial policy!", stressed
Ukrainian president Zelenskyy angrily demanding again Patriot air defense rocket systems.

Ihor Terekhov, Mayor of the eastern Ukrainian city of Kharkiv complained of persistent Russian
air strikes on the city- just 20 in the month of June. In Kharkiv Ukraine experience shortage of
several hundreds soldier to fight against Russia but French far-right activist Jordan Bardella
declined sending French troops to Ukraine; French acting prime minister Gabriel Attal countered
him with the argument "the National Rally is not part of the French government, it is opposition!". Such a dispute!
Such a quarrel !

A court trial started in Munich against Hendrick XIII Prinz Reuss for his coup d'etat attempt
in Germany back in December 2022. The German police evaluated the international situation in
422 pages report! German interior minister Nancy Faeser was bluntly accused of "doing nothing"
and "not implementing AI for criminals' face recognition".Television showed her limping on 2 crutches. Currently
Germany hosts European football championship but this cannot help the
stagnating German economy: by contrast Russian economy is booming and thriving despite

the EU-sanctions: one of the latest are on Russian gas and the ban to Russian ships
to dock in EU-ports.
German industry minister Robert Habeck traveled in vain to China to polish souring
bilateral relations. China is the second best trade partner to Germany after the U.S.A.
There is much concern on cheap Chinese products; but while the EU imposed 38% toll
on cheap Chinese cars the U.S.A. blew the expansion by whole 100%! And in Germany
Malu Dreyer-Minister-President of Rheinland-Pfalz resigned "because of exhaustion".
Conference of German Minister-Presidents in Berlin led to compulsory real estate insurance.
The German Bundeswehr ordered at Rhein- Metal artillery munitions in the value of 8.5
billion euro till 2025 – to boost its own reserves and for Ukrainian help. Romania too
joint the cavalcade by donating one of its Patriot air-defense system to Ukraine.

The EU-Commission warned 7 member states for far excessive budget deficit 7-11% :

Romania, Slovakia, Poland,Italy, Malta, France,Hungary…while the EU-limit is 3% of the respective country's GDP. The EU claimed "more power to the center-right and less power to the center-left".

Hungary started its 6 months' Presidency of the European Union with the slogan "Make Europe great again!" The Hungarian Presidency means EU-support to Ukraine will become smaller and slower. Former U.S. President Donald Trump said:"The more money we give to Ukraine the more money Ukraine will demand from us!". German Chancellor Olaf Scholz said "Russia must not win this war and Ukraine must not lose it!". How? All in all Ukraine has only 20 F-16 pilots: currently trained in Denmark and The Netherlands. Afterwards we will witness new rocketing of fuel prices.
In the end of the month Russia lost a second precious radar system after an Ukrainian hit; Russia in turn bombed the city of Lviv in Western Ukraine by 25 missiles many of which intersepted by Ukrainian air defense systems. Russia targets mainly energy facilities.

UK-reform politician Nigel Farage said "Europe and NATO provoked Russia by expanding eastwards" and "he had predicted the war 10 years earlier". He faced strong criticism for echoing Vladimir Putin's justification of the war. He insisted on his arguments: "The sooner we take this stand the closer the end of the Ukrainian war will be". Farage has been Member of European Parliament since 2014. Labor criticized his stand and Kiiv protested: "The virus of Putinism is stronger than the covid-19 virus". Kyiv but not Zelenskyy! All this comes at the dawn of UK elections scheduled for 04.July 2024. Donkeys are known for their camouflage! UK Prime Minister Rishi Sunak-already wearing spectacles-condemned Farage's comments made to the BBC-Panorama: saying "Reform leader's comments 'play into Putin's hands" and "dangerous to Britain" while Labor described them as 'disgraceful' . "This kind of appeasement is a danger to the British security" "This comment only encourages Putin further in his aggression". With his Panorama remark Nigel Farage practically justified the Russian war on Ukraine! It looks like playing with fire.

Hungarian Prime Minister Victor Orban accused Ursula von der Leyen of "Hungaro-phobia: she was elected with Hungarian votes". He criticized also the EPP-leader Manfred Weber: "He has only one aim in his heart – to harm Hungary!" Hungary has always blocked any EU-help to Ukraine .

Russian missiles hits are said to have destroyed already half of the Ukrainian grid; Ukraine in turn destroyed 3 Russian oil refineries, boasting to "have intercepted 12 out of 16 Russian missiles fired". For the month of June alone Russia dropped 2,400 glide bombs on Ukrainian targets. Each side rigorously testing ability to continue the fire; half of Kharkiv-city is with out electricity, claimed the city's Mayor.
Already on the peace summit in Switzerland the Saudi Arabian foreign minister said "Ukraine must find a form of compromise! The Russian threat of tactical nuclear weapons resembles to a saber-rattle."
It is exactly one year since Wagner mercenary Chief Eugeny Prigozhin started his "March for Justice" on Moscow- a direct rebellion against Putin regime ending with amnesty. President Putin dismissed all allegations of ammunition shortage as "absolute lie". 2 months later Prigozhin's air craft was downed killing 10 people on board: all top Wagner officials. Earlier Prigozhin served 9 years in Russian prison. By December 2022 Wagner troops accounted 50,000 soldiers.

German CSU Parliamentary group leader Dobrindt(1970) proposed repatriation of all
Ukrainian refugees back to Western Ukraine, "which is safe enough!" 71% of the East-
Germans are against Ukrainian immigrants and against economic sanctions on Russia.
German economy is on place 24 world wide, said CDU-president Friedrich Merz in an
interview and added "The German budget is 1,000 billion euro-it leaves little space for
mis-management" . The wife of the Spanish prime minister Pedro Sanchez accused of
corruption .
In cricket Afghanistan beat Australia only to show that Afghans can practice sports too.
German Chancellor Olaf Scholz expressed concern over the upcoming elections in France:
The far right National Rally of populist Marine Le Pen high approving rate made it number one
in the French opinion poll- far ahead of the current President Macrone's party. France is the first
country in the world to grant the right of abortion in its Constitution.
Scholz will however continue his contacts to his friend Macrone regardless of the election result;
optimistically cautious but a bit nervous too! It is blunt pre- election campaign to help Macrone.

Both sides-Russia and Ukraine rigorously testing bilateral ability to continue the war race this
time by direct hit on the Russian annexed Sevastopol. Oil and gas re-export pass by over third countries the
sanctions imposed on Russian commodities.
The EU foreign affairs council in Luxemburg enforced new sanctions on Russia,targetting 61
companies and 20 Russian ships, forbidden to dock in European ports. According to the IMF
German economy grows 0.2%, while the U.S.A. 2.4% and China 4.6%. Chancellor Scholz was
heavily criticized for failing to boost German economy. Former German Chancellor
Gerhardt Schröder-also SPD-became manager and advisor in an unnamed Russian oil
company earning 10,000 euro monthly.

Kremlin accused the U.S.A. for delivering American missiles to Ukraine-6 of them hit the
Crimean city of Sevastopol. Russian spokesman Dmitri Peskov threatened the U.S.A. with "consequences" but
didn't elaborate. A play with the fire ! The U.S. Ambassador in Moscow was
forced to give explanation to the Russian MID.

9 NATO member states started military exercises in the Baltic area :
for Sweden it is for the first time.
Julian Assange -aged 52 - released from London prison Belmarsh where he spent 1,901 days
and re-united with his wife Stella Assange and his 2 sons. Australia Prime minister Anthony
Albanese expected him on a Sidney air port and than pardoned him. He received also the Nobel
price for journalism
Former U.S. vice-president Mike Pense tweeted protest against his release; however a court trial
in the U.S.A. would release in public all Assange Wikileak information he had gathered secretely.

Japanese Emperor Naruhito and Empress Masako started 3 days state visit to London for talks
with British King Charles III:on trade, education and military co-operation.
He had studied water engineering at Oxford University. The talks of both close
friends will comprise topics of common interests and common threats they are exposed to,
incl.on how to steal publically.
He even didn't visit 10,Downing street.

Massive LGBT parade in Maidan square in Ukrainian Capital Kyiv; we have to question
the answers. Ukraine started negotiations for EU-membership !

Ukrainian special forces hit and destroyed Russian radar communication station-the newest one which Russia possesses .
High political volatility in NATO connected with Dutch Mark Rutte's appointment as a NATO secretary General which comes into effect July 2024. Jens Stoltenberg left NATO in good hands.
Both Ukraine and Moldova started talks with the EU for their EU membership. The talks may take a decade; all officials interviewed spoke fluently exuberant Russian-just like me.
Serbia signed an agreement with the EU for tightened border control and against irregular migration.

Visiting the Donetsk region President Zelenskyy discovered massive abuse of duties by local Ukrainian officials and administrators (BBC). Many of them even absent for 6-7 months in key areas. In 24 hours Russia shelled 25 Ukrainian villages. "If North Korea sends troops against Ukraine "they will simply convert to cannon fodder in an illegal war", said General-Major Pat Ryder, U.S. defense official.
The ZDF tv showed again German interior minister Nancy Faeser on crutches; celebrated for her strong anti-immigrants attitude and policy.Her new immigration bill came into effect from now on wards: the naturalization period was reduced from 8 to 5 years, the repatriation of foreigners became easier.

A court trial started in Russia against Evan Gershkovich on espionage charges. Officially he worked for the Wall Street journal, unofficially for the CIA. The Time magazine named him "one of the 100 most influential people in the world". Born 1991 in the U.S.A. in a Family of Jewish emigrants from Russia.

The EU-Commission signed a "10 years security pledge" for long-term military help with Ukrainian President Volodymyr Zelenskyy signing ceremonially in Brussels. He signed also bilateral agreements with both Estonia and Lithuania. The pledge provides a German military training in Sachsen-Anhalt where up till now 22,000 Ukrainian soldiers have already been trained esp. in tank skills. The EU released the first package of military support to Ukraine of 1.4 billion euro financed from the frozen Russian assets abroad. Zelenskyy thanked but insisted "to move faster".
Estonian Minister-President Kaja Kallas met in Brussels with outgoing NATO
Secretary General Jens Stoltenberg and insisted on Ukrainian membership into NATO.
New peace talks with Russia are not scheduled yet.

British opposition pledged UK revival of its relations with the EU, said Mike Galsworthy, spokesman of the "European movement-UK" because we have not the same hostility to the EU as the Conservatives.

Hungarian President Victor Orban visited his French counterpart Emanuel Macron for coordination while German Chancellor Olaf Scholz defended the current EU 3 top jobs allocation. Italian Prime minister Giorgia Melony remained disappointed and criticized sharply the current EU-practice; she felt herself skipped,so angry that she refused to speak to anyone in Brussels to express her dissatisfaction with he decision! No position to her despite her sweeping 53%-win of votes in the EU-elelctions. Both Italy and Hungary don't support the EU-nominations of the trio.

Despite South Korean protests North Korea sent 10,000 military personal "to help repairing the hit Russian infrastructure". Additional 10,000 newly recruited Russian troops were sent to the front lines. Russia accused South Korea of sending military-technical goods and war supply to Ukraine.

In a pre-election speech Republican candidate Donald Trump said "I will achieve peace between Russia and Ukraine the very first day I am elected as a President of the U.S.A."
German FDP minister signed an agreement with China "for mutual electronic data exchange"; Chancellor Olaf Scholz criticized him sharply.

G-7 education ministers met together to discuss improvement. Italy came out with a concrete detailed plan how to improve current Ukrainian education level.

All of the sudden President Zelenskyy launched a new peace plan for ending the war with Russia; the timing was carefully chosen to coincide with the weekend to avoid comments and critics. No details of The Plan : he urged instead NATO for the weaponry deliveries as promised! He was been "thinking"and "preparing" the "comprehensive" plan. The announce was made at Slovenian President Natasha Pirc Musar visit to Kyiv during the week end. The details will be discussed on
a second peace conference later this year. Zelenskyy insisted on the EU weaponry deliveries to Ukraine as promised earlier. On the AfD week end summit Alice Weidel put it bluntly:"Ukraine does not belong to Europe!"

Russia re-started the production of intermediate range missiles previously abandoned in 1988. The news was announced by Vladimir Putin at the National security council meeting. The Russian troops keep advancing all over the front line, killing many civilians. In return Ukraine launched 6 missiles to the Kursk region across the border and destroyed several plants there.

In the U.S. presidential debate even Democrat vice-president admitted "poor presentation of Joe Biden" in the race against Donald Trump! Even the Democrats consider Biden as "weak"!
Trump vowed "to kick crooked Joe Biden out of the White House".

Panama paper scandal, starting in 2016: 11,000,000 papers leaked on off shore financial secretes of politicians and other leading public figures who concealed their wealth both machinations and money laundering.

On his X-site Ukrainian President Volodymyr Zelenskyy claimed "800 Russian guided bombs on Ukraine in the last week".

JULY 2024

Ukrainian tourists attacked massively the Black Sea coast and occupied the expensive hotels there. Speaking Russian to each other and not their "native" Ukrainian language.

Hungarian populist PM Victor Orban started his rotating presidency on the European Parliament for 6 months. He vowed to fight for "peace, order and development while the Brussels elite brought war, migration and stagnation". Orban opposes heavily the Ukrainian candidacy to the EU and vowed to block it. Under his presidency Austria, Hungary and Czechia formed in Vienna a far right block in the European Parliament under the name "Patriots for Europe"-alliance, waiting for Portugal and 3 further EU-members to join.

The French parliamentary election ended with victory of the far right National Rally of Marine Le Pen winning 33% while Emanuel Macron's party is beaten to the 3rd place.
Definitive results after the second round of the elections due on 07th of July 2024.
Macron decided to stay in independently of the second round out comes. His counter part Jordan Bardella is aged 28 years. Melenchon and Macron withdrew their candidacy for the second round "at the door steps to power".

L'Assamblemente Nationale

Outgoing Dutch Prime Minister Mark Rutte urged the nation "to help Ukraine in these hard times"; he dubbed Putin's peace plan as "absolute crazy" : exactly the tone Ukraine likes to hear.
For the UK elections on the 4th of July ca. 300,000 Brits,- mostly retired- failed to register because they live abroad, mostly in Southern Spain.
The German Marshal Funds changed its address to:
1744, R St NW, Washington D.C., United States of America, tel. +1 202-745-3950/ gmfpress@gmfus.org
U.S. president Joe Biden met his counterparts of the NATO governments members to a summit in Washington D.C.

By rallying Ukrainians and, seemingly against all odds, delivering a searing rebuke to Putin, Zelenskyy has done more to enable peace than most Nobel Peace Prize laureates have done in their careers. That's why he is among the 2023 Nobel peace price candidates.
David Lami – UK Foreign minister sttarted an EU tour of 3 countries – Germany,Sweden and Poland to agitate against the war in Ukraine.He visited also the Ukrainian Black Sea port of Odessa to gain personal impression . The Indian Prime Minister Narandra Modi visited Moscow for talks on cooperation and bilateral trade between India and Russia; he does not support the Ukrainian

cause. His visit helps President Putin's international image and brings him out of his international
isolation. In his 5-day visit to Russia Modi visited the nuclear technologies museum to gain personal
impressions of them.
 Kiiv was attacked by 40 Russian rockets: 30 of them were downed, boated Kiiv's Mayor
Vitaly Klichko, former box champion. The United States donated furter $2 billion military aid to Poland. US President
Joe Biden delivered poor presentation in a tv debate with the presidentional candidate Donald Trump. It is believed
Biden suffers from the mental disease of Parkinson of slow motions and slow wirr-warr speech.
The Ukrainian President Volodimir Zelenskyy attended the NATO member summit in Washington to
mark the 75th anniversary of the military coalition. NATO promised long-term military aid to
Ukraine despite its poor military presentation on the battle field against Russia. Donald Trump expressed his deep
sympathy to Russia and to his Russian friend Vl. Putin. At the NATO summit its Secretary General Jens Stoltenberg
was awarded with the Liberty Order for his stanch long-term duty
and service to NATO; this is the highest U.S. award: "Russia will not stop at Ukraine with its conquery
ambitions but Ukraine can stop Russia!", he stressed in his speech. It was decided 5 more "Patriot" rocket launchers
to Ukraine; "we will support Ukraine as long as it takes independent of the price!",
Joe Biden stated in a feeble. The U.S. started its delivery of 15 F-16 fighter jets but Ukraine has no airfields where
they can land, so they stay in hangars. "More "Patriots", more MARSH missiles fore Ukraine", demanded Zelenskyy
again and again. It became true the children hospital in Kharkiv was
hit by Ukrainian rocket and not by Russian one as it was chanted again & again. The European Union
started massive military drill 40 km away of the Russian city of Kaliningrad which was a sheer provocation. Ukraine
managed to hit the electric station in the Russian city of Rostov. With 35,000
soldiers the German Bundeswehr cannot not send troops to Ukraine; more over there is a bird flue epidemy in
Germany. The right German AfD-party managed to establish right-wing party in the European Parliament.
It is clear Ukraine is already loosing the war with an army of 33,000 soldiers-thus smaller than the
German army of 35,000 soldiers. "Nevertheless Ukraine will be irreversibly EU & NATO member ",
stated NATO Secretary General Jens Stoltenberg. It is said that "Tomahawk" missiles & SM-6 stationed in Wiesbaden
and elswhere in Germany are serious deterrent to the Russians. Russian deputy Foreign Minister Sergey Yavkin
put bluntly his indignation , saying "We'll give proper military reply to this pogrom"; And really soon began joint
China – Belarus military exercises , giving properly a chance to German Interior minister Nancy Faser to speak
and agitate bluntly against China. U.S.
president Joe Biden who mixes the name s of Vl. Zelenskyy and Vl. Putin – an open outlet of his clear mental disease
of Parkinson spoke blunt non-senses.

The assassination attempt on German Rhein- Metal chief Pappe for his weapon delivery to Ukraine was foiled;
it was for his weapon deliveries to Ukraine. With 2,500 km range his High-Mars missiles can hit targets deep
inside Russia-bot civilian targets and military spots. German Foreign minister Anneline Baerbock took no stand to
assassination attempt and said nothing. By contrast the Pentagon enjoyed the saga of 1,200-1,500 losses of Russian
soldiers on a weekly base. "Russia intensifies its attacks on Ukrainian targets to provoke NATO", the Pentagon
commented bluntly while Hollywood celebrates its 101st anniversary of its foundation. Again the Pentagon estimated
the Russian losses of 1,200-
1,500 soldiers losses on a weekly base. "NATO will survive only by Russian defeat!", the Pentagon
commented and "NATO will be different to Ukraine under the presidency of Republican Donald
Trump" while Russia increased the emigrants' flood to Finland to destabilize it. U.S. President
Joe Biden criticized him sharply for his ambitions towards the White House. Yet again at a
Republican rally in in Milwakee an assassination attempt was made on candidate Trump:
he survived with a minor injury of his right ear.
The attempt increased rigorously his popularity among middle-rank
Americans to be seen on www. Realdonaldtrump.com. The attempt was impossible without

Democratic security breach. The assassin was killed on the top of a roof by snipers. "There is no place for such kind of violence in the U.S.A.!", President Biden stated hypocritically. He was diagnosed with Covid-19 and disappeared from the political horizon after isolation in Delaware. Kremlin spokesman Dmitryy Peskov commented lapidarily " Biden must improve the American internal security instead sending weapons to Ukraine designed to kill Russian lives."
President candidate Trump is considered as social politician: he promised to reduce the pension age down to 63 years and many other social contributions. His presidential campaign is financed by Microsoft owner Elon Musk and Bill Hatman-another Republican sympathizer.
Ukrainian President Volodimir Zelenskyy visited Ireland for talks with Irish prime minister Simon Harris after rebuff from the Democrat conference in Salt Lake City.He demanded from him demining the mining fields in Ukraine and help to the Ukrainian cyber security. At the NATO conference in Wiesbaden, Germany, Zelenskyy demanded 25 more "Patriot" multiple rocket launchers but his demand was rejected.

Roberta Metsola became the new President of the European Parliament for the coming 2.5 years. The EU-deputies get 8,800 euro monthly salary plus 4,900 euro grant-in-aid plus 350 euro daily day-to-day money : thus altogether 17,000 euro monthly while the Children money in Germany is only 285 euro.
German conservative politician Ursula von der Leyen-CDU-was re-elected as President of the European Commission with 401 votes "for": 56% of the vote because the deputates united against the right front in the EU-Parliament- the party of the Italian president Georgia Meloni and French Marine le Pen and German AfD.

At the Republican
Convent in Milwakee Hungarian President Victor Orban put bluntly:"We buried already $200 in Ukraine; what we have to achieve there ?!". The German military budget dropped down to 1.25 billion euro yearly. The German overall budget was fixed to 480 billion euro, 1.85 euro for defence. The German foreign minister Anneline Baerbock was not present at its discussion in the Bundesttag: she was on a visit to Africa ! Such importance ! The German magazine "Compact"with 40,000 circulation was forbidden.

The Council of Europe criticized sharply the Hungarian President Victor Orban for his peace efforts: as a rotating EU-president he visited in the middle of the summer he visited Kyyv for talks with Volodimir Zelenskyy. Afterwards he met with the Russian President Vladimir Putin in Moscow and China President Xi Jin Pin in Peking .
No peace chance at all : Ukrainian tourists boosted their massive Black Sea coast attacks occupying many expensive hotels there, speaking fluent Russian to each other thus not their "native" Ukrainian language.
A new slogan was coined :"Trump trades": Presidential candidate Donald Trump phoned up President Zelenskyy to discuss peace talks. His proposal was rejected. Instead peace talks Ukraine hit by drones the Russian airfield of Milerovo and destroyed it; a massive attack on Russian city Rostov-na-Don followed. President Zelenskyy phoned up German Chancellor Olaf Scholz and displayed to him "his"peace plan. In vain: Germany said nothing. Euronews concluded "Ukraine is losing the war." On 22.of July 2024 U.S. President Joe Biden pulled out candidacy for president in the next mandate and appointed his vic-president Camela Harris as a new Democrat candidat in the U.S. November election. Donald Trump dubbed him "the worst president in U.S. history". Biden's pull-out from the presidential race was the most difficult decision in his life. And Putin's ? Putin obviously takes decisions easier than he does.

German foreign minister Anneline Baerbock defended the U.S. rocket dislocation in Germany "for eventual hit on Russian targets deep inside the country" and greeted the holiday camps for Ukrainian children in the Carpaten mountains. She praised openly the Bitcoin: "If Germany will not introduce the bitcoin China will and thus will over speed us", she admonished. She withdrew her candidacy for the German Chancellor election rally against Olaf Scholz (SPD) and Friedrich Merz (CDU). Neither her education nor "business" experience allow her to make such daring avanture proposals. Olaf Scholz by contrast was earlier German finance minister.

Ukrainian foreign minister Dmitryy Kuleba visited secretly China for talks with his Chinese colleague Wang I to solicitate behind the back of Moscow. His proposals amounted to "dirty deals' but Kuleba was satisfied "of no Chinese weapons to Russia". Russian rockets hit a private Ukrainian park in the city of Ismail. U.N. Secretary Joseph Borrel concluded "by the U.S. presidential election in November the Ukrainian electric grid will be completely destroyed by Russian fire". German Chancellor Olaf Scholz flew for 3 weeks holiday.

Mihailo Podolyak-a frantic fanatic advisor of president Zelenskyy-refused any peace talks with Russia "because this will be a contract of the devil", said Associated Press:"despite the fact that 55% of all Ukrainians both in Ukraine and abroad are ready for peace". Spokesman Dmitryy Peskow confirmed Kremlin readiness for peace talks.

The 1st tranch of 1.5 billion euro of frozen Russian assets in Europe was sent to Ukraine. "The aim is not Ukrainian war victory anymore but how to avoid Ukrainian defeat", Joseph Borrel repeated. Russian president Vladimir Putin warned "for a 2nd cold war". He denounced the proliferation of Western medium range nuclear missiles in Europe. The will be placed by the West by 2026: Tomahawk, SM-6 and Taifun. The need 10 minutes time to reach Russian targets deep inside Russia while the Russian rockets need only one minute to hit Kharkiv from the Russian city of Belgorod.

Italian President Georgia Meloni too visited China for 5 days to discuss bilateral trade and relations and was shown modern Chinese factories and plants Dmitryy Kuleba by contrast has nothing offer or show to his Chinese counter part Wang I.

Ukraine sent 3,000 internal prisoners and other criminals to fight on the front and to replenish the thinning Ukrainian army which use to mourn 30,000 deads from the war begin. 42,000 more prisoners from all Ukrainian jails are waiting to join the army. So it looks Ukraine is one single huge state prison ?? President Zelenskyy inspected Ukrainian army units to boost moral but in vain. Later on he visited a military hospital in Rodne and dispenced orders to wounded Ukrainian soldiers. German defence minister Boris Pistorius flew to Hawai for vacation. He said "Germany has to introduce the Bitcoin. If we don't introduce it, China will !"Quite an expert !

Massive protests against U.S. missiles dislocation in Germany against Russian threat: the first Nato country to protest against this escalation of war.

AUGUST 2024 – 900 DAYS OF WAR

Associated Press reported for the first NATO fighter jets delivery to Ukraine as it follows:
10 from Denmark
24 from The Netherlands
6   from Norway
40 altogether
It seems rather futile because Ukraine has no air fields where the lavish donation can land !
Massive Ukrainian exchange of the prisoners of war with Russia with Turkey as mediator.
Ukrainian tourists massively visit the Olympic games to inspire
Ukrainian sportsmen and the Ukrainian audience.

Massive electricity black outs in whole Ukraine since March.
Ukrainian fire sank the Russian U-boot "Rostov-na-Don"in the Russian port of
Sevastopol together with 4 Russian air defense stations in Crimea and an oil refinery there.
Full scale attacks with 75 Ukrainian drones on Russian targets. Belgorod, Rostov-na-Don and Krasnodar regions are beloved targets for Ukrainian attacks.
500 Russian spies expelled from the European Union since the begin of 2024. Russia did not comment. The European Central Bank will decrease its leading interest with 0.25% by September 2024. Massive contradiction in Germany between Chancellor Olaf Scholz and his finance minister Christian Lindner. Russia did not comment again. The Mayor of the Japanese city of Hiroshima commemorated the 79th anniversary of the American atomic bomb in World war two and urged Ukraine into peace.

Windows covered with wooden planks in the Ukrainian city of Kharkiv-20 km from the Russian border.
Ukrainian infantry flooded the Russian regions across the border and penitrated 25 km deep into Russian territory bombarding barbarically the Russian Atomic power plant of Kursk and the Russian gas pipe line to Europe. Russian President Vladimir Putin named this
"a provocation". He ordered an emergency situation in the Kursk region and dispensed ca. 100 euro to the Russian civilians hit.
 Ukrainian president Volodimir Zelensky kept silence for 8 days. It seems
a deep controversion between Zelenskyy and his advisor Mihailo Podolyak who looks like
a frentic fanatic chauvinist like many other Ukrainian political and military leaders. The U.S. said "the attack was not coordinated beforehand with any U.S. officials".

The bitter fights continued with Russian tanks hit already on the transport trucks.
"Every mean is legal & right destroy Russia, which is obviously the aim. The bigger the pressure on Russia the sooner the peace", Ukrainian president Zelenskyy said despite he rejected several

peace talks proposals from the international community. However Zelenskyy insisted "Russia black mils the world!"

The Ukrainian troops advanced to 60 km
from the Atomic power plant of Kursk and 500 km from the Russian Capital Moscow.
The European Union concluded "Ukraine has the right to defend itself from Russian attacks".
Poland increased its defense budget to 4% of its GDP: the biggest in Europe and the biggest military aid donor to Ukraine. The EU aid to Ukraine amounted to 108 billion euro- for what? For which gain?!
All these comments inspired further Ukrainian attacks on Russian soil: they hit a Russian military convoy and burnt it alive with the Russian soldiers inside. A Russian military airfield and an ammunition depot . Altogether 82 Russian villages and towns in the Kursk region surrendered to the Ukrainian Army. Russian soldiers surrender massively and willingly into Ukrainian prisonership & custody. A real hot summer ! The Ukrainian army started to build up a puffer zone around the encursion of Kursk to defend itself from eventual Russian counter attacks across the common border with Russia

The Covid-19 epidemy spread out all over Europe and even in the international Olympic games in Paris – it contaminated the European population by 20% even in the middle of the summer.
Even the American President Joe Biden was hospitalized for Covid-19 infection !
An arson set afire the Atomic power plant in Zaporizhia- both sides accused each other for the brand. Vl. Zelenskyy repeated his beloved sentence "Russia blackmails the World!"

Ukrainian troops hit & destroyed a bridge near Kursk to hamper Russian military deliveries to the front line and succeeded a lot with this strategy. Now Ukrainian army operates entirely on Russian soil. It continues to attack Russian infrastructure and managed to destroy a second strategic bridge
to cut off Russian military supplies to the front line and set afire an important Russian military fuel depot.
No single word from the Ukrainian President Volodymyr Zelenskyy- obviously the ultra right chauvinists of Mihailo Podlyak (which means vile mean) have taken command of the Ukrainian army with all the consequency to follow.
Ukraine started building a puffer zone around Kursk to counter eventual Russian counter attacks.
Full political chaos in Germany; it decreased its help to Ukraine from 7.5 billion euro down to 4 billion euro for the year 2024.I don't flung into details but Germany decreased its supply of spare parts and accessories for the Ukrainian tanks now in advance towards Russia.

The U.S. President Joe Biden nominated officially and formally his vice-president Camela Harris-former prosecutor- as a Democrat candidate for the presidential election in November.
In a long long he praised his staggering achievements in his boring life career taedium vitae.

After hitting a Russian amunnition depot and a fuel store Ukrainian army managed to destroy a third Russian bridge which disrupts the military supply to the Russian army. Ukraine displayed further superiority on the battle field. Now it occupies 700 square km Russian territory in the Kursk region. President Zelenskyy praised his troops and thanked them for changing the dynamic of war. German Chancellor Olaf Scholz decided to cut half of the German support for Ukraine for the year 2025. Dutch tv providers cut at will Euronews programs to broadcast ads instead news.

Ukrainian forces continued their advance on Russian soil taking new 1,200 square km.
11 from 45 Ukrainian drones hit Russian Capital Moscow – where they got so much fire
power from ??! At the same time Russian forces advanced in South-East Ukraine; very
wicked complicated situation. Unlike ailing U.S. President Joe Biden the Russian President
Vladimir Putin was shown exuberant and vivid stepping down briskly his air craft stair case:
demonstrating Russian courage and enthusiasm against visible cranky American President Joe
Biden who negotiated with the Democratic Party to keep his post till November 2024 when new
American elections will take place despite the encouraging support of his Democratic colleague
Barack Obama – former U.S. President in decline. Wait and see in November 2024.

A false alarm was howled with roar in the German air base Geilenkirchen near Aachen.
The Germans blamed futile the Russians for an ostensible drone attack at the airbase; a
witch hunt which turned out as a false later on. At the same time the Indian President Narandra
Modi visited unhindered Kiiv and hugged the Ukrainian President Zelensky for the cameras.
Officially India is neutral in the conflict. Modi urged Zelenskyy to peace talks with Russia -
something which China did already two months earlier. No Ukrainian reaction was reported
which closes up to rejection of the proposal. President Zelenskyy marked 33 years of Ukrainian independence:
"Now buffer zone!",he vowed.

Russia attacked again massively Ukrainian energy infrastructure
and destroyed many electricity facilities; Kiiv remained in darkness.

3rd day in row of heavy Russian bombardment. A rocket hit a hotel in Pokrovsk
President Zelenskyy praised the Ukrainian counter attack to Kursk as"essential for the
forthcoming peace talks with Russia: we are open for dialog but only in the position of the stronger
party". The fights continue only 30 km away from the atomic power plant of Kursk. The Ukrainian Army bombarded
it but denied to have done. The scars are distinctly shown. The IAEA Grossi
visited the plant and warned "it is not military objected and should not have been bombarded.
The atomic reactors in Kursk are similar to the Chernobil reactor which exploded 1986.
Russia claimed to have killed 5,000 Ukrainian soldiers in the battles around the reactors.

British Pime minister Keir Starmer visited Germany and discussed the war in Ukraine with the
German President Steimeyer. No concrete results were reported.
Actually Steinmeyer was not present-he flew to Paris for the Paraolympic games. The talks were
led in fact with the German Chancellor Olaf Scholz Full political chaos in both
Germany and France. President Zelenskyy sent his peace plan to the U.S.A. for approval.
Cyprus stopped the in-take of Syrian emigrants for 14 months.
The EU-foreign ministers met together in Brussels-thus not in Hungarian Capital Budapest-
in sign of protest to the Hungary foreign policy inside the EU and beyond. No concrete results
reported.

***The North-Stream pipe-line Ukrainian saboteur managed to escape back to Ukraine
over the German - Polish border. (CNN) In a televised interview the German
Chancellor Olaf Scholz promised a tough fundamental investigation of the Ukrainian
scheme and perfection of its sabotage role.***
Ukraine's President Zelensky said " Russia incursion is part of my victory plan" which
he intends to show to Joe Biden.

A Russian rocket hit a chemical plant in the town of Soumi: a sulphuric and Nitrogenium clouds covered the sky as result. Contradicting reports on the battles in Pokrov and Konstantinevka.
NATO Secretary General Jens Stoltenberg "permitted Ukraine to hit objects deep inside Russia", which actually unleashed the full-scale war in the region.

SEPTEMBER 2024

Germany will introduce the Bit coin : "If we don't introduce it China will overspeed us!"
Serbian president Alexander Vuçiç denied to have maintained close relations with Russian President Vladimir Putin. He insisted to have not spoken to Putin since 2022. Serbia has not joint the EU-embargo on Russia and did not condemned the war there.

Ukrainian tourists have massively visit the Olympic games in Paris earlier in July 2024 to applaud & inspire their sportsmen. The massive electricity black outs in their native Ukraine date back to March 2024.

The European Central Bank decreased the leading interest by 0.25%.
Russia bombarded massively Ukrainian Capital Kyiv using ballistic missiles
the other side of the war is mirrored by www_medusa_com obviously sponsored by former oil oligarch Mikhail Khodorkovsky who served his long times in Russian prisons-with myopic glasses and with the slogan "Make Kremlin sad!". Kremlin keeps the eternal rests of former Soviet leader Vladimir Lenin in a mausoleum in the center of Moscow.

In the German elections in Thüringen AfD came to 32% of the vote, the ruling CDU to
bitter 23% only. The Greens made only 5% with 2 chairs in the State Parliament only. In Saxony the CDU made it first, the AfD- second. AfD- Massive part of the medal . "Bitter election hang-over",admitted German Chancellor Olaf Scholz.
Massive political and party quarrel all over Germany with concern of the AfD success.
Massive propaganda against the winner AfD. AfD leader Björn Höcke named his victory "historic". According to the AfD 200,000 young Germans emigrate abroad annually in a search for a better life there.
German Chancellor Olaf Scholz appealed "not to forge any coalition with AfD"! Which is a huge contradiction to the election results ! He prepares to rule over Germany till October 2025! Than to candidate for German Chancellor again ! The main election losers are SPD, FDP & the Greens with their foreign minister Anneline Baerbock.
CDU claimed "election fraud because of computer failure" and demanded new election excluding any co-operation with the clear election winner AfD. So much also Polish media.
The AfD calls bluntly for a stop of German military aid to Ukraine and to settle the conflict by by diplomatic negotiations and not by weapon deliveries to Ukraine.
The Thüringer CDU exempts any talks with AfD and forged alliance with BSW & SPD.

There are over 200,000 rejected emigrants and asylum seekers in Germany with prison capacity for only 8,000 of them (BBC).

Russian President Vladimir Putin traveled unhindered into Mongolia for talks with the leadership
there despite the international arrest warrant against him. A colorful military ceremony was given to Putin when
he touched down into Mongolian Capital Ulaan Bataar. Ukraine protested but futile !
Putin intends to build a gas pipe line to China over Mongolian territory

Dutch Prime minister Dick Schoof visited Ukraine and promised a 200,000,000 euro military aid against Russia
while Russian President Vladimir Putin promised "safe bomb shelters for Russian school children attacked by
Ukrainian bombardments on the Kursk region". The Dutch schools
banned schoolchildren to bring phones into the class rooms. Dutch officials accused Germany of
polluting the waters of their common river of Rhine.

Russia continued its Belgorod & Bryansk bombardments without achieving any further land gains.
However television showed Ukrainian bakery selling freely sweets and candies.

2 Russian ballistic missiles hit the Ukrainian military base in Poltawa and killed 49 soldiers there.
200 more were wounded. A military school there was also hit and destroyed. High ranking
Ukrainian military and politician Oleksandr Litvinenko asked again the West for more long
range missiles in a television speech to the Ukrainian people.
125 blood conserves were dispensed to medicate the wounded Ukrainian soldiers. It became
known that the Ukrainian air defense systems failed to recognize timely the Russian rocket and
this was the reason for the high dead toll. Poltawa is in the middle of the high way from Kharkiv
to the Capital Kyiv.
Russian foreign minister Sergey Lavrov wisely concluded "The West needs Ukraine only to hurt
Russia and Ukraine has manifested clearly its incapacity to reach reasonable peace with Russia". Which is actually
true also in my eyes.

Both the German TV-channel ZDF and the German magazine "Der Spiegel" accused and
argumented that Ukrainian saboteur Volodymyr S. blasted the gas pipe line "North Stream".
The German state prosecutor issued an arrest warrant for him; nevertheless he managed to
travel on a diplomatic passport unimpeded and escaped into his native Ukraine. His sabotage
action occurred on 28th May 2024, so "Der Spiegel" which in translation means "Mirror".

Ukrainian foreign minister Dmitryy Kuleba resigned after 3.5 years of service. Probably to get
appointed as an ambassador in Brussels .President Zelenskyy congratulated him for his decision
as "Cabinet restructure". Obvious quarrel inside the Party. His advisor Mihailo Podolyak is
hysteric fanatic & lunatic. 6 other ministers replaced too as a whim.

Germany re-armed with U.S.-Israeli supersonic missiles IRIS-T SLM to defend its territory from
Russian rockets and drones; it is 3 times faster than the speed of sound . Chancellor Olaf Scholz introduced and
advocated the change. Germany has already delivered 4 such systems to Ukraine.
German onion Olympiad-the biggest onion weighted 2 kg.

The U.S.A. accused officially Russia of cybernetic crimes and intention to influence the U.S.
presidential election in November 2024 by hacker attacks. (ARD)

In a televised speech Russian President Vladimir Putin called "the Ukrainian incursion of
Kursk a failure with the aim to force Russian to transfer troops from the Donetsk region and to
hinder the liberation of Donbass".

He will use China,India and Brazil as mediators because "Ukraine holds no direct peace talks with Russia". He also praised Kamala Harris for her presidential candidate campaign: "She simply laughs so distinctively,so hearty that it is impossible to reject her! If all is fine with her than why should we obstruct her ?! Current U.S. President Mr. Biden supports her, why we should support her too ?!"
Obviously Putin's speech was an essential part of his peace mission.
Further on Putin said " The West aims to make us nervous, irritates us, provokes us , scandalize us persistently, makes us to transfer troops from one region to another in order to stop our advance. The defense of our territory is holly duty of our sacred Army!"
Ukrainian president Volodymyr Zelenskyy took no stand to Putin's speech but asserted "Ukraine cannot carry out new elections under the current martial law."He stated "80% of the Ukrainian territory is occupied by the Russian army ". He had partly shaven his head in a Punk hair fashion and had bred his beard long.

Ukrainian Defense Contact Group deliberated in the U.S. base in Ramstein near Frankfurt am Main, Ukrainian President Zelenskyy met with U.S. defense secretary Lloyd Austin and German Chancellor Olaf Scholz. Germany promised financial help, Great Britain – weapons but U.S.A remained reluctant to deliver long-range missiles to Ukraine because it will not get directly involved in the conflict with Russia but promised further $225 mn to bury in Ukraine, Germany promised 12 panzer Gauwitsers type 2000. Vl. Zelenskyy refused to speak to the cameras. It became clear the German Bundeswehr uses 7.62 mm patrons – the same caliber as the Russian Kalashnikows. A Russian superiority yet again ?
However Zelenskyy thanked for "the Italian peace formula" and demanded again Western permit to bombard Russian airfields deep inside Russia. For the moment Russia hit and partly destroyed the Eastern town of Pavlohrad: 3 children among the victims. He claimed "Russia set afire deliberately wild fires in the Ukrainian border areas"- first the grasses and than the ajar forests on Ukrainian soil. Currently Ukraine keeps up with the Joneses ass. One day after his Brussels visit Zelenskyy landed in Italy for furter talks with Italian officials.
.
Hungarian Prime minister Victor Orban criticized sharply the EU with the words "Migration has a corrosive effect on the whole of Europe and its entire legislation". He leads currently the rotating EU-presidency till 2025.Vitriolic EU-quarrels. The EU rushed to dub him "a Nationalist". He issued his statement at an EU conference in Italy but all ears were deaf deafened as talks in the wind. His practical decision was to load emigrants on busses to EU-head quarters in Brussels. Orban meant "emigrants will tear appart the EU.

However Zelenskyy thanked for "the Italian peace formula" and demanded again Western permit to bombard Russian airfields deep inside Russia. For the moment Russia hit and partly destroyed the Eastern town of Pavlohrad: 3 children among the victims. He claimed "Russia set afire deliberately wild fires in the Ukrainian border areas- first the grasses and than the ajusted forrests. Zelenskyy added "Ukraine has no choice but to fight & defend itself.

An U.S. court ruled the verdict on Donald Trump will be announced after the presidential election in November 2024.
Iran delivered short-range missiles and Shahet-drones to Russia despite the warning of Washington not to do so;the precise number of the missiles was not announced. The 2 U.S. officials confirmed the delivery but preferred to remain anonymous.

The Russian forces liberated the town of Kalinove- 25 km South-East from Pokrowsk. Only than the aim of the Ukrainian counter- attack became clear- to create a buffer zone on Russian soil. That's why Ukraine rejects the Russian peace proposal – on & on & on & on …

A meager anti-Russia demo took place in the Czech capital Prague: Prague pronounced as the Dutch Capital The Hague; the 100 demonstrators demanded more international help to Ukraine. Czech defense minister said the Czech republic has already donated 259 million euro worth of military hard ware to Ukraine as tanks & ammunition.
The Ukrainians don't like the euro as a currency and prefer U.S. dollars instead. Which is my personal observation too: Germany has already accepted,receipted and welcomed 1,000,000 Ukrainian refugees and gave them working permits & German passports; Poland welcomed even 2,000,000 Ukrainian refugees of the same type:what more they ask for? The main aim is to harm
Russia: at any price,any value. Families, wives, children-all ?! They all demand whole defeat of Russia! Even the U.S. President Joe Biden keeps silence ! What about when the West would arm Ukraine with nuclear weapon ?!
Massive election participation in the Russian Kursk region with no results.

German Chancellor Olaf Scholz promised deep investigation in the alleged Ukrainian assault on the North Stream pipe line which paralyzed all the Germany earlier in the war.

The North-Stream pipe-line Ukrainian saboteur managed to escape back to Ukraine over the German - Polish border. (CNN) In a televised interview the German Chancellor Olaf Scholz promised a tough fundamental investigation of the Ukrainian scheme and perfection of its sabotage role.

* * *

German Chancellor Olaf Scholz insisted on Russian participation into future peace talks. Up till now Russia was excluded from participation. The West however refused to accept the election results in the Crimea "election". Russia and China started joint military drill in the sea of Japan . The Ukrainian town of Nikopol-near Dnepro- was heavily bombed and destroyed. For retaliation Ukrainian drones attacked Moscow and destroyed a sky scraper there.

In the Bundestag-debatte German Chancellor Olaf Scholz appeared very nervous & irritated. He was accused to be "frantic German descent Chancellor".
His SPD- minister of interior Nancy Faeser was visibly both bodily and mentally deranged -walking on right arm crutch – clearly visible & photographed by all media- but not able to medicate by mental crutches - with mentally deranged delusion emigration proposals to the entire EU.
Hopefully the EU will not accept her delusions !
600,000 homeless in Germany- from empty alcohol bottles to excrements : ARD, ZDF.
Germany – a German disaster :
"Deutschland , wir weben dein Leichentuch!"- Heinrich Haine , 1825 :
"Germany ! We weave your shroud !"
Dream: "A tree with 7 of my enemies hanging on it!",
This was but a prelude;
where books are burnt
human-beings will be burnt
in the end" : Heinrich Heine, 1856 , "God will forgive me – it is his job!". In German:
"Dies war nur ein Vorspiel;

wo Bücher verbrannt werden, Menschen werden verbrannt am Ende"!

Austria faces parliamentary election in the end of September 2024 : a celebration for the extreme right populists FPÖ.
U.S. President-candidate Donald Trump asserted "millions of illegal migrants to the U.S.A".

Sibiha became the new Ukrainian foreign minister; not known how. He met in Kyiv with the foreign ministers of U.S.A and Great Britain Antony Blinken and David Levy met and discussed president Zelenskyy goal to hit targets deep inside Russia. Rather clumsy ! Zelenskyy presented
detailed plans of 245 Russian targets he aims to bomb. Blinken took no stand but promised
$380 mn for repairing the damaged Ukrainian electric grid and $180 mn humanitarian aid to Ukraine.

Russia and China started joint military drills in the Sea of Japan. For this reason Russian President Vladimir Putin delivered an ample speech in which he "condemned the whole series of U.S. provocations against both allied countries-Russia and China".

ECB sank its interest rate to 3.50% for credits. ECB means European Central Bank in Frankfurt am Main , Germany where all credit cards failed to work whole a day long.
The Russian Army managed to liberate 10 more towns in Kursk region. Too little too late.

British prime minister Keir Starmer – Labor – stated "Vladimir Putin started this war and he can stop it any time!"He is on his flight to Washington D.C. for talks with American President Joe Biden. Vladimir Putin him self stated "if British-American "Storm Shadow" missiles are used against Russia we will regard this a war, as an aggression and we will rethink our response!" (Euronews).

Joe Biden however brushed off Putin's speech, Keir Starmer didn't even mentioned it at their Washington meeting : he simply dismissed Putin's threats.
Literally he stated "I don't think of Vladimir Putin too much", which means "I dont't care at all".
Both ignored Putin's threat of a war and allowed Ukraine to use Western missiles to Russian targets deep inside Russian territory. Ukraine was deeply satisfied by this decision .
Keir Starmer said nothing in a typical hypocritical British style. (ARD)
Both politicians seem to have calculated wrongly on Ruissia despite agitation to their people.
Russian U.N. Ambassador Vasily Nebenzya told the world "U.S.A. and Britain are in direct war with Russia by delivering long-range missiles to Ukraine ". Which brushed off Russian warnings about the war with the West. The long-range missiles can turn the table of the war outcome.
Nato Admiral Rob Bauer confirmed rather reluctantly their position.
Admiral Rob Bauer-Chair man of NATO Military Committee -permitted to Ukraine to hit targets deep inside Russia. It is exactly what Keir Starmer was seeking from President Biden. A quarrel. NATO Admiral Robert Peter Bauer (born 11.XI 1962 in Amsterdam) is a Dutch soldier of the Royal Netherlands Navy. From 5 October 2017 to 15 April 2021, he was Commander of the Dutch Armed Forces.Now as Nato Admiral he advocates Ukrainian war on Russia:"Our allies should have our permit to hit air fields,fuel & ammunition depots of the enemy. Polish Defense Minister Radoslav Sikorsky agitates against paying social benefits to Ukrainian conscripts who fled to & hide in Poland:"We pay to these deserters not to fight! They must go back to Ukraine & fight there against the Aggressor !" 2.5 years after war begin politicians finally hatch of the core nature of these deserters !" And it is really so: Poland pays the Ukrainian soldiers for not fighting, not ware faring against Russia: Such an absurd !

2nd assassination attempt on Donald Trump while he was playing golf on his ranch Palos Verdes in Florida: a Soviet

AK-47 Kalashnikov sub-machine gun was in use afterwards left in the shrubbery. Its muzzle was found in the same shrubbery - alleged Zelenskyy supporter against Russia. Both Biden & Harris extended sorrow, condolence and relief that he remained unhurt. Local U.S. police recognized the Assassin and apprehended him 25 km away from the assassination venue. Another U.S. assassination attempt was made back on 30.03.1981 – this time on Ronald Reagan–a Republican too! What about us? Humble street covers ?

Both German NRW Minister President Wüst & Bavaria Minister President Markus Söder
withdrew their candidates for a German Chancellor and supported Friedrich Merz as an CDU Chancellor Candidate in the forthcoming German election. ZDF showed German Chancellor Olaf Scholz visiting Russian-held Uzbekistan in his election campaign against Kamala Harris- U.S. Democrat . Wüst -MP NRW - decided not to run in the forthcoming German election against CDU Friedrich Merz. The EU introduced a new post-an EU-Defense Commissionaire. German Chancellor Olaf Scholz visited Kazakhstan because he is greedy for its row materials & other resources . However he ate a humble pie only.

Ukrainian President Zelenskyy praised the "Ukrainian courage in the distractions of Kursk, Tversk, Belgorod & Bryansk "and thanked the soldiers with superlatives: "The Ukrainian victory plan over Russia is ready! We had hit deep into Russian territory!" Russian President Vladimir Putin declared "Russian high-tech advance in the Russian war on Ukraine and modernization of the Russian Army and Navy: not individual any more but serial! We need and select motivated, prepared, highly intelligent people with good education and readiness! We achieved our goal to weaken our enemy !".The photos I saw were disastrous ! More over Russia started to locate Korean missiles & Iskander rockets in Toropets- near the front line.

EU-Commissioner Ursula von der Leyen visited Kyiv for the 8th time in a year and promised 35 billion euro help for kindergartens and native Ukrainian missiles. The loan will be payed back from the frozen Russian assets abroad. Russia uses to target the Ukrainian infrastructure esp. power plants and the Ukrainian electric grid: 80% already destroyed, said President Zelenskyy. Russia warned that its missiles can reach Strasbourg within 3 minutes. Ukraine prohibited the use of Telegram-Channel amid wear of malware. Moscow said "The number of the Russian victims since the start of the war amounted to 680,000 both killed and wounded". It evacuated 1,200 people from a hit & exploded ammunition warehouse near Krasnodar (BBC). British feminists accused and alleged Harrods superstore owner Mohamed Al Feyed who died one year earlier aged 94. His son Dody al Feyed died in a suspicious care crash on 31-08-1997 in Paris.

In the elections for a Landtag in German province Brandenburg the AfD landed at 2nd place with 29% of the vote barely behind after the ruling SPD-party with 30.9%. It has no other choice to forge a coalition with BSW (= Sahra Wagenknecht Union).Alleged to have gotten 5,000,000 euro donation. Alleged also of close relationship to Kremlin with no evidence to the allegations. FDP(=Liberals)
marked catastrophic 0.8%. The SPD crown man – acting German Chancellor Olaf Scholz,meaning Olaf Stolz- flew to New York for a meeting with Ukrainian President Volodymyr Zelenskyy. In a summary they concluded: nothing ! The German Christian-Democratic Union CDU appointed officially and formally Friedrich Merz as Chancellor candidate in the forthcoming election in September 2025. His line is not very clear. Greener Thursday following next Thursday in Germany not clear description

Ukrainian army demolished ammunition depots both in Toropetsk and in Oktyabrsk; Zelensky repeatedly asked the West for its permit to hit targets deeper in Russia. BSW (=Bündnis Sarah Wagenknecht) is for German weapon stop to Ukraine. During his U.S. visit Zelenskyy thanked to a military plant in Pensylvania for its weapon supply of 3,000,000 artillery shells to Ukraine (!?), "which saved many Ukrainian lives". Whom U.S.A. & Germany will target first: Ukraine,Israel, Palestine or Lebanon on the Eshafot. Delivering a broken English speech to the U.N. he used to wear myopic spectacles- result of his permanent hiding in underground bunkers. He presented his so called "victory plan against Russia" based entirely on Western long-range missiles exports to Ukraine

Ukraine started to test domestically Ukrainian manufactured missiles and hit Russian ammunition depots near Krasnodar & Toropeevka destroying both 3,000 tons of explosives and 18,000 artillery shells. **Tisoretsk** just like Tsolov.Slowly I become suspicious on how Ukraine knows their exact co-ordinates. Seemingly it seems Euronews blows up the news and that not moderately but shameless: if so much Ukrainian successes why Ukraine does not win the war finally? *We witness excursions of President Zelenskyy to Normandy, Rome, Paris and finally New York. Ukrainian tourists flooded both Western Europe & the Black Sea expensive hotels, Ukrainian sportsmen competed unhindered at the International Olympic games in Paris and exports unhindered Ukrainian grain to all over the world while EU-Commission President Ursula von der Leyen visited unhindered Kyiv 8 times (= eight times) 2023-2024, so is difficult to believe at all there was a war at all and Ukrainian propaganda Machine blew the balloon of lies & propaganda to a cosmic space dimensions ! All the billions worth of capitals & military & economic help for the empty Ukrainian p r o m I s a s to investigation on the Dutch air craft downing over Ukraine with 198 victims over Ukraine back in 2019.*

At the UN-summit European Commission Foreign Affairs Chief Joseph Borrel praised and applauded Ukraine for the destruction of the three Russian ammunition depots alongside their common border and promised further 35 billion euro support to Ukraine both militarily and economic: "Russia obviously aims to put Ukraine into the cold and dark by destructing Ukrainian infrastructure but we (UN) will not allow that; no sense to support Ukrainian infrastructure today and expose it to demolition tomorrow! Ukraine had suffered severe disadvantage because the lack of weaponry so far", he said but than hesitating :"How to say it?" Pop up, mixing up in one mug Ukraine, Israel, Palestine and Lebanon, so how to believe him ,how to trust him fairing away from all of reality in the World ?! Alongside with him was German foreign minister Anneline Baerbock-Green-and promised tough de-escalation of the war any time soon. Not so former U.S.President Donald Trump summarized the current situation in few words only:"What does President Zelenskyy ? Nothing – every time he comes to us he used to go home with further $60 billion from us equivalent to 63.63 billion euro. As a President of the U.S.A. I will bring them both to the negotiation table to discuss the topic for as long as they bring an agreement!"
American and Russian astronauts left the Russian Space station Soyuz after spending in Space 374 days and landed safely in Khazakhstan. More than a year! Amid them the notorious Russian cosmonaut Oleg Konalenko (1971): The first citizen in the World to spend over 1,000 days in Space :
logged 1,000 days off Earth, has orbited the planet 16,000 times and flown 420 million miles. A paragon of long-term peaceful co-operation between the two superpowers! They all persuade own goals, own ambitions and they all make our World better & safer . What about Ukraine? Nepotism ,cronyism , stately sponsored corruption and seemingly deep reverence to the West & Western officiousness .
Certainly this is not the end of the war but certainly end of my book and certainly end of the year
2024 as well. Zelenskyy's so called "Victory plan" meant no negotiation, no peace talk at all
"because Russia understand only the language of power. So he concluded wisely "Russia has
to be beaten off" and "Russia must be forced into peace" . He talked also to the president
candidates Donald Trump and Kamala Harris. Bitter battles for the city of Vuhledar. President
Putin threatened the West with nuclear weapons. "The translation of his speech in English was very clumsy, moot and vague so that we cannot know what precisely he said ":
(Armin Coerper, ZDF -Moscow).
26-09-2024 Strike in German ZDF television program.
The German Green Party split in two.
The German industry grow declined with 0.1% .

U.S. President Joe Biden announced $7 billion further help to Ukraine. Only than president Zelenskyy was allowed to present "his victory plan to him". His "victory plan"besteht from 3 points, one of them
U.S. permit to hit with American weapons Russian targets deep inside Russia.
The Dutch Air Force replaced its F-16 fire jets with F-35; the F-16 went to Ukraine while Vl. Zelenskyy was still in the U.S.A. : another rat to smell: "We will win the war!", said Zelenskyy with aplomb clearly
intricating the U.S.A more and even more"The U.S. help must have come 2 years!" Zelenskyy met
the Democrate candidate Harris who promised both prolongation of the war & further American help.
By contrast ex-President Trump and current President candidate schemed up a very reserved stand

to Ukraine cause- a full,sheer contradiction between the generations, so ZDF after finishing its strike.
A very short………
At his long long speech to the U.N. General Assembly Ukrainian President Volodymyr Zelensky
spoke unconvincingly and stuttering; it became not clear what he demanded exactly?! He missed
the word "PEACE" in his long long speech
Beatles John Lennon and his widow Yoko Ono exhibition in New York where I visited her New York apartment in May last year (2023) .

AfD Alice Weidel candidated officially & formally for a German Chancellor candidate in December 2024 despite all odds created by German CDU and other German parties. Hard upon hard !
Finally the Province Constitutional Court appointed König for a President of the Landtag.
AfD protested.
A Russian rocket hit the police station of Krivij Rih- the home city of Ukrainian President Zelenskyy.
A glorious victory but only partial one ! We all demand full victory trough out !
In the Austrian election the extremist far right was the winner: both over smarting & overwhelming
even neighboring Germany!
Only now Serbia introduced compulsory military service for all Serbian men. We understood
it comprehensively.

OCTOBER 2024

As Russia intensified its attacks on Eastern Ukraine President Zelenskyy started to prepare a new security agreement with his EU-allies. Russian attacks included Zaporizhie, Cherson & Donetsk
pushing back the Ukrainian army and causing mass destruction.
Vl. Zelenskyy had handed in already his "victory plan" to the U.S. presidential candidate Harris
and demanded more financial and military help from the West to bury millions & billions in Ukraine.
Up till now $735 billions were already buried in Ukraine.
In a NATO ceremony Jens Stoltenberg gave the Secretary General post to Mark Rutte-57-former
prime minister of The Netherlands. Rutte said "NATO is not thinkable without free independent
Ukraine. Ukrainian independence ranks high on the NATO priority list!" Stoltenberg presented him
with a Norwegian hammer for use on special occasions ! !

Slow but steady Russian advance in East Ukraine after Russian troops captured strategic important
city of Vuhledar. Ukrainian President Zelenskyy took no stand but demanded more men to stop it:
his television showed enthusiastic Ukrainian soldiers kissing their flag to stop the Russian advance.
Israel declared U.N.O. Chief Antonio Guteres for persona non grata & issued arrest warrant against
him "for his antisemitic U.N. attitude": ZDF, ARD, Euronews. New NATO secretary general Mark Rutte-
aged 57- took no stand. On the contrary Dutch secrete service took an attitude again against me
as a Journalist and intimidated , bullied me. Bulldozed me ! Dutch Mark Rutte scheduled further continuation
talks with Zelenskyy in the German air base in Ramstein-40 km from Frankfurt am
Main for the next week.
NATO secretary general Mark Rutte-aged 57- made a surprising visit to Kyiv and promised $9 bn
help to Volodymyr Zelenskyy. It was not clear where he will take the money from; on the 2nd da of
his Kyiv visit he promised even $14 billion , building a bridge for Ukrainian NATO membership , deepening of
the bilateral relations between NATO and Ukraine and better military co-operation".
Zelenskyy demanded the same degree of help which Israel gets from the West.
Ukrainian terror groups set afire 2 Russian fuel depots – in Voronezh and in Perm, Ural.
Ukrainian secret service managed to kill André Korotkyy-director of the Russian Zaporizhie
Atom power plant. Details still leak through.
German CDU-politician and German Chancellor candidate declined proposals for peace talks with
Russia. Finally he is still in opposition !
Crude oil price rose to $80 a barrel internationally.

On the Israeli intimidates Iran replied "If Israel wants war so Iran is master of war", Iran replied.
U.S. Vice-vice president Vance supported this stand. Jewish names like Vance are as
common as Circus Vance- former U.S. Minister. U.S. President candidate Donald Trump advised Israel to attack &
destroy the Iranian atomic reactors. President Biden took a moderate peaceful reconciliatory position. 88 Francophone
countries criticized France for its weapon deliveries to

Israel. Crude oil price rose to $80 a barrel internationally.
Qatar transfers $30 mn to Palestine monthly.
The Netherlands started helping Ukraine to produce drone for the battlefield.
The Dutch Defense minister Brekelmans announced this decision during his visit to Ukraine. The Netherlands fills in 400 mn euro into the project. Also he confirmed that the Dutch F-16 fighter delivered earlier are already in Ukrainian service. The airfields of their dislocation are not known.
The capture of the east Ukrainian city of Toretzk formed the basis to Russia to conquer the
whole of Donbas.

In Strassbourg Hungarian Prime Minister Victor Orban stated "Ukraine has no chance to win this
war and the EU must search and seek other means and ways to dissolve the problem!".
Massive quarrel in the EU-Parliament in Strasbourg criticizing sharply Hungarian President Victor
Orban because his Ukrainian & EU-policy: the LGTB's are better protected than Europeans.
Hungarian left-wing opposition got a better tribune than in their native Hungary.
Speech time was limited to one minute for each speaker.
Victor Orban named "the allegations as absurd" and "condemned Soros as a Jew.
He accused the EU "taking more money from Hungary than the EU-"helps were"".
As an EU-president Orban was allowed to speak 7-9 minutes flinging into sore details,
so the broadcasting of his speech "was interrupted for technical reasons!". Hungarian provokers
rained up banknotes on him accusing him of corruption before led out by Parliament Quaestors.
EU-President Ursula von der Leyen abandoned her neutrality as a President and attacked him
sharply and groundlessly at a quaff, yet again with quaestors' intervention at a scuffle.

The Eu needs the Hungarian vote otherwise Hungary will block the EU 5 billions Ukrainian aid.
Ukraine surrendered Toretsk-city to the Russian army amid massive Ukrainian evacuation of
civilians, Ukrainian army spokesman admitted. The capture of the east Ukrainian city of Toretzk formed the basis
to Russia to conquer the whole of disputed Donbas. Rather controversial !

Crocodile tears Ulf Röller – stuttering myopic fat crack-brained bearded
ZDF Brussels correspondent ! Police error ! Police disaster !

Ukrainian President Volodymyr Zelenskyy expected to Berlin for talks with German Chancellor
Olaf Scholz. Freely on Friday when mass media expected for a rest. In fact he arrived for a
half day visit in London for talks with British prime minister Keir Starmer and than left to Paris-
also for talks. On Sunday he is expected in Berlin- also for talks. Always talks ! Smell a rat !
………… said German interior minister Nancy Faeser. Is she healthy or suffers demencia ?
.
12-years-age marriages in Africa and not only there!: As a pupil I learned Africa at 300 mn
population now it is over 900 mn !
German Chancellor Olaf Scholz however promised further German weapon deliveries to
Israel:"Ja, we had delivered German weapons to Israel and we continue further German
weapon exports to Israel too!", he re iterrated among applause of the German Parliament
The Bundestag.
The German Bureaucracy continued to block cannabis sales country wide despite the German
permit law supporting thus the illegal German black market more and more and any more to
flurish. Russian rockets hit the port installations of Odessa, 7 men were killed; one expensive Ukrainian Patriot-
launcher destroyed in Dnipropetrovsk.

Ukrainian president Vl. Zelenskyy started his Europe tour to present his "victory plan to defeat
Russia" to his allies, according which the war must end in 2025. Europe approved further 35
billion euro loan to him. The frozen Russian assets are said to amount to 210 bn euro. The next
peace talks will be held with Russian participation. Zelenskyy visited the Pope at the Vatican and
than German Chancellor Olaf Scholz in Berlin. The Pope accented on the humanitarian aspect of the war while
Olaf Scholz promised 1.4 billion euro help after further 4 billion are already planed in the German state budget.
Quite a schedule ! Rather a scam …An eye watering spectacle of historic proportions ! The ARD -television asked
however "how long will we further support Ukraine
without any strategic plan for the war?!" Ukraine continues to lack TAURUS-MARSH missiles which
it will use to interrupt the Russian logistic supply chains to the front.
Russian attack on Ukrainian atomic weapon depot:
Since when Ukraine harbors atomic weapons ?!

German CDU-chief Friedrich Merz thanked Bavaria Minister President and CSU-chief Markus
Söder for his stanch & franc pre-election support. Both demonstratively shook hands & hugged
each other as shown on ZDF. The German Chancellor election is in 2025 while the U.S.
Presidential election is due in November 2024.

Half of the Ukrainian electricity is claimed to be produced by Ukrainian nuclear power plants;
Ukraine is complains "Russia deliberatedly bombards them in order to switch them off!".
Russian secrete services accused of blowing the ammunition plants in Czechia for their alleged
exports to Ukraine. Dutch sources claimed "an Ukrainian F-16 managed to down a Russian
SU-34 fighter jet', but this was not confirmed independently.
Polish president Donald Tusk announced the Polish operation "East Shield" to protect East
Polish frontiers against Russia & Belorussia . The EU strengthened its sanctions on Iran
"because drastic Iranian weaponry exports to Russia". It banned also traveling of 7 Iranian
officials and 7 Iranian entities to the EU, their bank assets frozen. Good intelligence !

KNDR (North-Korea) blasted off all rails, roads and bridges to South Korea and logically
with them all relations to the South (ZDF).
Congressman Mike Turner from Ohio, chairman of the House Intelligence Committee, urges the White House to
hold an "immediate" briefing after reports that North Korea sent its soldiers to fight in the war between Russia and
Ukraine, a development which crossed the "red line " .
North Korea helping Russia fight the war in Ukraine is scary for several reasons, says Dan Rice, a former special
adviser to the commander of Ukraine's military. He tells "CUOMO" this could turn the Russia-Ukraine war into a
world war. #ukrainewar #russia #northkorea

Golf countries' meeting with EU-activists in Brussels; what Volodymyr Zelenskyy did there?
Maybe translating from Arabic into Russian ?? The Gulf countries are : Saudi Arabiya,
Qatar, Kuwait, Oman and the UAE.
Russia is more willing than ever to sabotage and spy on Western countries. Even a military conflict with NATO has
become a serious option, warns the secret service in Germany. The British are also sounding the alarm bell about
the "increasing recklessness" with which Putin's regime operates.

Finally president Zelenskyy presented his "victory plan" to the Ukrainian Parliament: it includes
among others permit to hit Russian targets deep inside Russia,faster entry in NATO and faster
entry into the European Union. The very next day he visited Brussels for the NATO defense minister meeting
there. So he presented them again his "victory plan" which rejects any territorial gains for Russia and the permit

to hit Russian targets with EU-ballistic missiles which both the U.S.A. and German rejected again. So Zelenskyy retreated back to Ukraine empty-handed and disappointed:
with "only" 35 billion euro credit to buy new destructive assault weapons. After presenting "his victory plan" he stated "sending 10,000 North Korea is a step towards World War".
The Russian State Duma accepted unanimously a new bill against pedophiles, LGBT and change of sex. It intends also to punish propaganda aiming to limit the size of children "in traditional Russian families". The bill must be ratified by President Putin. The President of the EU-Commission Ursula von der Leyen blamed "both Russia and Belorussia of leading of a hybrid war against the West". Putin himself replied "the West is trying to undermine Russia political life by amicable ideology" and vowed "to protect traditional values".

U.S. President Joe Biden finally found time to visit Berlin where he was decorated with the highest German order – Distinguished Service Cross -but mentioned Zelenskyy "victory" plan with no single word: same as in both Paris and London . The very next day Chancellor Scholz arrived in Istanbul to sell 40 EURO fighter jets to Turkey which are fabricated in Germany.

The ECB rose its leading interest rate to 4% despite the EU-inflation sank to 1.7%.
The Swedish concern IKEA marked its 50th anniversary despite critics of have used forced labor of political prisoners of the former GDR.

In a TV-interview president candidate Kamala Harris said wisely :
"Who soever President of the U.S. is ,he domains the office".

U.S. Defense secretary Lloyd Austin made an unannounced visit to Kiiv by train, where he expressed his concern of North Korean troops deployed by Russia to fight in Ukraine. Additional fighting camp was established in Russian far east for training additional North Korean soldiers to fight against Ukraine. North Korea had delivered already 2,000,000 artillery shells which Russia can not produce on its own even in a year (CNN). North Korea brought up 12,000 soldiers help to Russia. Neither North Korea nor China were even touched tangable by the Gorbachov's Perestroyka in the 1980ies which is my personal but objective point of view.
While Ukraine suffers serious man power shortage South Korea summoned the Russian Ambassador to Seoul for explanation of the war escalation (Clair Boldowson, CNN).

Ukrainian drone group targeted a crucial Russian arms factory more than 500 miles from the border:
The state-owned Sverdlov plant is one of the largest manufacturers of explosives used by Russian forces in the war. It has been under US and EU sanctions since 2023 for acquiring goods in support of Russia's war effort, producing explosives, industrial chemicals,
detonators and ammunition (Yahoo).
Russian army pilot defector Maxim Kuzminov shot dead in Spain already in April 2024. His defection to Ukraine was well paid by Ukrainian Government plus protection for his Family (NPO1). His gun-riddled body was found in a garage in Alicante along side his new name false documents.
Always on the brink ! Germany opened new marine command point in Rostock (ZDF). Russia protested and asked the German Ambassador in Moscow -J.Lambsdorf-for explanation (ZDF). The German Lufthansa cancelled its flights to Beijing "because must fly over Russian territory".

U.S. Secretary of defense Lloyd Austin made a surprising visit by train to the Ukrainian Capital Kyiv. With a mackintosh and black spectacles he promised an U.S. aid package for $400 million mostly weaponry ,ammunition, artillery shells,air defense systems, armored vehicles and anti-tank guns.

Well ahead of the visible victory of Donald Trump in the ongoing U.S. president election campaign. It coincides with Antony Blinken shuttle diplomacy to the Middle East. Strange co-incidence ! Ukrainian president Volodymyr Zelensyy looked visibly very pleased by this visit obviously pre-coordinated. Only few days earlier U.S. President Joe Biden visited Germany already during the week end.
Mark Rutte, the new secretary general of NATO, says on X that it would be a "significant escalation" if North Korea sends troops to Ukraine to fight alongside the Russians. He has called South Korean President Yoon Suk-yeol about cooperation with the East Asian country and the security situation in the Indo-Pacific.

Kazan hosted the BRICS top with world leaders to demonstrate that Russia is not isolated internationally despite the efforts of Western Europe. Among the delegates attended the leaders of China, India, Brazil, South Africa, UAE, Egypt, Iran… President Vladimir Putin said "95% of the Russian exterior trade volume is materialized in the national currencies of its partners and not in U.S. Dollars". He said also "The Russian Army is strong, well equiped, highly HITECHed: we are ready to afront the West!'During his flight to Kazan Chinese leader Xi Jin Ping was escorted by Russian fighter jets, said CNN ; Russian exports to the sky !
Russian neighbor Turkey will candidate for the membership. Saudi Arabia is associated member.
 The former NATO secretary general Jens Sstoltenberg,aged 71 commented sarcastically. But the very next day U.N. Secretary General Antonio Guterres landed in Kazan for the BRICS top and all rumors stopped. At his closing speech at the BRICS top Vladimir Putin insisted "on a new democratic payment order "and criticized Ukraine "as a global treath to all Russian speaking countries". At the same time German foreign minister Anneline Baebock visited Beirut for her 4th time in office but achieved nothing.

U.S. President elect Donald Trump accused presidential candidate Kamala Harris of being a communist in the election smear campaign. He was also said to have phoned up Vladimir Putin and have advised him "to finish the war in Ukraine". Kremlin spokesman Dmitrii Peskov denied however such a phone call has ever taken place, reported "The Washington Post". German police arrested a 14 years old boy suspected "of planning a terrorist attack", said ZDF; the alarm signal came again from a foreign intelligence secrete service.

EU-foreign policy chief Josep Borrel visited Kyiv to advise Ukrainian president Volodymyr Zelenskyy and to discuss further EU-support to Ukraine and European unity.
 Both German Chancellor Olaf Scholz and EU-Commission president Ursula von der
Leyen remained absent from the world climate change conference in Baku.
U.S. secretary of state Antony Blinken arrived surprisingly in Brussels for urgent talks with Nato Secretary General Mark Rutte on speedy U.S. aid to Ukraine before January 2025 and how to help Ukraine to get out of the war. Putin however countered: "There are people in NATO who are interested in BRICS,
and perhaps the number of such countries will grow," , as reported by TASS. Putin also said that some NATO countries could consider involvement in the BRICS alliance, which he described as a "prototype of free, non-aligned relations between nations".
Nobody believes that Crimea will ever go back to Ukraine, said EU-foreign affairs Chief Jose Manuel Barroso to Euronews and
added "German opposition had calculated the German help to Ukraine amounted 12 billion euro in two years only". As to Reuters Ukraine attacked Moscow with at least 34 drones, the biggest drone strike on the Russian capital since the start of the war in 2022, forcing flights to be diverted from three of the city's major airports and injuring many people. Russian air defenses destroyed another 50 drones over other regions of Western Russia. The Ukrainian army however downed a record high of 145 Russian drones over Ukraine, said Euronews. Senior Russian commander Vlodyslav Volozhin died in a car explosion in Sevastopol, said Euronews. Further on South Korea delivered 21 K9A1 rapid-fire houwitsers to Poland to strengthen its defense against Russia.

The first contingent of Canadian troops arrived in Latvia welcomed by Nato secretary general Mark Rutte – with visibly colored hairs on his head. The drill was conducted within strict communication limits. German car maker Audi closed a filial in Belgium kicking out 4,000 workers to the street.
Mark Rutte uses to color his hairs like the former British finance minister Gordon Brown.
France completed the military training of 2,000 Ukrainian volunteers and sent them to fight against Russia. This is not simply escalation of the war but also internationalization of it. Nothing new: already before French minister-president Macrone insisted on bombardments of Russian cities and bases deep inside Russia – but by Germans not by French military
Russian president Putin has a new peace plan. he newswas leaked by Systema, part of Radio
Free Europe, a U.S. government-backed organization that broadcasts news, information and analysis to countries in Eastern Europe, according to the Huffpost. Putin peace plan foresees surrender of all conflict territories to Russia; incl. the coal rich Donbas and iron ore rich Kriviy Righ- the birth place of Volodymyr Zelenskyy.
A popular German proverb says:
Je später die Nacht desto schöner die Gäste: The later the night, the nicer the guests:
One hour phone conversation between German Chancellor Olaf Scholz and Russian President Vladimir Putin. Just like me Putin is a fluent German speaker. Olaf Scholz initiated and coordinated the phone call two days earlier but the press reports remained
meager & poor:"The current war is result of the mean dishonest NATO-policy", concluded Putin wisely. The phone call let him feel less isolated internationally.Volodymyr Zelenskyy criticized sharply the phone call dubbing it mean and nasty and said "it is like opening   of Pandora's box"; he refused any peace talks with Russia. Very near sighted of him ! After a long bear sleep Scholz came to the right conclusion. Zelenskyy couldn't hide his anger, malice,
disappointment that Putin had come out yet again from his "international isolation",comented German ZDF.
In an interview with the Ukrainian radio he complained "that his country has received only half of the weapons promised
by the United States.".

Ukrainian drones attacked the Krasnodar Krai region in southern Russia on Friday, with a military airport as the apparent target, RBC-Ukraine said. Volodymyr Zelensky claims in an interview with Ukrainian radio that his country has received only half of the weapons promised by the United States, but media say Joe Biden should deliver the military aid before leaving the White House.
All of the sudden Volodymyr Zelenskyy proposed "diplomatic solution of the war and peace with Russia"; he lied "Ukraine has always insisted on the peaceful solution of the war". His lie came on the 1,000th war day.
Further lie was "war end already in the year 2025".
His big fat blue lie came exactly one day after the phone conversation between Vladimir Putin and German Chancellor Olaf Scholz ! By contrast the First German Television ARD reported exactly the oposite of this !
We have to wait and see.
In a TV-interview the Green Chancellor candidate Robert Habeck spoke frankly and openly for the German energy and economy crisis and promised further TAURUS-MARSH missiles deliveries to Ukraine.
Current German defense minister Boris Pistorius counts as Chancellor favorite.

On a Republican rally U.S. president elect Donald Trump announced triumphally :"We will frack,frack,frack and we will
drill,drill baby drill!" A clear statement of his economic purpose.

18.NOVEMBER 2024- WAR DAY 999.99

80,000 Ukrainian soldiers reportedly fallen.
U.S. President Joe Biden allowed Ukraine to use American missiles against Russian hinterland "to end the war".
France and Britain followed. Tearful Euronews scenes to justify it. EU-foreign affairs chief Joseph Borrel congratulated the U.S. permit and even thanked the U.S. feeble batty president Joe Biden for his feeble decision & his
batty feeble cry. Both Slovakia and Hungary condemned the feeble decision of batty U.S. President Joe Biden.
By contrast Germany delivered 4,000 further mini-TAURUS missiles to Ukraine.
North Korea vowed retaliation against American troops in in South Korea.
So the war internationalized far way already before today ! Kremlin spokesman Dmitryy Peskow named it
"a new qualification of the war". Slovakia president Robert Ficco said "this decision was made in order to
delay the peace talks". Both Slovakia & Hungary condemned feeble batty Joe Biden cry.
 British prime minister Keir Starmer vouwed "UK will double its support to Ukraine!"Why not – promises are always so easy. French president Emanuel Macrone accused Russia for the escalation of the war.
Russian President Vladimir Vl. Putin threatened openly the West with Russian nuclear weapons by putting lower the treshold of using nuclear weapons against the West.
It became clear 7,000,000 Ukrainians sought refuge abroad mostly in the European Union.

German Chancellor Olaf Scholz is on the G-20 conference in Brazil wrongfully reported as "Brussels".
Full mess: G-20 conference in Brazil , conference in Baku : both with the same name but different aims.

British air craft carrier "Queen Elizabeth" – 284 m long - entered the Elbe at German port of Hamburg for demonstration:
Quite a Starmer trick:"We cannot allow Putin to win this war! ! Or not a Starmer trick?"
"Biden too old for tricks", said U.S. President elect Donald Trump.

Slovak President Robert Fico announced "he will block Ukrainian membership to Nato!". Hahhah! He will not import war ! Two years earlier the President of the European Commission Ursula von der Leyen advised us live on television how to protect ourselves from Corona virus. Even now she continues to fail constantly advising us "how to protect ourselves from the Putin-virus". Quite a remark ! Russian spokesman Dmitryy Peskow replied:"Not a burden! Not at all ! Russia will simply replace its rockets strikes from deeper hinterland: Than we can strike the Ukrainians faultless! Without punishment!". Russian president Vladimir Putin endorsed the new Russian nuclear doctrine allowing Russian nuclear hits on the West. He sad also "the U.S. authorization of long-range rocket strikes has fueled oil in the fire!".
One day after the permit Ukraine bombarded and hit Russian ammunition depot in **Karachew.**
Russian foreign minister Sergej Lavrov said "this attack was not possible without American help and American training!". Vladimir Putin signed new shape of the Russian nuclear weaponry doctrine.

Ukraine declared "Ukrainian victims number amounted to 80,000 soldiers". This is not true – they lie. The real

victim number is much more higher. Many Ukrainian cities and towns remained without water because lack of electricity for the water pumps. In Northern Europe 2 undersea optical cables were cut off in a clear sabotage attack. The EU announced the end of Joseph Borrel 5-years term as its foreign affairs Master.
What about of Volodymyr Zelenskyy 7 years term as a President of Ukraine ?
German steel concern Thyssen-Krupp wrote in 1.5 billion euro losses – 1,500,000,000 !
The U.S.A. closed its embassy in Kyiv "because of security concerns for its personnel". Washington advised its citizens to take shelter elsewhere. Several EU-embassies followed this U.S. pattern.
Ukraine started to place U.S. delivered anti-personnel mines though banned by 1997 Ottawa convention.(CNN). But Ukraine has not signed this treaty being the most mined country of the world with 300,000 hectare terrain mined .
U.S. President Joe Biden stepped on significantly his military aid help to Ukraine after Donald Trump won the U.S. Presidential election in November 2024.Biden suffers from progressing his Alzheimer disease that's why
Trump used frequently to dub him "the sleepy man" at least for one zillion times.
Feeble senile U.S. president Joe Biden is suffering from
dementia praecox & Alzheimer ever since an ample time.
Hard words, word bandages !
Angry British farmers protested against the hated Labor prime minister Keir Starmer who raised taxes. Ukraine however increased the use of British Stormy-Shadow missiles; the possible use is discussed of the American "Abraham" tanks .
The Russian Secrete Service FSB arrested a German saboteur in Kaliningrad . The arrest occurred already on 30.X.2024.
President Zelenskyy admitted to the German ZDF television "Ukraine may lose the war" ….

Russia downed 2 British Storm-Shadow missiles used by Ukraine in the Dnipro region; Russia used in this case ballistic missiles RS-26 fired from Astrakhan on the Caspian sea, said BBC amid conflicting reports.
Ukraine managed to hit the Russian Army Head Quarter in the Kursk region.
Russia condemned the Ukrainian Western friends as "irresponsible".
Kyiv named it "Russia is using us as military testing ground of polygons!".
Vladimir Putin addressed the World with the words "this was our symmetric response" and "Russia has the right to defend itself against any aggression", BBC reported. Afterwards the video-link "broke"; to test the West. The NATO - Ukraine Council discussed the crises during the week-end. French foreign minister Barrot met his British counterpart David Lammy in London to discuss the war in Ukraine. Both warned of possible "Putinization of the world"; not very clear what they meant. Maybe the Russian war machine. Strong , independent Russia is obviously thorn in their flesh.
NATO Secretary General Mark Rutte flew to Florida for talks with the American president elect Donald Trump; Trump criticized sharply the European military aid to Ukraine. 10 years earlier Rutte served as a prime minister of The Netherlands.
On the 3rd grain summit in Kyiv president Zelenskyy said :"Ukraine is feeding 400 million people in 100 countries world wide by its grain production exporting 6 million tones grain monthly by its Black Sea ports before Russia started the war . Now with 321 port facilities destroyed by the war Ukraine faces difficulties with shipping its grain".

German steel giant Thyssen-Krupp planned to cut 11,000 jobs;
Bosch planned to cut 3,800 jobs, Ford-2,800.
Further German companies are expected to follow the pattern while U.S. President elect Donald Trump vowed to impose 10% tax on all EU-imports.
Chancellor Olaf Scholz was officially appointed for SPD Chancellor candidate in the forthcoming German elections in September 2025. CDU-candidate Friedrich Merz was rejected "because he lacks political and governing experience". He was said to be "very cold & unpleasant for the highly responsible post".
Defense ministers from few European countries came together in Berlin; they discussed the threat U.S. President elect Donald Trump posed to Europe to abandon the NATO and the EU in January 2025 when he officially will enter the

White House. Minutely they were: France, Britain, Germany, Poland and Italy. They accentuated their missiles & fighter jets production apart from the U.S.A. and also apart from its research, development & know-how.
G-7 top of their foreign ministers followed – Antony Blinken inclusive. All met in the Italian town of Fiuggi.
Ex German chancellor Angela Merkel published her memoirs in staggering 700 pages:
she speaks Russian as fluent as I do.
She is widely blamed of making Germany too dependent on Russian gas.

The U.S. President Joe Biden, who suffers **dementia praecox & Alzheimer unlike me and must** leave office in less than two months, has spent his final weeks in the White House working to help Ukraine as much as possible. His successor, President-elect Donald Trump, has criticized U.S. aid to Kiev and could change Washington's policies toward Ukraine and Russia when he returns to the Oval Office on January the 20th 2025.
The Speaker of the Russian Parliament – the Duma - VyacheslavVolodin- criticized in a speech sharply
Biden, Macron, Scholz "and many others like them". Russia expelled 2 further German ARD journalists from Moscow with the Russian names Ivan Blagoy (Blagoyin) & Eischman,ARD said. German
foreign minister Annalena Baerbock named the "Russian claims false & lying "and ordered the Russian Ambassador in Berlin to explain the case.
FORD is about to cut off 2,800 jobs in Cologne, Germany, with moot reasons & explanations. The workers expressed concern about their futures. It became known that the cut optic fiber cable in the Baltic Sea was cut by a negligence Chinese trade ship – "Yi Peng-3" and thus not in a sabotage act.
In a television interview president Volodymyr Zelenskyy insisted on even more Western help both politically and militarily as if the current help was not sufficient. Literary Zelenskyy used the word "more Western pressure on Russia" and **"risky"** rather than "military". Swedish prime minister Ulf Kristersson reassured him "he will get it" on the background of state debt rising in several EU-countries such as France and Germany: why not Sweden to follow their pattern ? To unleash a new form of war ?!
Later on Sweden has formally asked China to cooperate in connection with suspicions of sabotage allegedly committed by the Asian country in the Baltic Sea. Swedish Prime Minister Ulf Kristersson announced that his government was demanding "clarification" on the severing of two submarine fiber optic cables. One cable connects Finland with Germany, the other cable Sweden with Lithuania.
President elect of the U.S.A. Donald Trump appointed Robert F. Kennedy junior as his Health Secretary!
This is exactly the news I expected and longed.
Radio Genoa – a far right extremist Radio broadcast in many languages at 102.5 FM.
The renovation of the Notre Dame Cathedral in Paris cost $900,000 while the useless financial and military aid to Ukraine amounted up to $900,000,000,000 – only to compare to !
Visiting Kazakhstan Russian President Vladimir Putin praised the political experience of the clever
U.S. President elect Donald Trump. Putin said also that Russia would use all weapons at its disposal against Ukraine if Kyiv were to acquire nuclear arms. " Some Western officials suggested U.S. President Joe Biden could give Ukraine nuclear weapons before he leaves office", reported The New York Times.

Russian defense minister Belousov arrived in North Korea for talks with his North Korean counterpart "
and "to expand the cooperation between both countries on the military field.

The Ukrainian Ministry of Defense reported more than 2,000 Russian soldiers were killed in a single day. This has broken a record that was set just a few weeks earlier. A ministry report said Moscow's forces lost 2,030 men between November 28 and 29, the first time more than 2,000 were reported in a single day. Euronews reported however exactly the opposite.
A new commander of Ukrainian army was appointed – General Mihaylo Drapatyi. President Zelenskyy assumed the surrender of some Eastern territories to Russia "with the aim to recover them back on the diplomatic table of negotiations with Russia"- something which he refused to negotiate up till now! SPD

congress in Berlin without the current German defense minister Boris Pistorius 85 days ahead of the forthcoming German elections. The German military producer QUANTUM became busy with production of German drones for Ukraine. 118 333 – the German telephone Auskunft.

Sweden has formally asked China to cooperate in connection with suspicions of sabotage allegedly committed by the Asian country in the Baltic Sea. Swedish Prime Minister Ulf Kristersson announced that his government was demanding "clarification" on the severing of two submarine fiber optic cables. One cable connects Finland with Germany, the other cable Sweden with Lithuania.

The political crises in Germany deepened: This time the resignation of the F D P Secretary Bijan Djir Sarai, an Iranian born on 06-06-1976. Further coalition with the SPD is not possible any more. The place of Sarai was taken by Marco Bushman – a justice minister in the coalition of German Chancellor Olaf Scholz.

1ST DECEMBER 2024

A short summary of the November events includes the election of Donald Trump for U.S. President for 2025-2029;
U.S. permit to Ukraine to fire U.S. and EU missiles on military objects deep inside Russia;
engagement of 12,000 Nord-Korean soldiers on the side of Russia; engagement of Iranian-made Shahed drones against Ukraine.;
Failure of the second peace conference for Ukraine-simply did not take place.

In a DVD speech around 2017 President Putin stated the following 5 truths on Russia:
Russia was not the first to invent the nuclear weapon;
Russia never used the nuclear weapon on the battle field;
2002-2004 the U.S. abandoned unilaterally the nuclear treaty;
The Japanese pupils are taught that the A-bomb was not implemented by the U.S.A. but by its allies;
On an earlier stage Ukraine has agreed to surrender its Eastern territories to Russia.
Full stop .

German opposition party CDU declared "it will attack Russia with German Taurus-Marsh rockets already on the first day it would be elected in". Current German SPD Chancellor Olaf Scholz countered "Germany plays no Russian roulette with Russia". The new EU-foreign affairs Chief Kaja Kalas will however exactly play Russian roulette . This became clear already at her first visit in Kiiv.
A new NATO summit is inching on among its member.
Already on November 13, the United States opened a new permanent military base in Europe near NATO's eastern border with Russia. This air defense missile base has been in the works for more than ten years.
German Chancellor Olaf Scholz – with 80 days only in further service as a Chancellor – made a surprising visit to Kyiv and promised president Zelenskyy a new German military aid amounting to 650,000,000 euro excl. TAURUS-MARSH nor powerful Cruise missiles while Germany is ripped by massive strikes at Volkswagen factories all over the whole of Germany. The Ukrainian ambassador to Berlin named Scholz's refusal "a blank check to the Russians".Already "his phone call to Vl. Putin earlier in November 2024 was undermining international efforts to isolate Russia "! Scholz tried every mean to avoid escalation of the conflict but ended
his short speech with the Ukrainian words "Slawa Ukraine" (Glory to Ukraine!)! Which led the German opposition party CDU to conclude wisely "all of Scholz words & deeds are simply preelection maneuvers ! "
Finally Ukraine agreed "to surrender the Eastern regions to Russia if it would be accepted into NATO".
Vladimir Putin does not want part of Ukraine to come under NATO control, an expert said.

Earlier Volodymyr Zelenskyy indicated that he is willing to cede areas already captured by Russia to Moscow, but he wants NATO guarantees for the rest of the country.

Russian President Vladimir Vl. Putin visited a hospital in Moscow to speak with wounded Russian soldiers in an orthopedic clinic and promised "medication & rehabilitation will be fine". According to the Wall Street Journal the wounded and killed soldiers amounted nearly one million – both Russians and Ukrainians. It reads 1,000,000.
NATO Secretary General Mark Rutte said on a conference in Brussels that "NATO has to deliver more weaponry to Ukraine, strengthen Ukraine militarily and only militarily strong Ukraine can sit at the peace negotiation table and share military intelligence dates with Ukraine to protect it against Russian sabotage acts" . Ukraine started already to intersept Russian Shahed drones and to redirect them back to Russia; obviously by Western ideas, engeneering & technic. The West named this "cyber warfare".
Mark Rutte speech in Brussels looked very much like sabre-rattling

In the German Bundestag Chancellor Olaf Scholz admitted clearly
"The German help to Ukraine amounted 28 billion euro – 28.000.000,000 euro" ,said Chancellor Olaf Scholz ".

This was shortly before he was grilled by the German Bundestag on the shrinking German economy. While Scholz prepares German soldiers for Ukraine as peace keepers in an eventually established demilitarized zone - if any- Volodymyr Zelenskyy commented vitriolically on the tumults in Georgia far away from Ukraine. Chancellor Scholz was grilled by the German Bundestag for the shrinking German economy for 3rd year in row but he preferred aid to Ukraine instead. On the peace OSCE conference in Malta attended both Russian and Ukrainian foreign ministers and other officials of both countries.
The head of the Ukrainian military command of the Kherson region, Oleksandr Prokudin, gave an interview with the Financial Times that 300 boots Russian had convened to cross the Dnipro river. At the same time President Volodyr Zelensky attended a **second hand church opening** in Paris, as shown on Euronews.
Russian President Vladimir Putin signed a treaty with Belarus promising military help incl. nuclear weapons to keep Belarus under Russian nuclear umbrella. Belarus is heavily dependent on Russian economic help.

Hunter Biden- son of the acting U.S. President Joe Biden- was convicted in both Delaware and California for "illegal possession of fire arms and drug abuse". President Biden declared "full and unconditional help for his son Hunter Biden" and pardoned him by his presidential power.

Meanwhile South Korea introduced martial law:
I make no mistake: South Korea;
the Pentagon is monitoring the situation. Volodymyr Zelenskyy realized quickly that Donald Trump is already President elect of the United States of America and decided to become a friend to him; very clever move! He is said to have shepard most of the Ukrainian wounded soldiers again to the front to fight.
German AfD leader Crupalla stated by contrast bluntly :"Ukraine is n o t the 17th state of the German Federal Republic ! We buried in Ukraine 28 billion euro = 28,000,000,000 euro." One week after Olaf Scholz's visit to Ukraine German Chancellor Candidate Friedrich Merz – C D U - visited Kyiv too – to promise war; only war!
Switzerland started to dump its nuclear waist in neighboring Germany!
Ukrainian secrete service started dispersing videos and leaflets urging North Korean soldiers to desert; They contain also detailed instructions how to desert and description of the living conditions in Ukrainian captivity. Dispersion by both Ukrainian projectiles & drones: where has Ukraine so very much drones at its disposal??
Massive American protests against the appointment of Robert Kennedy junior as a Health Secretary by Donald Trump.

The United States conducted its first ballistic missile interception test on Guam, preparing the Western Pacific outpost for defense against China's threats. However China is in the Eastern hemisphere!
The Aegis Guam System, which defends America's westernmost territory, launched a Standard Missile-3 Block IIA

interceptor missile from Andersen Air Force Base and successfully intercepted a medium-range ballistic missile. This is the first ballistic missile defense conducted from Guam, according to the US Missile Defense Agency.

President Zelenskyy declared "his country Ukraine is open to all Western helps and all western troops against Russia". Clear speech .
Ukrainian deputy prime minister Olha Stefanishyna
said,"The West must step in its military & industrial help for Ukraine; Ukraine itself has to implement the Danish model of military industry". Which means stepping in its own military industrial production; a piece of hot air balloon !
The oil price hit $60 a barrel equal to 57 euro.
The European Central Bank sank down its leading interest down to 3%.
The Secretary General of NATO Mark Rutte summoned Europeans to reduce their incomes & to increase their defense spends, make more sacrifices in their pension system and in their health care if they want to live in peace. He wanted very clearly the European countries must increase their defense spends and expenditure.
The Freedom of Russia Legion, wh ich consists of Russians fighting for Ukraine, announced on Telegram that it is in possession of a powerful weapon: advanced ground drones equipped with machine guns,so Euronews.

German Chancellor Olaf Scholz faced no confidence vote in the German Parliament – The Bundestag.
So The Bundestag was dissolved. The new elections were scheduled for 23rd February 2025.
Helping Ukraine too much Germany neglected its own people – in 2024 22,400 German companies went bankruptcy . Scholz refused however sending German soldiers and German TAURUS-MARSCH rocket systems to Ukraine – a step which German opposition
leader Friedrich Merz will fulfil already as a part of his election campaign. Merz has no experience as a minister on any minister
portfolio. Why not exercise as German Chancellor ?!

Russian President Vladimir Putin warned the West in a televised speech "to stop Western instructors to the Ukrainian mercenaries"
pushing Russia to a red line whose crossing Russia cannot afford any more. All is flowing towards Ukraine: money, weaponry,
instructors & advisors. He drew a parallel with the Soviet era cold war and praised also the Russian Army for taking 197 villages
off the Ukrainian territory; but at which cost?

Top Russian general Igor Kirillov was killed by remote control bomb in Moscow; he was head of the Russian nuclear,chemical &
biological defense forces since 2017. The Ukrainian Secrete Service claimed responsibility for the assassination: the remote control
bomb was implanted in a vehicle near his house entry; they accused General Kirillov of chemical weapons use in Ukraine. He was sentenced in absentia for war crimes by Ukrainian court "so Kirillov was a legitimate target for the Ukrainian secrete services".
This is the highest military rank Ukraine managed to kill in the Russian rear; so Russia claimed "retribution with no mercy".
Russia claimed also "An American biolab in Ukraine". The Uzbeck bomb planter was arrested soon afterwards; he claimed "a legitimate Russian target for planing chemical assaults against Ukraine. He was hired by the Ukrainian secrete service, said ZDF.

The minimal wage in Germany rose to 15 euro an hour while the maximal tax on food was limited to 5%. Minimal annual income reads 68,000 euro. Children doles – 255 euro monthly. Economic growth for 2024 – zero percent Polish president Donald Tusk made a surprising visit to the West-Ukrainian city of Lemberg (=Lviv) to hug Ukrainian president Volodymyr Zelenskyy while German media kept silence on his visit. Poland starts EU-Presidency in January 2025. (Euronews). Lemberg (Lviv) and Western Ukraine keeps a long record of traditional ties to its Western neighbor Poland so Tusk's visit is not a surprise to me. In the television interview given for the Polish visit Ukrainian president Volodymyr Zelenskyy spoke his usual sipi d sour non-senses polished as a glancing shimmer. .

On December 17, 2024, NATO fighter aircraft from Sweden, Finland and the Netherlands intercepted and identified two Russian bombers of the long-range Tu-22M3 'Backfire' type, escorted by Su-27 Flanker fighter aircraft, over international waters of the Baltic Sea. The operation was part of regular NATO air patrols. It was confirmed that the Russian aircraft were carrying inactive supersonic cruise missiles, as visually determined. During the mission, the Russian bombers were escorted by Swedish JAS 39 Gripen, Finnish F-18 and Danish F-35 fighters, demonstrating the rapid and coordinated response capabilities of NATO air forces in the region. According to the US, North Korean soldiers have been killed in Russia's Kursk region in the battle alongside Moscow's forces against Ukraine. Without giving numbers, Pentagon press secretary Maj. Gen. Pat Ryder said Monday that North Korean soldiers had been "killed and wounded" in the first U.S. confirmation of casualties from the secretive state.
EU-conference in Brussels- the last one for 2024 "with president Volodymyr Zelenskyy as a permanent visitor to Brussels", as the German ZDF- television channel put it: "he was more frequently in Brussels than in his native Ukraine" – the city of Krivij Rijg , where his father teaches cybernetics at a domestic university. NATO secretary general Mark Rutte praised on the conference the Ukrainian enthusiasm and promised "NATO support to Ukraine to lead the peace negotiations with Kremlin from the position of strength". Rutte promised air defense systems and **"other weapons to Ukraine"** in his fanatic speech. At the conference Zelenskyy exercised his command of English language and expressed his unwillingness for peace talks with Russia. The German Bundeswehr set the ambitious goal to increase its stuff of soldiers up to 230,000 men. Which is rather unlikely ! "Germany spoke of its untimes". "The threat is that the Russian bear is coming closer & closer!". Washington Post journalist Catherine Belton admitted "Russia is losing 2,000 soldiers every day of the war". Putin himself said, he has nothing against peace talks with Ukraine but president Zelenskyy has to be re-elected first, currently he acts as a dictator. Putin's Press conference lasted 4 hours with a rapid temp which U.S. President Joe Biden can never achieve as a performance. Former French President Nicholas Sarkozy – aged 69 - sentenced by French court for corruption & bribery in his office times. The Bank of England rose its interest rates up to 4.75%. while the Russian Central Bank rose its interest rate to 21% "because of an economic boom & stability despite the war".
President Volodymyr Zelenskyy rejected once again peace talks with Russia :"Cease fire without clear plan is impossible; president Putin is crazy!" And he repeated amid strong officious laughter: "Putin is crazy!" and "No security guaranty – no cease fire ! " and "Putin loves to kill!"..
A Saudi Arabian doctor rammed his car into mass of visitors in Magdeburg Christmas Market, Germany killing 9 people & wounded
250 more .German interior minister Nancy Faeser shed down some crocodile tears. Amid a waterfall of tears German Chancellor Olaf Scholz visited the scene immediately but did nothing. Ukrainian hit on Kazan-city – 100 km away from the Russian border. Ukrainian boxer Olexander Usyk won a box match despite the war. 100,000 euro = the annual award to members of the European Parliament.
Glorious Russian Army re-conquered the city of Pokrovsk – a Christmas present to Russian President Vladimir Putin; Russia will celebrate its orthodox Christmas on 07. January 2025. A bit awkward. Slowakia's minister president Robert Ficco visited surprisingly
Russia to arrange Russian gas for his country. Slovakia imports Russian gas transit over Ukraine but now Ukraine refused to renew the transit gas contract for Slovakia ! An interesting event with two words only : "YES" or "NOW". Crystal clear form of the long-standing rumour that Ukraine practices the steal of Russian gas to Western Europe. President Zelenskyy protested against the visit both with

hatred and malice. Vicious talking cuts like knife.

Russian President Vladimir Putin on Sunday vowed to bring more "destruction" to Ukraine in retaliation for a drone attack on the central Russian city of Kazan .Russia accused Ukraine of a "massive" drone attack that hit a luxury apartment block in the city, some 1,000 kilometres (620 miles) from the frontier. Videos on Russian social media networks showed drones hitting a high-rise glass building and setting off fireballs, though there were no reported casualties as a result of the strike. "Whoever, and however much they try to destroy, they will face many times more destruction themselves and will regret what they are trying to do in our country," Putin said during a televised government meeting .

ussian President Vladimir Putin on Sunday vowed to bring more "destruction" to Ukraine in retaliation for a drone attack on the central Russian city of Kazan a day earlier.

Russia accused Ukraine of a "massive" drone attack that hit a luxury apartment block in the city, some 1,000 kilometers (620 miles) from the frontier.

Russia is deploying "human waves" of North Korean soldiers, the U.S. said and at least one soldier captured by Ukraine died of his injuries. According to White House National Security Council spokesman John Kirby, some North Korean soldiers have taken their own lives rather than surrendering to Ukrainian forces. These suicides, he said, were "likely out of fear of reprisal against their families in North Korea in the event that they're captured."

Russia and Ukraine exchanged prisoners of war 150 to resp. 189 to celebrate New Year in their homes. Even on the New Years Eve Russia continued bombarding Kiiv and destroyed its Darrnytsky suburb.The German DAX -Index rose up with 20% and knocked the record 20,000 mark.

JANUARY 2025

Russia stopped its gas deliveries to Western Europe as the contract for gas transit over Ukraine expired with the year 2024. Russia is said to make 5 billion euro of revenue by gas exports to Western Europe. Ukrainian President Volodymyr Zelenskyy vowed to end the war with Russia within the forthcoming 12 months. A short summery of the month December 2024 shows that the second conference on Ukraine was brushed off and did not take place at all-a stale mate in the European relation . Car bomb explosion at president elect Donald Trump hotel in Las Vegas. Volodymyr Zelenskyy praised his Ukrainian troops for eradicating a whole Russian battalion of infantry in the disputed Kursk region where the Ukrainians seemingly prevail.

The Ukrainian Ministry of Defense has announced a new order of 180,000 units of HEI-(high-explosive incendiary and rail ammunition) of 35 mm for the anti-aircraft tanks Gepard. In addition to ammunition, Rheinmetal has also supplied advanced air defense systems to Ukraine, such as the Skynex system, which uses programmable AHEAD munitions that can explode in mid-air to maximize the impact area. The company is recognized worldwide as a leader in the production of complex gun-based air defense systems and is the sole supplier of a full range of fire control systems, protected and integrated missile launchers, as well as air surveillance and detection radar technology. President Zelenskyy omitted several of his nightly addresses to the Public in order not to contradict to BBC & other information media.

Many people in Canada want to be the 51st state of the United States of America; Greenland to follow. The United States can no longer suffer from the huge trade deficits and subsidies that Canada needs to stay afloat. Justin Trudeau knew this and resigned. If Canada merged with the United States, there would be no tariffs, taxes would drop significantly, and they would be completely protected from the threat of Russian and Chinese ships that constantly surround them. Together, what a great nation we would be!!!"

Meanwhile president Volodymyr Zelenskyy insisted to U.S. President elect Donald Trump "to use pressure on Vladimir Putin to dissolve the Ukrainian war". All of the sudden Trump demanded colonial power Denmark its colonial island Greenland to be handed in to the United States of America. The U.S.A. had asked Denmark already in 1946 to sell Greenland to U.S.A.for $100,000,000 . Trump himself "warned his opponents if they don't comply with me I will tariff them at a high level!" Greenland is the biggest island in the world located closer to America than to stranger Denmark- only 600 miles away. The U.S. have already a great military basis there located in strategic north port of Gander. Denmark as a current owner stated "Greenland is not for sale!".

Ukraine has launched a counterattack in the southern Russian border region of Kursk warning that Russia is "getting what it deserves." Andrii Kovalenko, the head of the Ukrainian Center for Countering Disinformation, an official body, said Ukrainian forces had launched surprise attacks against Russian forces in several locations across Kursk, months after launching its incursion in the region. In a short Telegram post Sunday, the head of the Ukrainian Presidential Office, Andriy Yermak, said: "Kursk region, good news, Russia is getting what it deserves." The Ukrainian military first launched an incursion into Kursk in August 2024 and has held much of the territory it took, despite efforts by Russian and its recent deploy of its North Korean troops against Ukrainian unit troops back across the border. Quite an assistance !

The so called Ukraine conference group came together in Ramstein, Germany to discuss its help for Ukraine during

Donald Trumps official duty over United States starting on 20. January 2025. The U.S.A. added new $500 million aid to Ukraine. For the U.S. defense minister Lloyd Austin this is his 25th conference at the group.

Slovakia got angry upon Russian gas delivery stop by Ukraine. Zelenskyy countered : "Russia is aiming to access all its profit
markets possibly accessible both industrially and geographically!"
Ukrainian president for 8 long years Volodymyr Zelenskyy dubbed the move "Russia is aiming to access all markets possibly accessible both industrially and geographically.
Germany increased the minimum wage to 15,- euro an hour. Not too much. Bündnis Sarah Wagenknecht (BSW) protested against the presence of 37,000 U.S. rangers in Germany and urged them bluntly "Yankees, go home!" The pecuniary money from this funds will go for basic pension increase up to 1,500 euro monthly; as a matter of fact Germany is the main industrial hub in Europe and number 3 in the world.
2 North Korean soldiers were captured by the Ukrainian attack on Kursk region. They were interrogated by South Korean translators. President Volodynyr boasted this "as a great success for Ukraine". Usually the North Koreans prefer to fight to death than to land in Ukrainian captivity. Up till now the number of the North Korean soldiers kill by Ukrainian forces rose to 370, the wounded are over 3,000. South Korea showed interest in the arrest and demanded their delivery to South Korea for further ample interrogations by South Korean army officers.

Germany delivered 55 more houwitsers to Ukraine; Ukrainian president Volodymyr Zelensky only mocked :"Ukraine needs no aid, no mediators: Ukraine needs allies!". This is in stark contrast to the fact that earlier Ukraine admonished China to mediate in the full scale war. China delivered 12 points peace proposal which Ukraine bluntly rejected "as humorous" and "compromising".
Switzerland declared its readiness to host tree-lateral peace talks between Russia, Ukraine and United states of America as soon as Donald Trump enters the White House as a 47th President of the United States of America; Ukraine however keeps silence. An American journalist stated already "we don't know whether the strong man in Kremlin really wants to put his signature under a document or he is simply fooling around." President Zelenskyy took no attitude at all – he was busy with the two North Korean soldiers captured by the Ukrainian troops and dislocated to the Capital Kiiv.
Nato increased its readiness & willingness to "security on the Baltic See' having in mind the "Russian undersea cables cut". German Defense Minister Boris Pistorius – SPD – visited in an unannounced visit - for 5th & last time Kiiv to promise again 5 more German hauwitser deliveries to Ukraine and other sophisticated weaponry lavishly. Germany is the second big weapon supplier to Ukraine after the U.S.A. However a friend warned me by phone from the front line "the Ukrainian war could take 10 years or even more". Sorry for my comment!. Pistorius promised also "to ship more of the German financial support to Ukraine to the European Union!". Quite a caricature appeared in the media. One day after his visit British Labor Prime minister Keir Starmer visited Kiiv too. He signed with Zelenskyy a
100-years partnership treaty while the Ukrainian air defense sirens wailed. Starmer promised 3 billion British pounds of military aid to Ukraine for 2025 and 2.2 billion British pounds as a loan from the frozen Russian assets in Europe. He gave long-term guaranties for the territorial integrity of Ukraine. On Mikhailivskaya square Starmer commemorated the soldiers fallen for Ukraine by laying flowers.
It leaked to the media that Volodymyr Alexandrovich Zelenskyy- a capricorn in the Zodiac- was earlier a theater actor, a comedian; why not to exercise as president of Ukraine ?! He was appointed to president of Ukraine back in May 2019- non stop to our days. Under the leadership of Dutch man Mark Rutte Nato increased its military control over the Baltic Sea by more military frigates and fighter jets to shy Russia timid and to please him again; As to Rutte he has no military rank at all. Former prime minister of the marshy swamp of the Netherlands… He stated however "To prevent a war we have to prepare for war" and he put it bluntly "NATO countries must shift to war time mindset!" . Next Nato conference is planed for August 2025 in the Dutch Capital The Hague. Cybernetics attack on the Dutch Technical University in Eindhoven; Eindhoven is the city of Phillips. Ukrainian drone attack

on Moscow energy units; Moscow wowed retaliation "for the Western made weaponry attack" while Donald Trump declared "he wants peace in the Middle East" thus not in Ukraine. Currently Ukraine runs 1.6 million men active personal plus 2.7 million men reserve personnel, claimed Wikipedia. Also Wikipedia UKAF still have 56 operational fighter jets as of March 2022.

Till the 1830ies Ukraine was known as "The Little Russia"...

The Iranian President Pezershkian flew to Moscow to sign up a 20-years military contract with the Russian President Vladimir Vladimirovich Putin.

>>>>>>>>>>>

On the 20th of January 2025 Donald Trump entered the Oval Office of the White House as the 47th President of the United States of America for whose reelection multi billionair Elon Musk spent $92 million while the top conference of the industrial countries is planned for 25th of January 2025 in Davos, Switzerland.Trumps promise of "Ukrainian peace within 24 hours"seems to be a very very distant dream ….

And this is the end of *part 2* of my book **"THE RUSSIAN-UKRAINIAN WAR"**:

20. JANUARY 2025

Donald Trump entered the White House as the 47th President of the United States of America.

Russia stopped gas delivery to neighboring Moldova to push social & economic turmoil there.
A cool strategic calculation. Ukraine proposed hypocritically Ukrainian coal as a compensation.
There was a mounting pressure on Donald Trump "to end the war in Ukraine".

Andriy Yermak – the Ukrainian Army chief of staff gave an extensive interview to Euronews in
which former NATO secretary general Jens Stoltenberg said bluntly:"The Bucharest agreement is nothing more than piece of paper !". Quite a conclusion ! And Mark Rutte – the current Nato Scry. General?
The Russian troops conquered the town of Vasilka- another important gain which enhance
Russian control on Donbas. At the same time President Zelenskyy visited a memorial in neighboring
Poland as shown on television.
The EU defense industry program sounds very much like Cold War Two: I personally
coined this term.
As usual Russian marine shadow fleet damaged yet another under sea transmission cable in the
Baltic sea- a good NATO reason to increase its marine presence there.
And again as frequently as usual Dutch police use narcotics to harm their victims short memory-
esp. before their court trials; so they cannot testify before their Courts. Actually Press Court Trials
designed esp. for the Press to silence up . A century long improved practice…

Danish Prime Minister Frederickson visited Germany to pledge German support in the raging
Greenland-USA scandal, while Coca-Cola was accused of contaminating its Coca-Cola
products – mostly Coca-Cola & Fanta – mainly in its Coca-Cola factory in Belgium.
Coca-Cola apologized and withdrew its Coca-Cola products from the markets.
Donald Trump was greeted by President Ronald Reagan at 1987 White House reception.
Ronald Reagan Presidential Library.
Ronald Reagan Presidential Library.
40,Presidential Drive, Simi Valley, CA 93065
In a speech, Reagan referred to the Soviet Union as an "evil empire" and as "the focus of evil in the modern world".
In 1983 Reagan ordered the U.S.invasion of Grenada.

Trump's peace proposal for the war in Ukraine, in which he sets three conditions, is being talked about this week.
The aim is to reach a final peace by May 9, a symbolic date for Europe and Russia. The first of these conditions

concerns Ukraine's NATO membership, with one of the most important conditions being that the country gives up its ambition to join the Atlantic Treaty, an explicit demand from Russia.

Ukrainian drones said to have hit Russian Luckoil fuel depots in the Volgorod region – quite a distance !
As to the plane crash over Washington, D.C. President Trump accused the Biden administration "of hiring inappropriate staff with **intellectual, epileptic and psychiatric deviations**".

FEBRUARY 2025

Russian rockets destroyed the city of Poltawa in geographical center of Ukraine. Kiiv confirmed the use of long rockets with 250 kg explosive against targets deep inside Russia. Ukrainian forces attacked strongly and destroyed significantly the Russian city of Sucha, Kursk region. Ukraine dropped down the recruitment age for men in the Ukrainian army from 25 to 18 years of age.
The German minimal salary amounted up to 1,300 euro net monthly.

Mark Rutte agitated again for higher expenditure of all NATO countries.
French Minister President Emanuel Makrone agreed and added "the European weaponry must be produced and used inside Europe itself". EU-Council President Antonio Costas fully agreed with him.
The Swedish Stated prosecutor admitted "the undersea optical cable rupture was not an act of sabotage" and let the captured ship free to continue its journey across the Baltic sea.
Donald Tump agreed to shut down the USAID, many of its officials set on a leave.
An Ukrainian war lord was accused to have helped Russia with his battalion in action and was executed by fire squad.
On the defense top in Brussels became clear that European Nato members have 372 types of different weaponry while for the United States this figure is on 32 (ARD)

U.S. President Donald Trump launched up his Gaza peace plan which I support fully.
He applied also for the Nobel Peace Price what I support truly too. No more details: facts!

Russia and Ukraine exchanged 150 prisoners of war from each side. The deal was brokered by the United Arab Emirates (UAE). Prisoners' swap is a rare form of cooperation between Russian and Ukraine.
Russia launched up a new space ship for military purposes to supervise. Poland increased its military budget to 4.7% of its GDP.
Massive shootings both in Belgium & Sweden with 11 people at least shot dead. Than followed by another shooting in Örebro, Sweden, West of Capital Stockholm leaving 11 people dead. As a matter of surprise Russia was not accused of the shooting: not yet.

The three former Soviet republics of Latwia, Lithuania & Estonia cut off their contacts from the Russian electricity grid. For the festival of it EU-Commission She President Ursula van der Leyen paid an week end visit to them and their Capitals. The decision came at the back ground of the overall European energy crisis for which we all pay double price. A kind of mental suicide we Europeans have to pay for. No single word on the crises from Germany – Germany is convicted of ablaze of its own election campaign. Quite a show!
This are the www.patriots.eu. Lavishly financed by the European Parliament. As Geerd Wilders put it "The Scholz-Macrone era is over. We step in! They are history!"

Ukraine hit the Russian city Rostov-on-Don by 76 drones.
Ukrainian troops increased their attacks against the Russian city of Kursk.
The German Commando point confirmed " in Schwesing bei Husum are Ukrainian soldiers trained on how to use Patriot anti-missiles defense systems", said ZDF. So it is a core of a war against Russia.

The European Investment bank President Nadia Calvino transferred 1 billion euro to miscellaneous Ukrainian banks for recovery already before the war ends – if – for reconstruction. So is there a war there or no war? With such free bank transfers!? It reads 1,000,000,000 euro as a lump sum ! We here in Europe are scavengers exploring the street containers for garbage food and suddenly 1,000,000,000 euro! So Ukrainian banks operate rather freely to accept the European Investment Bank donation of 1,000,000,000 euro to several Ukrainian banks simultaneously. Calvino posed for a joint photo with Volodymyr Zelenskyy like a real whore. This all well ahead of the European top in Munich, Germany later in February 2025. The U.S.A. was represented by U.S. Vice President Vance. The U.S. Defense Secretary Pate Hegseth stated bluntly "Ukraine must retreat from the occupied territories and the European states must send peace keeping forces in"; thus not American troops – no single U.S. ranger! In a whole an hour phone talk with Vladimir Putin U.S. President Donald Trump reassuered him "No U.S. troops in Ukraine, no Ukraine in the 2014 border": A bitter pill for Ukraine , a triumph for Russia". ZDF & Euronews avoided any comment.
Kremlin spokesman Dmitryy Peskow stated "Russia will never swap the seized territories in Eastern Ukraine for the Ukrainian-seized Kursk regions. The Russian demands to Ukraine are:
1. No NATO membership
2. No EU membership.
3. Both sides found the phone talk important & decisive, "a historic shift"etc.
The phone call was said to be lasting 75 minutes incl. its translation times, BBC said,
"Trump is a great friend of Putin and he said again pleasant words to Putin in order to please him",stated the British Ambassador to Washington, Mr. Daniel Wittenburg : (Damian McGinnes??)
Car – hit attack in Munich one day only the annual Security Conference there ; as usual BBC reported first well ahead of the German ZDF- German native television
As usual police was unable stop the kamikaze attacker despite heavy police presence at the venue.

Already before the annual Munich conference Volodymyr Zelenskyy disagreed with the
American plan and criticized sharply Putin and his decisions in order to prolong the war; betting much on the annual Munich security conference the day after, attending in person. U.S. Defense Scry. stated "no Russian aggression against Ukraine took place during Donald Trump Presidency!" marking a diplomatic end of the war as BBC put it. British prime minister Keir Starmer phoned up president Zelenskyy to reassure him "no talks about Ukraine without Ukraine". The talks were scheduled to take place in Saudi Arabia.
Russia had even not put any delegation member to the Munich Security Conference while Volodymyr Zelenskyy ordered a barbaric drone attack attack on the Russian Chernobyl nuclear reactor exposing all of Europe at a nuclear disaster. Neither Russia nor Germany responded in words to the barbaric Ukrainian nuclear attack. BBC did. So who is exposing Europe at nuclear danger – Russia or Ukraine ?! EU-Commission President lost no single word onto.
As a fact Ukrainian drones bombarded barbaricaly the Russian nuclear reactor of Chernobyl increasing radiation level. Chernobyl is exactly 135 km northern from the Ukrainian capital Kyyv, very close to the Belorussian border.
In a television interview Volodymyr Zelenskyy looked very pale & bled (bledolik) demanding the increase of the Ukrainian Army from 82 to 100 brigades. Rather unrealistic. The news as it is. Europe must show relevance.
The media cut short Zelenskyy notion parroting Dmitry Kuleba – the former Ukrainian foreign minister
As to Russia it did not sent even a delegation to the Munich security conference.
As to Russia it established a new Russian navy base in Port Sudan.
So President Zelenskyy warned the West that "Russia doesnot want peace" and urged Europe to "form its own defense army".

The second half of the week Donald Trump spent in talks with Indian President Narandra Modi discussing with him topics of bilateral interest; thus not global problems.
The mutual trade balance of both countries amounts to $29 billion – 29,000,000,000 U.S. dollars .
With Donald Trump as a new U.S. the world got full of new news- both national & international.

The Munich Security Conference was chaired by a German diplomat.
The Munich car attack – bad advertising to the Munich EU-security conference the day after.

No condemnation of Russia so far. U.S. foreign minister Marco Rubio put it bluntly :" Ukrainian mineral resources in exchange of peace" . Wolodymyr Zelenskyy followed him at the conference in Saudi Arabia where the U.S. were represented by Marco Rubio but Europe was n o t represented there whatsoever. Zelenskyy was absent from the Paris conference though he lied "No talks on Ukraine without Ukraine!"And suddenly he was absent ! At
the conference in Saudi Arabia the U.S. was represented by its Secretary of State Marco Rubio and Russia – by its Foreign Minister Sergey Lavrov. Both Ukraine and the European Union were not represented at the peace talks because Kremlin doubts in their legitimacy. Zelenskyy in fact visited Turkey and the Paris peace conference didn't even take place, such a dissonance in Europe. Above all Donald Trump stated "Ukraine had had 3 years to end the war but president Zelenskyy
di not wanted this. Now the infrastructure is destroyed at 100% after 3 years of war. I will give Ukraine almost all the land they want but the regime in Kiiv is ilegimate – it is a martial law!" The discussion continued online. The peace talks in Saudi Arabia lasted only one day and ended with a speech of the Russian foreign minister Sergey Lavrov to the Russian
Duma (the Russian Parliament) in which he said "The Atlantic Alliance is bankrupt". Developing strategic ties with China he said "Xi Jin Ping is invited to Moscow military parade for the Victory Day 09th May 2025."
Sergey Lavrov reminded also "The Baltic states & Ukraine had collaborated with Nazi Germany millions upon millions
of time during the World War Two." He invited also Indonesia to join the BRICS-group.
President Zelenskyy lied bluntly "he had chosen not to attend the peace talks in Saudi Arabia because of complications" This is a blunt lie – neither Ukraine nor the European Union were admitted to the peace talks in Saudi Arabia" . And Zelenskyy lied "This was his choice".
The White House sent a special envoy to Kiiv – General Keith Kellogg- to consulate Zelenskyy.
But Zelenskyy accused Donald Trump "of living in a space of disinformation " and "helping Putin to leave his international isolation in which he was trapped due to the Ukrainian war". "Zelenskyy popularity sank down to 4%", so D. Trump. Trump dubbed Zelenskyy as "a dictator without election who spilled $350 billion US Dollars in a 3-year war"- $350,000,000,000 United states dollars. Zelenskyy him declared unconditional joint of NATO if Russia breaks the truce, so some Dutch media. Letland introduced German as a compulsory school language instead of Russian. Russian was compulsory school language for 75 years.

French President Emanuel Macrone started his U. S. visit with Donald Trump teaching "How can you be strong to China when you show weakness to Russia??!"Rather demagogue !
British prime minister sir Keir Starmer visit to Washington largely & lavishly advertised by British media despite the fact he has nothing to get neither from the U.S.A. nor from President Donald Trump personally. Wait & see!
In a rare press conference in Kyiv Volodymyr Zelenskyy stated "he will give up his Presidency in exchange for Ukrainian NATO membership!" Zelenskyy demanded also bigger European & NATO guarantees for Ukraine. Difficult to believe!
The news as it is : Emil Tzolov

World leaders met in an international summit in Kyiv to express solidarity , to express support to Ukraine.
As they traveled & met with no hinder in Ukraine the question rose : Is there war or all is only show?!

Trains run smoothly abandon of electricity, televisions run smoothly, even *AN UKRAINECAST* was established – so it war in Ukraine or there is none ??
The show in Kyiv was a Canadian one is not clear who represented the U.S.A. - the biggest Ukrainian supporter during Joe Biden administration. Above all a petrol bomb exploded at the Russian consulate in the French port Marseille. Russian authorities demanded an explanation of the terrorist attack. French president Emanuel Makrone flew to Washington to agitate Donald Trump for more American aid to Ukraine. his visit coincided with British prime minister Keir Starmer visit to Washington too; so who first ?!
According to other reports Keir Starmer attended the world leaders' summit in Kyiv.

On a ceremony in Moscow President Vladimir Putin handed in awards & orders to "soldiers who have fought for Russia and Russian glory for 10 generations ahead". The number of the Russian soldiers killed in Ukraine amounted to 350,000. 800,000 others were wounded, said Euronews.

At the 3rd anniversary of the Russian-Ukrainian war Ukrainian president Volodymyr Zelenskyy gave freely Press conference in Capital Kyiv – untouched by the "war" – and even tried to speak some English hunting his own aims & purposes. Canadian prime minister Justine Trudeau praised him and admitted "Canada will continue to train on its ground Ukrainian soldiers and other Ukrainian military staff": the news without make-up ! Canada has its own high-level optical forces, so Zelenskyy. "The war is changing into technological war fare!". Upon the question of his opinion on Donald Trump Zelenskyy hesitated… And amid ironical laughs Zelenskyy admitted only "good" in overall laughter . My personal opinion on the summit is Ukraine is supported only by Canada & Spain in 17 minutes exposure; all other countries submitted only 7 minute press time at all. Among their questions was "why Ukraine changed its mind on the war?". The elucidation lasted 4 minutes at all.
An EU-diplomat dubbed the whole summit as "rather cakaphonic" and placed 4 further main questions Zelenskyy failed to answer. Instead he flung into "Soviet era weapon manufacture ever since!" So what Zelenskyy demand? A 2045 future weaponry developed by the West for Ukraine and only for Ukraine ?! Zelenskyy replied:"Ukrainian weaponry production – artillery shells, drones even rockets & missiles ! " Quite a question Zelensky failed to respond at all. All pushed back into second place the German Parliament election which was "undemocratic" according to the German AfD leader Alice Weidel . AfD means :'Alternative for Deutschland", a translator's remark.
The Zelenskyy so called "Press conference in Kyiv" lasted over 3 hours mirrored by the media in over 8 hours'stretch.
The European Commission President Ursula von der Leyen brought 3.5 billion euro present to Ukraine at the summit: say & write 3,500,000,000 euro cadeau plus expensive flight tickets for all European delegates .
3,500,000,000 euro. The Ukrainian refugees to Western Europe outnumbered 6.6 million:
6,600,000 Ukrainian refugees! The news as it is by Emil Tzolov. No pen name in GOOGLE.com

After the German Parliamentary election Chancellor Friedrich Merz will reign with the German SPD but without ex-Chancellor Olaf Scholz – from the SPD too.
Germany was said to be the biggest export nation in the World (CNN)
 A highly unusual e-mail to the White House led me to 2 conclusions;
1. The White House has an e-mail address
2. The White House e-mail address is well known but unknown to me ! To whom ??

French prime minister's Emanuel Makrone visit to Washington degenerated into raw with U.S. President Donald Trump. Full scandal, to name it cautiously. Macrone claimed falsely "France has paid 60% of all Western helps to Ukraine which includes EU & U S A . A sheer lie !
At a Press conference Russian foreign minister Sergey Lavrov stated "Russia is ready for peace talks with Ukraine but they were boycotted by dirty treacherous Ukrainian tricks & deceptions".

After the Washington mission of Emanuel Macrone failed president Volodymyr Zelenskyy decided to fly personally to Washington and promoted to Donald Trump the so called "row materials deal"- deposits of rare metals & minerals in exchange of American long-term help to Ukraine. The Ukrainian vast mineral resources deposits comprise lithium, titanium and graphite among others all kept in the Russian conquered zone. All fit to the U.S. military, space & defense industry needs , as CNN put it bluntly.

His visit coincided with the visit of the British prime minister Keir Starmer to Washington. So easy to fly to America – hop on , hop off ! Hop on - Kyiv ! Hop off – Washington !
Seemingly no sign of war at all. Earlier Zelenskyy had rejected similar American proposals "because of security guarantees lack". Currently the American support to Ukraine amounts to $350 billion. Say & write $350,000,000,000. American help to Ukraine up till now while Europe gave only $100 billions.
U.S. President Donald Trump had already denounced Zelenskyy as a "dictator" several times up till now but Zelenskyy remained unimpressed. Currently Donald Trump's agenda is overburdened by law suits so he really has little time for Zelenskyy and his skills as an actor by which he began his political career.
If the contract is not finalized by Zelenskyy his Washington trip makes no sense, Washington said bluntly .
Donald Trump named the Ukrainian $500 billion dept "a mire bag, not sharing humanitarian values but Ukrainian mineral resources: Lithium, Vanadium, Zirconium, Graphite etc. which Russia possibly owes too. So an empty bag of Ukrainian proposals !
Well before Zelenskyy Washington visit U.S. President Donald Trump gave an extensive Press conference which I recorded and which is affordable in copy upon request. He said "We buried $350 billion in Ukraine and we have no chance to get them back while Europe demanded back its meager $100 billion to Ukraine" Trump said also
"Artificial Intelligence is very much energy consumptive so we have to double our energy production no matter how".

Further Trump said "we help Canada with $200 billion annually but the give back to us only 4%. Canada relies only entirely on U.S. aid that's why Canada must become the 51st state of the Unioted States of America."
"The U.S.A. GIVES THE BEST MILITARY EQUIPMENT TO UKRAINE: AMERICA HAS THE BEST MILITARY EQUIPMENT IN THE WORLD AND WE GIVE TO UKRAINE!"
"Ukraine gave very much victims in this war – over 1 million sodiers plus 2 million civilians President Joe Biden failed to prevent this war it never shouldn't happen".
No single word lost on Ukrainian NATO membership.
No single word on American military guaranty to Ukraine.
As to Keir Starmer he was just heading to Washington and
couldn't attend Trump's press conference but he will somewhen learn about it.
"CBS put a question to Camala (Harris) but she failed to answer it. ".

In his visit to Washington,D.C. British Prime Minister Keir Starmer named President Trump "a good friend" and solicitated for more American help to Ukraine. Donald Trump responded to "as non-senses" and refused to give any guaranty to Ukraine. He came back very soon empty handed. Russian President Vladimir Putin said "Russia has nothing against the Ukrainian-US – deal" So Donald Trump exempted !

In his Washington visit president Zelenskyy agreed to give Ukrainian minerals to the U.S.A. The revenues will flow into a joint U.S.- Ukrainian funds but the U.S. rejected again any guaranty to Ukraine.
The 5th visit Zelenskyy to the White House brought nothing and degenerated even into a quarrel. Trump accused Zelenskyy
"that he risks World war three". The mineral subsoil resources deal was not signed and the talks turned into "verbal spat":
Trump accused Zelenskyy of been not serious about peace "and have not the cards to dictate". As CNN put it "full chaos
and shouting match in the lovely Oval Office!"

Further Trump accused Zelenskyy of "gambling with his people and gambling with World War Three". Zelenskyy was ordered to leave the White House; he flew to London to meet Keyr Starmer over the week end. Many European leaders criticized sharply Donald Trump but Hungarian prime minister Victor Orban stood with him and even praised him. An emergency meeting of European leaders was scheduled for Sunday in the United Kingdom , Zelenskyy will attend "because the U.S. are not a reliable partner any more"…
Russia got very satisfied of the quarrel spat…

NATO secretary General Mark Rutte – a native Dutch in fact – commented onto by repeating the words "javelin , javelin, javelin…." President Trump reiterated his concept of $350 billion help Ukraine should be thankful for because "Ukraine is running off soldiers!"
As to Zelenskyy himself he landed in London at 11:00 Saturday while the EU-emergency top
was scheduled for Sunday afternoon, said Malcolm Riffkind – former British defense minister in a BBC interview. Zelenskyy repeated his slanders to America. Keir Starmer didn't tweet at all unlike many European leaders- who actually ? Germany has no acting government after the German election chaos ?!
In fact weather is a massive part of flying.
What Zelenskyy wanted was support & publicity; he got both in London after he failed in Washington,so
Sahra Fick – BBC Russian team- even deepened the shouting match. Quite a spectacle.
In his visit to Downing street President Donald Trump was mentioned with no single word.
Macrone said: "There is one aggressor-Russia; there is one victim-Ukraine. We will support Ukraine for as long as it takes".
On Sunday Zelenskyy arranged a meeting with British King Charles to get reported yet again.
Turkey was invited to the talks too, "because it has the second largest NATO Army" (BBC).

Karl Bildt-former Swedish prime minister looking very much alike Keir Starmer-
stated to the BBC "this war cannot end without (military) pressure on Russia. He dubbed the EU peace efforts as "amateurish". Such a well trained hypocrisy !
BBC commentator Rob Watson in his 60ies mirrored heavily gesticulating with his hands & arms, as I saw it. and president Zelenskyy came home empty-handed sleeping one night in London AA.

Polish prime minister was shown to hink towards the meeting-yes, hinking; so ill.
NATO Scry. General Mark Rutte arrived at14:10. Zelenskyy is expected to get additional 2 billion British Pounds of aid to continue the war, BBC said. As a matter of fact the summit was held at Lancaster House in London with the slogan :"Secure our future!".
Chancellor Olaf Scholz arrived at 14:30 despite the fact he will be acting German Chancellor for 3 further weeks only after this summit. Hid sly his face from the cameras.

The UK, France & Ukraine combined their efforts to present a Sunday peace plan by phone to U.S. President Donald Trump after he "kicked out Volodymyr Zelenskyy from the White House". This is the shortest summary I could produce on what has happened on the EU-emergency conference in London.

The Sunday emergency London summit ended without signing any documents.
The very next day President Donald Trump paused all U.S. military aid " to push Ukraine to the negotiating table". Keir Starmer countered hypocritically :"I want people to be proud on where they live, we fund 1.5 billion pounds to build thriving high streets, parks, youth clubs, libraries and cultural venues. Supporting local growth, breathing life back into your neighborhood… " So poetical ! According to Donald Trump "a humiliated prime minister". All European media emphasized on the word "pausing" carefully avoiding other words such as "stopping" & "freezing". The advisor to Volodymyr Zelenskyy Igor Novikov summarized it in one word: "We fight for our lives; we have no other choice!". Is this true ?

Donald Trump accused the Biden administration of spilling $350 billion of military aid to Ukraine plus U.S. military intelligence data spying on Russia, so he decided to "pause further U.S. aid". So poetical. Well bearing in mind the U.S. satellites from the space – the so called **STAR LINKS** – provided by multi billionair Ellon Musk free of charge. **The STAR LINKS can be only partly compensated by France & Luxemburg.**

Zelenskyy dubbed the Friday White House spat "regrettable" but failed to apologize, saying "Ukraine is ready to sign any mineral& security agreement with the U.S. " and insisted again on territorial guaranties.
J.D. Vance said , the minerals deal is better deterrent of Putin than troops from some random country. In a BBC interview former Swedish prime minister Karl Bildt named it " for Zelenskyy this was a stab in the back"
but declined to comment on Keir Starmer saying "he said what he'd said",and closed down the interview.

Zelenskyy continued to re-affirm "that Ukraine will not its weaponry without American & European security guaranty.

U.S. President Donald Trump spent 100 minutes time to address the Congress.
BBC News spent 100 minutes on a British raper aged 28. The news as it is !

In an officious fax to the White House Zelenskyy praised again Donald Trump and apologized for his recent Oval Office failure. The News as it is. Emil
Donald Trump promoted a black U.S. teenager into a CIA-agent already from his childhood on wards. Trump vowed also to "crack on the unelected burocrates". America - the country of the unlimited possibilities. The news as it is. EMIL.

After Washington paused the American intelligence help to Ukraine president Zelenskyy became softer and apologize in written to U.S. President Donald Trump.
French President Emanuel Macrone planed a second visit to Washington together with Keir Starmer and Volodymyr Zelenskyy to put U.S. President under pressure. Instead he attended a second emergency top on defense of European leaders in Brussels- again with Zelenskyy participation. Macrone warned Russia for French nuclear capability in order to make it "softer in the peace talks". He insisted "Russia must give up." He proposed joint European peace keeping troops to Ukraine. Russian foreign minister Sergey Lavrov replied "we will consider this as direct NATO involvement". The Russian peace demand is neutral Ukraine without NATO membership. The Ukrainian peace plan is one million men strong Ukrainian army – 1,000,000 – supported , trained and equipped by Western Europe. Rather unmodest plan. He plans also a visit to Mohammed ben Salman – the Crown Prince of Saudi Arabia – after his visit to the conference in Brussels, Belgium. Light spirited on visits.
"Ukraine has to negotiate peace with Russia because they have no choice.
Russia has to negotiate peace because they have no choice too: in a different way- only I know why",
said Donald Trump.

Yesterday is over. It is already today. I spent my time to pray to both God & Buddha to bless you & our relations. That's all. Emil, The Netherlands. The time now is
President Donald Trump established a new strategic national crypto reserve in bit coins his own Family has assets in. The news as it is: Emil. However my own advice is not to risk to lay down assets in crypto.

Russia fired rockets to Kharkiv & Krivij Rijg and hit hotels there sheltering European civil servants there.
In fact they were Western military advisors to Ukraine with crocodile tears onto.

At the Brussels top Ursula von der Leyen spoke English and even kissed Zelenskyy on his cheeks; Olaf Scholz by contrast delivered his speech in his native German. The negotiations took place behind closed doors. The

leading voice was of British prime minister Keir Starmer who obviously pulled the strings.
Moscow expelled 2 further senior British diplomats for alleged spying.
Canada elected Mark Carney for a new prime minister to knot his tongue as he did; former bank director
like Ernesto Che GevuEara. Che Guevara – a Cuban National Bank Director- was killed 1967 in Bolivia
as a Father of 5 Orphans: Aleida, Hilda, Cella, Camillo....and one more

Mark Carney is the new Canadian prime minister to knot his tongue as he did; former bank director
like Ernesto Che GevuEara. Che Guevara – a Cuban National Bank Director- was killed 1967 in Bolivia
as a Father of 5 Orphans: Aleida, Hilda, Cella, Camillo....+ 1 . The news as it is : Emil, hall mark of truth.
In America every thing can happen.
* * *
Once upon my times while I was in the Army I read secretly Che Que Vara diary published in Berlin.
I hid this document secretly risking my life – or my time?? I understood: 1. He was a medical doctor
to remedy social disease of society. 2. He was very ill despite his lung disease . 3) Nevertheless Guevara
partisaned his mirror never betraying a friend. 4.) Finally he was betrayed & executed by the CIA – Central
Investigating Agency of the U.S.A. in 1967. 5). Such a glory full partisan to die! I follow ! I have 20 years
more to fight. The News as it is: Emil Tzolov, Hall Mark of truth.
*
The peace talks in Saudi Arabia led to the conclusion that the United States is an unreliable ally. United Europe
must face the Russian aggression alone.
During the peace talks in Saudi Arabia became clear the real figure of the frozen Russian assets aboroad: they
are 358 billion euro yielding 32 million euro of interest. Many European countries proposed confiscation of the
Russian assets in order to compensate the inflation havoc but France and Belgium vetoed this proposal sofar.
President Putin visited the newly liberated Kursk region for talks with President Trump special envoy Steve
Witkoff. Both sides agreed for a 30 days truce. Basically Putin agreed to peace but showed some reservations
most of all he rejected NATO-membership to Ukraine:"Too dangerous to agree to", he said. His words were:
"Yes,but no!" And the list of the NO's comprised 30 positions. "The peace will be enduring only if war root
causes are addressed. Ukraine does not mean peace but uses the pauses for further mobilization & weaponry]
replenishment". Further Russian demand was to the complete surrender of the whole Ukrainian army and a
future disband it- not simple giving up the occupied Russian territories but surrender. So president Zelenskyy
accused Vladimir Putin "of sabotaging the peace talks!". British prime minister Keir Starmer accused too
Vladimir Putin "of not taking seriously the peace talks". He accused Putin of "trying to delay the peace"
despite the fact Putin met in Moscow the U.S. special envoy Steve Witkoff. BBC did not commented on this
meeting at al: So far ! Far & fair. As to the Ukrainian troops' pull back from the occupied Russian areas BBC
admitted "the Ukrainians pull back but this is retrieval not an encirclement as Russia claims!".
U.S. President Donald Trump was speaking at a joint Press conference with the NATO- Secretary General Mark
Rutte in the Oval Office in Washington,D.C. in which they rejected the British position.
As to Canada Trump said "we don't need them, they need us however!". So bluntly ! All the world was frantically
working during the week end by video links : Canada, the U.S.A. , Britain, France , Ukraine , Russia etc.
No week end in view at all.
The Captain of the Russian cargo ship which collided with an oil tanker appeared to Hull Magistrate Court;
Mr. Vladimir Motin was accused of negligence and man slaughter and will remain in custody till 14th April
when he will be charged by the London Old Baily. Aah these Russians – collide with tankers and spill oil all
over the world, BBC exclaimed !
Above all a fire broke out in a discotheque in the small town of Koçani- 59 young people died, 150 injured.
President Zelenskyy extended his condolence to the victims' families! What else? The news as it is. Zelenskyy
was invited to the G7 top in Canada in June 2025. Trade war between Canada & the U.S.A.- Canadian prime
minister Mark Carney visited in one day France, Great Britain and a Press Conference in one single day..

It got known the size of the Russian Army – 1.5 million soldiers, while the Finnish army is staggering 900,000 soldiers under compulsory conscription and the biggest artillery in Europe.

In the phone talk with Donald Trump Russia insisted on security guarantees which means no Western weapon deliveries to Ukraine, recognition of the Russian territorial gains and stepping back to Russia of the Zaporizhija nuclear reactor which is actually a Russian one. It is the biggest in Europe. The Finnish president Cai-Göran-Alexander-Stubb -born on the 1st of April 1968 commented rather flamboyantly on the phone talk "Russia cannot decide neither on the NATO nor on the EU- membership of Ukraine!" .

On the phone Vl. Putin promised not to bombard neither Ukrainian power plants
nor Ukrainian energy infrastructure; on tv Ukrainian capital Kyiv was shown lavishly lit up by electric lamps. Unbelievable! Whom to trust ?On the phone indicated by Euronews I got no contact at all….
After an ample maze of news it became known that Vl.Putin rejected Donald
Trump's conditions on truce; "A vast humiliation to the American President", commented BBC. Euronews took exactly the opposite position. The only thing true was that EU-officials were not admitted to mingle in the phone talk; immediately afterwards V.Zelenskyy flew unrestrained to Helsinki for talks with the
Finnish president. From Finland Zelenskyy phoned up the U.S. President Donald Trump; on the conversation substance was not reported. A few words were spent on this meeting with a difficult balance. Russia however managed to destroy the power plant supplying the Ukrainian railways with electricity . Donald Trump commented "the phone call was useful" while German defense minister Boris Pistorius said exactly the opposite:"Number Zero" and "Putin plays a play!"; he advised Europe to take measures to arm Ukraine even further despite the fact his mandate expires on Easter. The EU-defense commissioner Cobillius urged Europe "to arm itself even stronger". The same position took the EU-Commission President Ursula von der Leyen in her 7 point "strategy paper".

Further peace talks were scheduled for 4 days later on again in Saudi Arabia; the U.S. delegation was lead by the U.S. Secretary of State Marco Rubio and the U.S. special envoy Steve Witkof. The U.S. stopped funding Radio Free Europe (=RFE, where I worked earlier) currently located in the Czech Republic.
French president Emanuel Macrone visited Berlin for talks with Friedrich Merz; he is however not a German Chancellor yet. Germany decided to keep its military budget to 1% of its GDP; only to compare with the Polish military budget of 5.8% of it GDP. Poland and the three Baltic states signed a treaty for canceling the anti-personal land mines ban already signed by 160 UN member states. Russia has not signed the treaty yet.

Still in Finland president Zelenskyy
As a matter of fact more details emerged on the phone call Zelenskyy placed to U.S. President Donald Trump-still hiding in lavish Finland with its 900,000 soldiers strong army - where he flew in unrestrained already at the begin this week: Zelenskyy proposed to the U.S.A. to take control of all Ukrainian power plants, all of the energy sector. All for the Ukrainian power plants' security.
This came from Finland where Zelenskyy is hiding after his White House spat attack back in February 2025.
It is not clear if Zelenskyy's Washington deal includes also the Zaporizhjie nuclear power plant which is actually Russian property liberated from Ukrainian occupation back in 2022. EPP Chairman Manfred Weber
praised the deal. "It will secure European safety-all over Europe", he lied to the media: "There is no cease fire, this is the reality", he stressed. European Commission Foreign Chief Kaja Kallas promised 5 million more artillery shells to Ukraine: this means 13,699 shells daily! 5,000,000:365=13,699 shells daily.
"The stronger Ukraine is on the battle field the stronger it will be at the negotiating table!" she emphasized with her usual stress exercising her nasty awful English: her initial proposal was 40 billion euro but finally the EU top in Brussels approved only 5 billion; not clear where the 5 billion euro will come from. 5,000,000,000 euro.

After his Finland visit president Zelenskyy flew to the Norway's capital Oslo to advertise again his failed policy.

Germany awarded Ukraine with 3 billion euro new military aid; till 2028 it will grant further 8 billion euro aid.
5,000,000,000 +3,000,000,000 +8,000,000,000 = 16,000,000,000 euro.
U.S. President Donald Trump awarded Boeing with a new F-47 fighter jet contract.
Heathrow shut down because of power cut; the airport is said to consume more electricity than the whole of neighboring Capital London. Massive German Neo Nazis demonstrations in both Dresden and Capital Berlin.
The news as it is . Emil, hallmark of objectivity.

During the peace talks in Saudi Arabia both the Russian and the Ukrainian delegations were lodged in one and the same hotel – The Ritz Carlton Hotel in Riyadh.; thus not Azizi in Borj. As a matter of fact the seize fire lasted only 30 hours but the both sides agreed not to attack their energy facilities but no one kept his promises. By hitting Russian energy hubs and oil depots the Ukrainians over smarted their enemy slowing down the Russian advance temp and increasing the Russian victims to 1,000 soldiers each day so the Russians were not pleased to talk about this. They were interested in keeping their Black Sea lanes open which is not very easy and to destroy more Ukrainian Black Sea port facilities in order to block Ukrainian exports. The main issue was stopping military actions both on the ground and in the air.
Both sides finally agreed on safe Black Sea navigation.

The talks were more on technical issues thus not on diplomatic ones , each delegation of 25 men strong.
At the same time Kaya Kallas visited Israel to polish her bumpy English.
All the same NATO Secretary General visited Poland and warned Russia not to attack Poland: "If you attack Poland the NATO reaction will be devastating" , ZDF 26-03-25 , 17:10. His warning was probably in English which he masters.

Neither the Germans nor the Dutch reported with no single word on the WH CHAT scandal.
Instead MAYBRIT – ILNER reports on Turkey. Aman van Waan ! Tulsi Gabbard – National
Intelligence Director - couldn't recall any details of the scandal. However „The Atlantic" weekly magazine reported on those facts. What it leaked out is that its Editor Jeffrey Goldberg is a devoted democrat.

Volodymyr Zelenskyy again in Paris. How many times ?? Obviously president Macron of France used the turmoil to smuggle through his ideas into the European Union . Both Donald Trump and Mark Rubio were at this time in Washington, D.C. Germany was represented by Olaf Scholz who's mandate as a Chancellor expires on the 20th April 2025.
Super fidels ! At the same time the Eifel Tower in Paris was lavishly illuminated with blue and yellow lamps – the colors of the Ukrainian national flag in flamboyant gesture of solidarity. It became not clear however if NATO Secretary Genal Mark Rutte was present at the Paris meeting. I could not see him on the group photo. The British prime minister Keir Starmer said "Vladimir Putin plays plays as usual , Ukraine is on his play book". Starmer pushed for further sanctions against Russia. It
became known the current size of the Ukrainian army – one million soldiers – 1,000,000 while the peace keeping troops from 7 European countries would number ca. 20,000 soldiers. Only to compare – the German unemployment army hit staggering three million men & women – 3,000,000. The peace keepers will be named rather poetically "Reassurance forces" . It became like a slogan ! A catch word! They called themselves "Coalition of the willing". Logically there must be "Coalition of the Non-willing" too: who will prevail and when ?? Meanwhile it got known that the number of European prisoners has drastically rozen – 1.5 million prisoners = 1,500,000. This only to compare facts.

At the same time Vladimir Putin was at the international top of the Arctic countries; he looked tired and older. He looks how to come out from his international isolation. However he turned out to be smarter and more inventive than his Western counterparts and proposed UN- mandate for Ukraine after the war ended.

His Ukrainian future vision is semi-independent territory under UN mandate.
Putin put also "it is a deep blunder to class Trump's Greenland ambitions "as a preposterous talk"" , said Yahoo;
The Trump administration sees Greenland's vast mineral ressources as vital for U.S. interests.
Putin took seriously Trump's efforts to claim Greenland for the U.S. The hint is clear-everybody can make what one wants into his back yard. Obviously Vl. Putin is active on several fronts simultaneously ..
Germany delayed again the chancellor nomination for the begin of May; it transferred its political chaos into neighboring France where Marine Lepen was forbidden to run for the presidential election .

APRIL 2025

German foreign minister Annalena Baerbock visited Kyiv for her 11th time; not clear for what.
Her mandate expires on 20th April – Easter. At the same time Russia was said to have launched a new barrage of drone attacks on Kharkiv but little was reported onto. Ukraine retaliated by hitting 2 Russian energy plants .
April began with the political beheading of the political actor Marine Le Pen by a conservative officious court inspired by president Emmanuel Macrone . He too has little time to stay in when the 2027 elections will sweep him away . Le Pen has only one scenario – to get acquitted.
The new Ukrainian foreign minister Andrej Sybiha took position to please the West. Both he and V.Zelenskyy started to plead for peace after 3 years rejecting it or at least impose Ukrainian conditions. So preposterous !

Democrat Corry Walker held the longest speech in the U.S. Congress history – 25:04 hours .
Poland started placing anti-personal land mines along its border with Russia in order to prevent eventual Russian invasion. The land mines are internationally banned by the Ottawa treaty. At the same time pop star Elton John continued to perform concerts in his native London at the age of 78. British style has been always exuberant !

Germany delay its Chancellor election for May 2025. The coalition treaty between the ruling parties CDU & SPD amounted to 144 pages of text in German. It is essential who'll be the Chancellor of Exchequer. Chancellor Olaf Scholz loiters. The CSU signed the coalition treaty first , CDU & SPD loiter on and on. Former German Chancellor Gerhardt Schröder went to a German court demanding more bureau space for his friends & satraps. Schröder is an advisor to a Russian oil company with 10,000 EUR monthly salary above his Chancellor rent.

The defense ministers of the Coalition of the Willing came together to discuss how to help Ukraine which is obviously losing to the Russian spring offensive. The Coalition of the Willings is no official entity but has over 2 million soldiers Europe wide under its command. John Healey – British defense minister- threatened Russia with further 4.5 billion pounds military aid to Ukraine in order to intimidate Vl.Putin. Only-he has not that money.
As for a joke a mistaken British embryo was implanted to mistaken British mother;
in Britain every mistake can happen ! Including a royal divorce or suspicious royal car crash death.

U.S. President Donald Trump commented on the high rise of U.S. import tariffs with the words :"I did it because some one has to do it!" Extraordinary Ukrainian prime minister on duty Denys Shmihal beat off all his peace proposals with the words "we are not a buffer zone". I fully sympathize with him. What about Keir Starmer ? He was involved in the heroic sinking of the Russian battle ship "Moskva" some 2 years earlier .When he has any dirty talk he refuses to go to the toilette. Ex German Chancellor Gerhardt Schröder failed with his pecuniary court trial.
As a consultant at a Russian oil company he gets 10,000 EUR monthly over his Chancellor pension.
The U.S. special envoy for Ukraine Steve Witkoff met Russian President Vladimir Putin in St. Petersburg to discuss for the 3rd time the Ukrainian war. At the same time in Germany deliberated the Coaltition of the Willing, the Ramstein Group
and the Ukrainian Contact Group. EU financial ministers' gathering in Warsaw. The last one can close the door.

All four came to nothing. Iran used the turmoil "to enrich uranium for a civil use" reaching enrichment level of 60% (BBC).

12. April 2025 in a mass British turmoil I predict current Labor Government will collapse and British prime minister Sir Keir Starmer will be ousted soon.

Ukrainian military site **MILITARNYI. Com** reported on a hit of Russian air crafts hangar in Tyotkino, Kursk region. So seemingly Ukraine too does not stick to any seize fire just as the Russians. Reportedly – and not for the first time Russia launched 97 drones into Ukraine; 57 were "intercepted". And the rest ? ? NATO Secretary General Mark Rutte visited the Odessa region in Ukraine but reported no irregularities.
German Chancellor-Candidate Friedrich Merz agreed with further German Taurus-MARSH rocket launchers delivery to Ukraine despite the objection they could be used for bombardment of the Russian Crimea bridge. His Father is said to be former German Nazi.
Greece decided to buy 16 further Taurus-Marsh missiles "in order to defend itself against any aggression". It is not clear how many Western rockets Ukraine had engulfed from the West so far; no numbers were released yet. It is well known Greece is a NATO member and doesn't bother too much of its security. The news as it is.

Ailing feeble former U.S. president Joe Biden in his 80ies refilled his time by criticizing Donald Trump and his first 87 days in office, accusing him of "damage and misadministration". It is not clear who stood behind Biden but his remarks are unproper and wicked. The media stressed on the importance of his short speech and repeated it many times like parrots having something entirely else in their minds ! An U.S. federal judge indicted Donald Trump of "contempt of the court" and introduced legal steps into accusing him formally. If so Trump might face legal procedure.

The European Central Bank – ECB- sank the leading interest down to 2.5% making thus credits cheaper. Who'll benefit from this is not clear – at least to me.
The U.S.A. stroke a deal with Ukraine for use of its mineral wealth. A special fund will be created supervised by both Washington and Kyiv. U.S. secretary of State Marko Rubio elucidated no further details but it leaked of importance is a graphite mine in central Ukraine . The U.S.A. will trade it in return for its military aid to Ukraine. U.S. vice president J.D.Vance visited Italy to discus … the Ukrainian war. He praised the Italian ceack down on migration. Italian prime minister Giorgia Meloni invited U.S. President Donald Trump for talks in Italy. Her invitation was accepted. Vance looked fat and fleshy while Trump – 40 years older – lashed Democratic Senator van Hollen for mingling into his Presidential duties. He rendered a sleazy account of his visit to an El Salvador prison.
It leaked also China delivered weaponry to Russia to fight in Ukraine; President Zelenskyy was infuriated and vowed "retribution next week!". In turn President Putin ordered 36-hours Easter seize-fire.
The German government placed submarine construction order for 6 billion EUR to a Kiel shipyard.

Two Russian cosmonauts and an American astronaut returned for Easter to the Earth after their joint 200 days' trip to outer Space. A paragon of peaceful coexistence! On the 20th April -Sunday-tennis player Alexander Zwerev hit his 28th birthday – the same day as Adolf Hitler! U.S.vice-president J.D.Vance used up the Easter vacation to visit the Vatican in a Sunday trip and to get blessed by Pope Francis. The very next day the Pope died aged 88; Vance learned the news in his aircraft bound for a state visit to India.

On 19. March 2025 Russia downed a French fighter jet over the Baltic Sea; the French armed forces joint staff reported on the incident only after Easter. Obviously they awaited a resurrection?!
It got known Egypt armed its air forces with Russian MIG-29 fighter jets – thus not French Mirage.

President Zelenskyy planed a peace talk with the U.S.A., the U.K and France for Wednesday after Easter. Russian President Vladimir Putin said "he had opportunity to speak many times to Pope Francis" and "he was an extraordinary person." U.S. President Donald Trump expressed his willing to attend to Pope Francis funeral scheduled for end of April 2025. Volodymyr Zelenskyy will attend too , after he was granted the charity to speak with the Pope earlier by phone. This became public only now and is not included in my earlier books. Former U.S. President Joe Biden will attend too in order to agitate world leaders against acting U.S. President Donald Trump.

After blessed by Pope Francis U.S. vice president J.D. Vance – not Cyrus Vance - arrived in India and signed a trade contract with worth $500 billion – it reads $500,000,000,000 . Rather impressive Pope bless. Vance visit lasted 4 whole days. He demanded bigger access for U.S. companies to the rich Indian market. In my view this will lead to inflation rise. The international pressure on the U.S. dollar rose from 25% to 40% ; calculation method unknown.

U.S. defense secretary Hegseth was accused for a second Pentagon security chat leak.
He denied all accusations massively supported by President Donald Trump :"It's an old story, try to find out something new", both said to the media.

The Russian attacks on Ukraine hold on. Führer Zelenskyy rejects for 5zillion times the Moscow peace proposals. Accepting them it will bring peace and prosperity to the whole of Ukraine. This can be achieved in surrendering of 50 miles disputed land on which lives practically no one . In a practical blunder president Zelenskyy dooms his people to 3-4 further years. For a peace he has nothing to offer – only cemeteries and ruins. Never the less he rams obstinately his anti-Russian no negotiation dogma gambling with world war 3 as U.S. President Donald Trump stated recently to the World.

Russia intensified its midnight missiles attacks on capital Kyiv using the absence of president Zelenskyy. Donald Trump accused him of being an obstacle to peace. Zelenskyy used his trip to South Africa to meet with president Cyril Ramaphosa. No details of their talks leaked yet. Trump remarked "if Zelenskyy does not make peace now he might lose the whole country in three years". He accused Zelenskyy of over confidence and arrogance in his approach". Zelenskyy fell back to a remark of former U.S. Secretary of State Mike Pompeo in which he said "the Crimea is Ukrainian". Trumps remark were muzzled by the media for more details. So Zelenskyy fired back on Trump's claim "he prolonged the war" and "he had nothing to boast about!" . Trump said negotiations with Ukraine are more difficult than with Russia. Zelenskyy prolongs the war un necessary by refusing to cede territory to Russia. Trump's peace plan foresees abandon of the Donetsk, Pokrovsk , Zaporizhie and Crimea regions and rejects Ukrainians NATO membership; the Zaporzhizhie nuclear power plant steps over to American control while Zelenskyy peace plan is unrealistic and obstinate. It's time for Zelenskyy to get the table. The Mayor of Kiyv-former box sportsman Vitalyy Klichko- agreed with territorial concessions to Russia:"It is not fair, it is painful but for the moment we have to compromise temporarily".
Polish President Andrzej Duda also summoned Ukraine to the negotiation table and ask for a compromise. British prime minister Keir Statrmer said approximately the same delivering a speech on board aircraft carrier "H.M.Prince of Wales".
Russia intensified its strikes on Dnipropetrovsk, Poltava, Kherson, Odessa, Sumi, Cherkasy, Pavlohrad and on Capital Kiyv. Hypocritically V.Zelenskyy said "he has no mandate to give up Crimea". Such a spectacle !

In Torgau-Germany- festivities took place to mark the 80th anniversary of the unification of Russian and American troops
to mark the end of World War Two and the defeat of the National Socialism. The Russian Ambassador Neçaev was not invited but he came as a private person. However he was forbidden to take the floor and to say few words on the event.

Such a vitriolic malice !!

According to Donald Trump each side of the war loses 5,000 young soldiers weekly in the battles; he said this has to stop.
In the middle of the negotiating preparations a car bomb assassinated a senior Russian general Yaroslav Moscalik while
driving his Volkswagen Golf 25 km East of Moscow in Malashikha . Another Russian general – Igor Kirillov – was already killed- again by a car bomb some time earlier again in Moscow- December 2024. So it looks like Moscow is not a safe area for generals. General Yaroslav Moskalik was deputy Chief of staff of the Russian army. Thus in charge in many military operations against Ukraine and many other secrete Russian military details. Now his "secrete" was blown . Moskalik was said to have led the Crimea annexation in 2014. Formally the news of his assassination was brought in by Svetlana Petrenko – a spokes woman of the Russian Army. It became clear the Ukrainian peace rejection consists of 3 points:
1. No country has to dispute the Ukrainian peace
2. No Ukrainian territory can be negotiated
3. No foreign country can forbid any future Ukrainian treaty or alliance
Obvious any territory dispute to Russia is still a taboo zone for Kyiv.

POPE FRANCIS' FUNERAL IN ROME

The preparations for Pope Francis funeral in Italy began with the start of Air Force NR.1- Donald Trump took off bound to Rome at 15:00 CET from the Washington Ronald Reagan air port.
Former U.S. President Joe Biden followed with a separate air craft to agitate against him at the out skirts of the official funeral ceremony. Rome is preparing its self with high police presence, sniffer dogs to sniff explosives and snipers and sharp shooters on the rooftops.

Euronews kept busy with the assassination of Russian General Yaroslav Moskalik till 28$^{th-29th}$ of April 2025 by repeating steadily the General was assassinated by detonation of remote control road side bomb in Malashikha near Moscow; according to the decorations seen he was not a "simple General": General Yaroslav Moskalik was deputy Chief of staff of the Russian army . Obviously in possession of many military secretes; now the secretes were blown up. CBS News' Holly Williams reported extensively on the scheme as "Vladimir Putin began a high-stakes meeting of his cabinet". All the world acts on a stage ! From Ural to Alaska !

Massive electricity failure all over both Spain & Portugal. German energy experts – such as Markus Rövekamp and others-
failed to explain the blackout for 55 million people (ZDF) : in Madrid, Barcelona, Sevilla, Lisboa, Porto etc. Air traffic,
trains, phone connections, water supplies – all collapsed !

The day after
power was restored to only 2.5 million people.
And we shed crocodile tears for Ukraine!

CNN accused unfounded "Donald Trump of being unpopular in his 1st term even more unpopular in his 2nd term". Something I don't agree with: all the world cannot overturn Donald Trump I am full fan of ! As CNN John King - seemingly younger than President Trump – concluded wisely " One hundred days and yet not wiser!". Reflection.

MAY 2025

May began with no German Government at all.
President Donald Trump marked his 100 days in office with growing unpopularity – ca. 40% of the opinion polls.
South Korean Intelligence said 600 North Korean soldiers were killed fighting for Russia in the war on Ukraine.
This cannot be verified independently, said BBC News but illustrates the globalization of the conflict.

The United States has signed the craved Mineral Agreement with Ukraine .
Scott Bessent – U.S. Treasury Secretary – signed the deal from the American side while Ukrainian deputy prime minister Yulia Svyrydenko-39- flew specially to Washington for the signature . It is not a peace deal, not a security guaranty , it is pure economic agreement but it will make Vladimir Putin to rethink his calculations. The deal signed is a very bad news for Moscow. U.S. top diplomat Marco Rubio welcomed the treaty and named it a milestone of the Ukrainian security and
prosperity. Ukraine posses only 5% of the global resources of rare minerals and they are in the occupied eastern provinces but obviously the U.S.A. is satisfied of the deal. The BBC named it "positive noises" while British prime minister Sir Keir
Starmer assessed it as "historic milestone to boost Ukrainian economy and security"; "wider frame work to come", said Ukrainian president Volodymyr Zelenskyy.
Both countries will share the profits of the deal and it will encourage further U.S. investments in Ukraine.
It is a business deal not a peace deal, the Ukrainian debts to the U.S.A. remain unpaid.

U.S. National Security Advisor Mike Waltz
left his post for a sheer havoc & tragedy for the ruling party both in Washington and Kyiv.
Donald Trump commented sarcastically "You may change even your religion " in a nasty foggy political Washington weather. Waltz began new job as an U.S. ambassador to the U.N. Marko Rubio became nationalsecurity a\ advisor parallel with his engagement as a Secretary of state.
Russian President Vladimir Putin did not comment on all these changes.

According to my own prognosis Marco Rubio will be the next successor of Donald Trump as a president of the U.S.A. Already now he attacks strongly the German Government as "sheer dictatorship". With right or without we have to wait.
President Vladimir Putin declared 3 days truce for the festivities of the 80 th Jubileum of Nazi Germany defeat in 1945.
Volodymyr dubbed this "a sheer cynicism". In the World War Two Ukraine was an ally to Nazi Germany and used to print Ukrainian banknotes with a Hitler swastica. The international public kept full silence.

At Victory Day President Donald Trump announced his decision to re-open the notorious Alcatras prison;
It was closed in the 1960ies. Donald Trump expressed also "his deep sympathy with Holliwood and imposed 100% charge for foreign film customers because "they steel our films!""

No American reports on VE Day.

80 years earlier – in 1945 – Sir Winston Churchill said "We celebrate our victory in Europe; we cannot celebrate everywhere yet!" Tea party followed after the parade in London; the Ukrainian detachments marched in result. Both Ukrainian troops and Ukrainian president Volodymyr Zelenskyy attended the parade in London.
The Czech prime minister Pëtr Pavel promise 1.8 millions artillery shells as a help to Ukraine. This is not necessary to them to march in London "war parades" which lasted 4 days. Ahead of the victory parade in Moscow Ukraine bombarded
the Russian Capital airport to prevent foreign dignitaries to attend the parade. .

A slogan rose up :"Don't seek Russian help to save
Greenland!", so Euronews.

After six months brake Germany established new government with Friedrich Merz as a German Chancellor and Frei as a financial minister. Nevertheless Germany continues suffering under its recession. Annalena Baerbock and her Green party are slightly represented in the German Bundestag but not in the German Cabinet. And this is the end
of the six months long German political crisis. Boris Pistorius continues his mandate as a German defense minister. Very soon he is likely to have to intervene.

Only one hitch: in the German Bundestag election Chancellor CDU candidate Friedrich Merz failed to achieve majority. According art. 63 (2) of the German constitution (=Grundgesetzt) he failed. So he was elected in the 2nd round.
All politicians world wide are shocked ! It is for the first time in the German political history ! The German political chaos deepens. A sheer triumph for the German far-right AfD. Euronews reported instead on Rumanian election till 14:00.
As a result France and Poland lost enthusiasm to meet Friedrich Merz as German Chancellor. He started his first day of
office with a Paris visit to discuss with French President Emanuel Macron the French-German nuclear arms cooperation.
ZDF-correspondent Diana Zimmerman reported extensively onto.

Because of Donald Trump's austerity measures on education, development and research 350 top scientists threatened to leave the U.S.A. bound to Europe. European President Ursula von der Leyen welcomed them with a short speech . Donald
Trump did not commented. In an exclusive BBC interview former president Joe Biden criticized sharply Donald Trump
and his current international policy; it became not clear what Biden-aged 88 – wanted to say. He accused Trump of "confiscation not peace, freedom & democracy which are our U.S. values". He accused Trump pushing Ukraine to retreat some land to Russia. No single word on the mineral treaty signed both by Ukraine and U.S.A. recently.
U.S. Defense Secretary Pete Hegseth single-handedly halted U.S. military aid to Ukraine in the early days of the Trump administration. "It's incomprehensible," a senior Ukrainian lawmaker told Newsweek. U.S. arms shipments to Ukraine were briefly halted in early February, Reuters reported. The news agency reported Tuesday that Hegseth's office had issued a verbal order to halt 11 flights carrying weapons and supplies to Ukraine shortly after the Trump administration took office.
Ramzan Kadirov-48 years old Russian forces activist retired his position for health reasons.

After a Washington meeting British prime minister Sir Keir Starmer -Labor, 62 years old-convinced the U.S. to reduce the American
tariffs to 10 percent, British steel and British aluminium to 0%. Donald Trump named this "a historic deal" and it is really a such one.
The American President insisted a 30-days cease fire instead the Russian proposal of 3 days only to celebrate the 80th anniversary of the Russian victory in the World War II. The celebration ended with a huge military parade in the Red Square in Moscow with world leaders from 27 countries including the Chinese President Xi Jin Ping and others. So Vladimir Putin demonstrated once again he was not isolated internationally. Ukrainian president Volodymyr Zelenskyy named the parade "a full scale cynicism" while Putin cited Sir Winston Churchill phrase "talking jaw to jaw is better than war!"
The EU-foreign ministers met together for a conference in Lemberg, Western Ukraine. They followed the Zelenskyy proposal to establish an international war crime tribunal for Russian war crimes in Ukraine. The Ukrainian name of Lemberg is Lwiw, the Russian name is Lvov. No extra security measures were taken because Lemberg is not in the war zone.
4 European prime ministers visited Kyiv to show support to V. Zelenskyy :prime ministers of France, Britain, Germany & Poland resp. Emmanuel Macrone, Keir Starmer , Friedrich Merz and Donald Tusk. So it is visible there is no war at least in Kyiv they demonstrated Dutch courage to visit it unlimited: They put an ultimatum to Putin – either to accept the Western proposal or to face even tougher sanctions. The Kremlin spokes man Dmitryy Peskow said : "There are no communication channels to the West, how to accept or reject their plan ?! Very clear logic – even for Keir Starmer.
Ukraine has disposed an alleged Hungarian spy network in Ukraine; the Hungarian authorities named this "an Ukrainian propaganda trick". Hungary has a small Hungarian minority living in Ukraine.

All of the sudden President Putin proposed direct peace talks with Ukraine in Istanbul for 15.May Thursday . Both sides make clear distinction between seize fire and truce. The Europeans are not united esp. because of the U.S. reservations, said ZDF. Zelenskyy
repeted several times:"I will wait for Putin on Thursday, 15th May, Turkey". However the chances for this diplomacy are slim.
Kremlin replied sour :"This is not the kind of speech to speak with Russia !" Well ahead of the peace talks in Turkey Poland ordered
Moscow to close the Russian consulate in Capital Warsaw. Only the consulate in Poznan remained open. Quite an anti-Russian
symphony ! Cardinal Robert Francis Prevost – bishop of Chicago- was elected as new 267th Pope under the name POPE LEO XII. Donald Trump welcomed his election 15 minutes before I did so. As a matter of fact his Vice-President J.D.
Vance is a catholic too – he converted to Catholicism in 2019. The Pope urged an end of the Ukrainian war in his inauguration speech. After the Mess the Pope met Ukrainian leader Zelenskyy for an enlarged talk. The ZDF dubbed mistakenly Friedrich Merz as an U.S. vice-president (18-05-2025, 19:08). Merz instead of Vance. My sharp ear hearing!

The deal U.S. President Donald Trump stroke with Saudi Crown Prince Mohamed Ben Salman
was for 160 Boeing air crafts for $600 billion – $600,000,000,000. The Crown Prince didn't even thank him for the deal
"because it was a private non U.S. one". Boeing employs some million workers world wide. (BBC News, ZDF in addition).

Mathew Watwaker-a NATO spokes man demanded 5% defense contribution to all its members deducted from all their country GDP. A bit overdone. Overdone dear Sirs.

In Constanz German special forces arrested 3 Ukrainian saboteurs set to attack German infrastructure .
Chancellor Friedrich Merz addressed the German Bundestag in non-sence 58 minutes speech for which I recall noth.
German ZDF-TV canceled its 17:00 news broadcast habit. More to follow to their call off. Some Elsinor tragedy - probably. No Shakespear involved . The news as it is.
Ford on strike at its German branch in Collogne.

Kremlin sent **Vladimir Medinsky** to Istanbul to negotiate the peace plan with Ukrainian president Volodymyr Zelenskyy.
Medinsky is a Russian editor of a book on the Ukrainian war. He led the Russian delegation back in March 2022. He is an ideologist of Russian full scale invasion into Ukraine.
 At the end of the week UK defense minister John Healey met his German counterpart Boris Pistorius to discuss further 2 million rounds heavy caliber ammunition delivery to Ukraine. Both criticized sharply Vladimir Putin and his approach
to the peace talks. Robert Brieger – EU military Committee Chair man promised too more ammunition to Ukraine. "with the aim to double the number compared to the previous year", he said to Euronews.
Both President Zelenskyy and President Putin did not come to the peace talks.
"The Russian delegation missed any decision makers", said snubbing Zelenskyy, himself on a visit in Albania – ca. 1,000 km away from Istanbul, dubbed by CNN as "theater like pathetic clown". Finally they decided a prisoners of war swap – a 1,000 prisoners from each side – and a continuation of the talks in June. **Vladimir Medinsky** seems to be a rather skilled negotiator after all!

One day later Kremlin spokes man Dmitryy Peskov asked who will sign eventual agreements from Ukrainian side?! Zelenskyy President mandate expired already in May 2024 - "so he is out of legitimacy", said Peskov. The conflict roots were not been touched by any side, said BBC correspondent John Inwood.

The head of the Ukrainian catholic church handed in to Pope Leo XIV a list of **momentous** Ukrainian prisoners of war and asked for their release. The late Pope Frances had had several times intervened for Ukrainian prisoners' release.
Former U.S. President Joe Biden diagnosed with cancer on score 9 of the Gleason scale. President Donald Trump extended
his condolence and sympathy to him and wished him speedy recovery (CBS). At the same time Amazon announced "Russians are survivors because they have one extra chromosome". Which could be true. True legend !

The long expected trunk call between Donald Trump & Vladimir Putin brought nothing despite of its duration of 2 hours -
translation time included- Putin simply did not disarray from his vacation at the Black Sea resort of Sochi with a subtropical scent. We have to wait for another phone call. President Zelenskyy failed to comment onto. The news as it is.
According to the CNN Putin was unmoved. After the phone call he visited the Kursk nuclear power plant so it is unbelievable that he mad the phone call in the Black Sea resort of Sochi. Zelenskyy turned off the Russian claims saying "He is obliged by constitution to defend the Ukrainian people "and "The prolonged negotiations only help Putin to buy time ". Which all might be true.

In a wealthy Madrid suburb Ukrainian secret service shot dead pro-Russian politician Andrij Portnov while driving his children to school; he was aid to the former pro-Russian president Victor Yanukovich.

The Polish Parliament condemned both Russia and Belorussia for encouraging illegal migrants to stream to Poland asking for asylum and thus destabilizing both Poland and Europe. There is quarrel between Poland

and Germany: Germany sends back the migrants to Poland but Poland rejects to accept them, so they stranded. In the full time both German TV channels – ARD & ZDF failed to report on the strifle , they kept busy with Peepy Long Stocking – a Scandinavian saga 80 years ago. Little reported on the current event Germany

sent its 45 tank brigade of 5,000 soldiers to Lithuanian capital Vilnus – Rudnikai to strengthen German presence there; Vilnus is close to the Russian border and some 1,000 km away from Germany. German Chancellor Friedrich Merz blessed the event in a television show-up. As a matter of reality the current soldiers number is only 400 men. Obviously Germany is not flush with cash yet nor any time soon. Ukraine rejected bluntly the Russian plan of demilitarized buffer zone in the disputed areas between Russia and Ukraine and claimed again the conquered narrow patch in the Kursk region. So hypocritical !

U.S.President Donald Trump announced $175 billion strategic defense system plan in Space called "Golden Dome."The Congress Budget Commission evaluated his program at $570 billion; it will speed up the arm racing at the venue of Space. Trump is set to accomplish his plan by the end of his term.
Further on his administration threatened the European Union to get charged by 50% tariffs on its exports to the United States. Instead to negotiate those charges the EU prefers to get involved in the Ukrainian war on the losing side. Such a short-sighted policy ! Such short-sighted politicians from 26 countries ! Too much interrogation marks !

Boris Bondarev, an expert in international relations and foreign policy and a former Russian diplomat, stated in a "Moscow Times "article that Russia's goal is to "exhaust both Ukrainian society and Western countries, and especially Europe, in order to end military support for Kiev."
Immediately after the start of the large-scale Russian invasion, Poland proved to be Ukraine's best friend of all its neighbors. Unlike many Western leaders, the Polish leadership did not urge Ukrainians to surrender, but believed that it was possible to stop Russia.

In a television interview CDU-political spokes man Armin Lasched guaranteed that Israeli Prime Minister Benjamin Netanyahoo will be not arrested upon his entry in Germany despite the International Arrest Warrent against him issued by the International Criminal Court ICC which accused him of massive genocide in Gaza. Armin Laschet assured him "he will be not arrested in Germany despite the arrest warrant against him . What about Vladimir Putin ? He too is accused by the ICC for genocide.
As to Armin Lasched – body weight 120 kg – he is spokesman of the CDU – Parliamentary fraction in the German Bundestag. 120 kg body weight equal to 265 pounds, an overwhelming politician

U.S. President Donald Trump-with no neck tie- wrote on X:"Putin is insane! Absolutely crazy! I knew him for a long time and I got along with him but now not any more because he sends rockets and kills people so I don't like him at all "and he threatened Putin with further sanctions. Kremlin countered with the words "the U.S. President is rather overloaded emotionally !" It looks very much like Cold War _ 2.
Diesel scandal at Volkswagen car factory in Wolfsburg,Germany.
Volkswagen Boss Martin Winterkorn jailed for 4 years. At the same time the British Monarch King Charles visited Canada to open the session of the Canadian Parliament in a gesture of show of solidarity with the Canadian people; he demonstrated support against the U.S. plans and ambitions to turn Canada into 51st
U.S. state.
French president Emmanuel Macrone toured Vietnam, Indonesia and Singapore to promise broad French support to them and intensifying their foreign trade with France. The three countries suffer from the heavy American trade tariffs which Washington imposed on them in May 2025.

The Western allies lifted all restrictions on Ukraine to use of long-range missiles against Russia, said the new

German Chancellor Friedrich Merz. Now Ukraine has permit to attack any military target deep inside Russia such as fuel stores and ammunition depots and thus to defend itself against Russian attacks beating them off in advance. The Western allies are France, Germany, UK and U.S.A., said Merz. He visited Finland and praised its bravery against potential Russian aggression. The scope of the TAURUS-MARSH rockets is 500 km (313 miles) and the permit of their use is escalation of the war. The former German Chancellor Olaf Scholz had opposed such a permit to the Ukraine. The Russian foreign minister Sergey Lavrov was not surprised at all:" We know of this permit already long long time ago", he said. With knowledge or without it the war escalation is a war escalation.
So simple. Already the very next day Ukrainian president Volodymyr Zelenskyy arrived in Berlin for talks with the German Chancellor Friedrich Merz . Merz looked a little bit perplexed. Zelenskyy looked furious and "wanted to bury Russia", as he said. He was received with military salutes and brass music. Merz agreed with the Ukrainian demand to hit with German missiles Russian targets deep inside Russia – something which we know already and which is escalation of the war. Friedrich Merz promised German help to Ukraine to facilitate its own missiles production and to thrust them against Russia. Merz stressed "infantry wins battles logistic wins wars". BBC said for him "he is very ambitious!"
Merz stressed on cooperation with the Ukraine on the field of military, industry, agriculture,
and also "Putin speaks the language of peace, he speaks the language of aggression". Merz thanked Zelensky for coming to Berlin while Zelensky thanked the journalists for coming to the news conference.
"We have to pressure Russia for a seize fire and Germany must increase its military supply to Ukraine" while Merz rejected discussing publically details. Both stressed the importance of the frozen Russian assets amounting to 50 billion euro. Zelensky insisted on Ukrainian participation in the NATO summit in June "Standing out of the summit means victory of Russia but not over Ukraine but over Nato" while Merz concluded "we have invested sufficiently in diplomacy". Zelensky accused Putin of delaying the peace negotiations . Merz promised again German aid of 5 billion EUR = 5,000,000,000 and additional military equipment
German help for joint military production of long range weapons both in Germany and inside in Ukraine while Zelensky expressed his hope for further seizure of Russian assets abroad. Moscow named this a sheer new provocation. For a first time Zelenskyy was dressed in a suit but without neck tie.

A short summary to close this chapter : Germany promised to Ukraine full military, industrial, logistical, humanitarian and other support because Chancellor Friedrich Merz is an adventurer. Germany is the second - largest supporter to Ukraine after the U.S.A. esp. these 5,000,000,000 EUR granted to Ukraine today.
Both sides showed no nuance of disagreement; they rejected the Russian proposal of buffer zone around Kursk, Bryansk, Belgorod & Sumi regions which Zelensky rejected with the words "we must make this war most painful to Russia". In the nuances of the reception the figure of the German unemployment became known – 3.9 million; 3,900,000. And in Ukraine – even more.

According to Zelensky Russia had allegedly amassed 50,000 troops along the Ukrainian border (which border?) and prepares them for a huge summer offensive. Which might be true.

In a televised interview the Russian foreign minister Sergey Lavrov set the peace talks in Istanbul for 2nd of June 2025 which is Monday. Literary Lavrov said in "Stambyul". He stressed on the root cause of the conflict which should be removed. The Russian delegation will be led again by **Vladimir Medinsky** – a prolific Russian writer. Meanwhile Jacques Baud published his book "How West Lead Ukraine to Defeat " .
In the meantime Turkish foreign minister Fidan visited Moscow and spoke with both Vladimir Putin and Sergey Lavrov. The Kremlin speaker Dmitrij Peskov declared "with the treaties forged with Ukraine Germany and the West entered direct war with Russia".
U.S. President Donald Trump set 14-days dead lock for Vladimir Putin to start the peace talks . Putin obviously is keeping his time limit. An Ukrainian drone killed the Mayor of Stavropol in the disputed regions. 10,000 Russian

troops entered the town of Tzetzevka. The Russian pre-condition for the peace talks in Istanbul is full stop of the Western weaponry to Ukraine.

The European Parliament discussed in Brussels the vote withdrawal of Hungary. The discussion started in 2018 because Hungary frequently misused its right of veto to block important European decisions regarding the Ukrainian war and "it leads Europe by the nose by vetoing it".

JUNE 2025

The month of June began with a railway bridge and Russian passenger train blown up by Ukraine in the Bryansk and in Kursk regions leaving 70 people dead. Neither Ukraine nor Russia claimed responsibility. Ukrainian ballistic missiles hit 4 strategic Russian air fields 1,000 – 4,000 km away from the front line one of them in Olenya, Murmansk, Irkutsk, , Ivanovo and Ryazan - destroying 41 fighter bombers parked on the tarmac before they even managed to take
off; this is was said to be one third of the strategic bombers Russia has on stock. The preparations for this attack had lasted 18 months . The harm amounted to $7 billion - $7,000,000,000 and The NewsWeek dubbed it "The Russian Pearl Harbor." The strategic bomb jets were capable of carrying nuclear explosives.
The speculations rose that these audacious attacks were launched from inside Russia after been smuggled there in proximity. A great humiliation for Russia one day before the Russian-Ukrainian peace talks in Istanbul. Nato secretary general Mark Rutte rejected any American involvement. He warned "that very soon Europe will be not able to defend itself against any new Russian aggression ".

In an ample press conference in Glasgow British prime minister Sir Keir Starmer said "if we want to deter a war we must prepare for a war". The UK is up to furnish 12 new attack submarines, six new ammunition factories and raise its defense budget up to 2.5% of its GDP. It sounds good but the construction of one of these submarine can takes 10 years.
"Nothing works unless we all work together! We deliver peace through strength". And he revealed his defence plan: "We never work alone. We work through our strategic strength: we praise Nato great again! The UK is steadfast ally to Ukraine".
Parallel to the peace talks in Istanbul a conference of Baltic and North-European prime ministers took place in Lithuania with participation of the Ukrainian head Volodymyr Zelenskyy. In his speech he condemned Russia in many ways and asked for more military and industrial aid to Ukraine. He plans 15 billion pounds aid to Ukraine; Lithuanian defense minister Da Vile Sakaliene accused Kremlin "of mocking at the United States of America" obviously aiming to escalate the conflict to international level.
The Istanbul peace talks brought nothing – Russia rejected all Ukrainian demands, esp. unconditional cease fire and return of the abducted Ukrainian children back home. Neither President Putin nor President Zelenskyy attended the talks. Both delegations exchanged documents through the Turkish side. The Russian demand was its claim on the regions of Donetsk, Cherson, Zaporizhiya and Luhansk-regions Russia unlawfully occupied but never fully controlled . Both sides remained deeply divided on key issues.

Britain released a new weapon factory – a "clear message to Russia", said British defense minister John Healey. EU foreign policy head and vice – president of the European Commission Kaja Kallas warned of growing relations of Russia and China:"The global security ties are extremely worried of such relations", she rattled .
U.S. Secretary of State Marko Rubio accused the German regime of tyranny in view of its treatment of the AfD party. Russia started suspicious maneuvers in the Baltic Sea – Poland protested in vain.The new Polish President Karol Nawrocky is against Ukrainian membership in Nato. As president he is supreme commander

of the Polish armed forces.

It became clear that Russia posses tactical nuclear weapons and the West – not. A sheer cross road .

Former German foreign minister Annalena Baerbock became president of the U.N.O. General Assembly for one year despite strong Russian objection. A largely ceremonial post , she'll get inaugurated on 09.September 2025.

The Nato defence ministers convened in Brussels ; U.S. defence secretary Pete Hegseth advocated again for 5% of GDP for all member states. They all discussed the option of 5% of the overall budget to be spent on reliable defence .

In Washington, D.C. President Trump received German Chancellor Friedrich Merz and praised him for his good English, for the high German defence spending and Merz commitment to resolve the Ukrainian crisis; finally Merz is 8 cm taller than Donald Trump. It became known that Donald Trump's grandfather Friedrich was born in Germany-Kreis Bad Dürkheim somewhere in Rheinland-Pfalz

Both leaders plan war and war escalation. The media spilled superlatives all over the carpets. Unlike me.

ZDF Washington correspondent Ulf Schmiese confused several times the names of the both leaders-unlike me.

Both leaders avoided the tariff issue-unlike me-the tariffs on German steel and German aluminum.

The discussions took place in a friendly and warm atmosphere.

Multi Billionair Elon Musk suggested "Donald Trump must step down and be replaced by his Vice-President J.D.Vance!". He accused Trump of ingratitude .So what is Merz doing in Washington and in the White House ??

Merz is the 4th European leader to visit Washington after Macrone, Melony and Zelenskyy.

The conversation lasted 40 minutes, afterwards Merz headed back for Germany. No Press-conference.

Merz only said "we have to push on Putin stronger, stronger, stronger to make him stop this war.

We are entirely with Ukraine!" It got known however that one day before his visit Donald Trump had had a phone call with Vladimir Putin. **Nothing and yet again nothing was reported on this phone conversation between the two state men.** Both have to meet again in ten days at the G7 top in Canada.

Trump designated the U.S. relations to Germany as "tip-top".

Meanwhile Ukraine attacked four Russian fuel reservoirs and set them afire.

And again meanwhile Russia offered political asylum to Elon Musk – Donald Trump's top man & top advisor, reported the Russian State Media TASS.

For the prisoners' of war exchange the Ukrainian side simply did not appear at the meeting point:

such Ukrainian demagogy! The Russian Army liberated the city of Dnepropetrovsk – the utmost West of the Donetsk region. The Ukrainian army denied such a happening as "propaganda". It dismissed the Russian numbers as "propaganda"esp.the firing of 500 Russian on Ukrainian target. Only there is one hitch – such Ukrainian targets seem to be endless. How could the Russians hit every day new targets? And new targets? And new targets? And new, a new, anew?! Ukrainian President Wolodymyr Zelenskyy named the situation "very difficult" but elucidated no details. So we have to consume his 1,001 night stories and clap applause to his narrative. The news was brought to public by CNN Berlin correspondent Frederik Pleitgen.

Nato Secretary General Mark Rutte – former Dutch prime minister – warned that "Russia will attack Nato within 5 years with missiles 5 times faster than the sound; there is no east or west , there is only one Nato; the European capitals are only few minutes away from the Russian hit", he said to Euronews during his visit to London. He urged the Nato countries to increase their defence spending to 3.5% of their GDP or to face a Russian aggression. His host Sir Keir Starmer agreed fully with him. Mark Rutte named this a "Quantum Leap". It sounds like the Chinese "Great Leap " in the Mao Tse Dung's times. Nothing is new. No new inventions.

The U.S. Health Secretary Robert J. Kennedy Junior fired 17 of his team because of sloppy work. Could happen !

In the aftermath of the rebellion in Los Angeles U.S. Defence Secretary Hegseth said "he and Trump can send U.S. troops everywhere in the U.S.A." And beyond, I would say!

Vice-President J.D. Vance said "the blood feud between Trump and Elon Musk is not going for the good of Musk".

And this is the end of the Story ! Nothing new: already 1977 Judas Priest released a song called "Dissident Agressor"! So simple !
In the Berlin Willi-Brandt House German SPD Chairman Rolf Heinrich Mützelich advocated for "talks with Moscow to avoid any armed confrontation". The party top and the German SPD defence minister Boris Pistorius ridiculed him instead to take any constructive discussion: the political chaos in Germany continues even after the resignation of Chancellor Olaf Scholz in May 2025.
Rolf Heinrich Mützelich himself – aged 65 - is rather controversial but pragmatic, a critic of Volodymyr Zelenskyy.

Dr. Bittner-SPD- German jurist and author- wrote on 08.August 2022- from a machine translation:
"The political situation is appalling and the persecution of dissenters in connection with the Ukraine war is taking the form of unbridled fascism. It is unacceptable that state terrorism is being carried out here under the eyes of the world public. The persecution of critics and opposition figures by Ukrainian government organizations must be stopped immediately. The federal government (of Germany) is called upon to lodge a protest with the Zelenskyy government against the discrimination against German nationals in Ukraine… and to stop all aid for Ukraine. The list of the CCD must be deleted immediately."
CCD means Common Core of Data database maintained by the National Center for Education Statistics NCES.

German defence minister Boris Pistorius came for the weekend to Kiyv. He declared "the full German support to Ukraine."
Pistorius pointed out "the new German government is sticking with Ukraine and even it will increase its support to Ukraine "es koste was es wolle": "Whatsoever the cost might be!"" . The President of the European Union Ursula von der
Leyen also expressed support for Ukraine :"Es koste was es woll!" She too is a German. Her German is better than mines:
because she is a native German. Finally Boris Pistorius promised 900 billion euro help to Ukraine mostly in the form of
joint missiles & drones production in Ukraine, reported finally the German ARD (First German Television). No videos shown; obvious secretes available.

The very next day Zelenskyy hosted a conference in the eastern Ukrainian city of Odessa with the leaders of Eastern European Nato countries. They condemned Russian invasive politic and decided to stand together against Kremlin At the same time
German Chancellor Friedrich Merz hosted Danish prime minister Metta Frederiksen, greeted her with a military honors and military orchestra and discussed with her the Ukrainian war reiterating aid to Ukraine and firm policy against Russia. The top
of their agenda was the war in Ukraine and the European security. No further details were released for their joint meeting.
The Odessa conference was absolutely redundant in the face of the fact G7 top in Alberta, Canada and Nato top in the Netherlands are impending in June 2025.

100 prominent members of the left wing of the German SPD-party published a manifesto against the stationing in Germany of U.S. medium-range missiles and stressed upon diplomatic talks with Moscow not a military confrontation with Russia. They criticized the current German policy of confrontation against Russia. They criticized the planed defence spending increase of 5%
The manifesto illustrates the deep division within their own party SPD, reigning now in coalition with Christian-Democratic Union CDU of Chancellor Friedrich Merz.
At the same time Russian President Vladimir Putin gave a command to strengthen the Russian army to face the growing

European coalition seeking confrontation with Russia.

In a talk show Euronews revealed the number of Ukrainian refugees in Europe – 4.3 million= 4,300,000 refugees. The British budget deficit rose to 100 billions pound – double as much as its defence spending, said British member of Parliament Mel Stride in an Euronews interview.
On 15. June 2025 President Trump marked his 79th birth day with an imposing military parade in Washington, D.C. 6,000 soldiers and 128 army tanks took part in the parade. The very same day Trump flew to Alberta, Canadia to attend the 3-days G7 top in Alberta; a venue for bilateral talks rather than show of unity.
Ukrainian president Volodymyr Zelenskyy too attended the top in his intrusive style in the Canadian Rocky Mountains despite the fact that his native Ukraine is n o t among the leading 7 industrial nations of the world. He lodged in the luxurious Hotel in **Kananaskis. U.S. President Donald Trump said "we wouldn't be here if President Putin attended too"** His talks with German Chancellor Friedrich Merz – a hard-liner were scheduled already for the first day. Their talk lasted exactly 20 minutes.
The Middle East war shifted the center of the talks far way from Ukraine focus so that Trump
left the G7 top prematurely , so new sanctions on Russia couldn't be discussed and president Zelenskyy could not speak with Trump; he spoke with the Nato Secretary General Mark Rutte who also attend the G7 top. Zelenskyy demanded more military help, more political pressure on Russia and more military heavy armor against it. "We are not looking at a cease fire – we're looking for a better than a cease fire" said Trump to journalists accompanying him backwards on board of his air craft; thus not his helicopter. Aboard Air_Force_1 Trump gave a short Press conference and stated "Macrone always does it the wrong way!" Said bluntly Trump simply refused to sign the G7 final document.

The reason for leaving prematurely the summit Donald Trump handed over to his spokeswoman **Karoline Leavitte**.to explain the details which led him to his decision. Anyway Trump re-assured the G7 he would attend the Nato summit in The Netherlands . But the fact is clear – the G7 got G-6 and Volodymyr Zelenskyy has to come in vain let alone to go back home with some profit. " In fact Trump left the summit because he wanted to celebrate his birthday in a closer circle and because he is skeptical of more sanctions on Russia as they will hurt the U.S.A. too", put it the BBC reporter on the G7 summit James Landale. Practically " Trump deserted the summit." "Obviously President Trump had lost his taste for diplomacy", commented the BBC impartially. The G7 ended without signing any treaty, any declaration, any joint statement on Russia's invasion in Ukraine and this was a bitter disappointment for Volodymys Zelenskyy, as BBC commented.
And this the end of Part 3 of my book. Above all Russia set a new peace condition to Ukraine- to destroy all the weaponry it got from the West and iused it on the battle field. As to Donald Trump he simply fired his intelligence director (Suzi Gabor ??)

In Bulgaria police arrested 3 Ukrainians for kidnapping a minor person and asking a ransom for his life, so ABV.bg.
Russian President Vladimir Putin declared his readiness for peace talks with Ukraine. Ukraine its self agreed to allow Ukrainian citizens to have double citizenship to motivate their coming back to Ukraine after the war. It is the first time in Ukrainian history for such a decision fluctuating in the centuries past.
The Israeli defence minister Israel Katz compared Iranian Ayatollah Ali Homeini with Adolf Hitler and denied him the right to exist , saying bluntly "He is a modern days Adolf Hitler".
Spanish Prime Minister Pedro Sanches refused the NATO bid of 5% defense spending of its GDP.
As an over touristed Fatherland he blew alarm whistle of overcrowded home land .
A classic paragon of discrepancy inside of NATO itself.

The Russian summer offensive continued.
Only than European media implied there was such a military campaign.

In the eve of NATO top in The Hague German Chancellor Friedrich Merz delivered detailed "Government explanation " to the German Bundestag – the German Parliament.
He promised "political security both in inland and abroad" ; he criticized the current Iranian regime, the Hamaz and the Hezbollah and flattered both Israel and the United States of America.
He praised also the foreign ministers both of France and Great Britain.
Further in his speech Merz praised Kiyv and its peace proposals towards Russia.
He accused Russia of intimidation of the entire European and American space.
He praised the Baltic Brigade 45 and its establishment by German advice and help .
He criticized both German and EU bureaucracy and promised its decline, degradation & limitation.
Only at the end Merz addressed the German economy and its growth provided by the industrious German people. His speech duration was 33 minutes. The left wing of the coalition SPD insisted on negotiation with Russia but in vain. Merz exclaimed The German Bundeswehr must stay the largest army of Europe whatsoever it may mean!"
AfD Chief Tino Cruppala contradicted to Merz in many aspects and nuances.
He said "we're not informed sufficiently on the nuances – only at the final point when bills come!"
According to him "one German tank cost as much as one German school".
He used the words "meine verehrte Damen und Herren "instead of the usual standard words "Meine geehrte Damen und Herren". It happened ! AfD politicians shown laughing happily during his speech.

The German ZDF showed B'90 leader Anton Hofreiter sleeping during the German Bundestag debate.
From all I concluded German Chancellor Friedrich Merz did not attend the NATO–Summit in The Hague where I used to report from.

NATO summit in The Hague where president Zelenskyy delivered a speech. Afterwords Zelenskyy was invited to a lavish NATO -dinner in The Hague where many streets were blocked or banned for traffic.

.. Summary .
The NATO member countries agreed with the American demand to raise their military spending to 5% of their GDP. Only Spain disagreed and made exception. It makes $700 billion.

NATO Secretary General Mark Rutte – a Dutch man just like me – was very officious to Trump and even named him at one point "DADDY" because he is only 51 and Trump 75. On the NATO photo Dutch King Wilhelm Alexander posed at Trump's right side and the Turkish Prime minister Recep Tayyp Erdogan on his left side.
So this NATO summit was nick-named THE TRUMP SUMMIT.
 At the Press Conference -impacted by some journalist questions – Trump promised 12 more F-35 fighter jets for Great Britain and more U.S. Patriot-launcher to Ukraine. His talks with the Ukrainian Minister-President Volodymyr Zelenskyy took place behind closed doors. We'll never learn what the two men discussed and how their discussion ended but Ukrainian NATO-membership was excluded. 25 minutes after the Press Conference Trump took off home from a military airfield near The Hague thus not the Amsterdam International Airport of Schiphol. Never before I have seen so strong massive police presence in The Hague as today.
Not even at Bill Clinton Sofia visit in the 1999ies. Only now the World understood what the "Coalition of the Willing" means and I will not comment on it. Abe tazi Kaya Kalas e mnogo gadna be ! Ebati Liglata! Ligla w progress! .
Zelenskyy himself had breeded vast hidden ambitions to address again the TRUMP SUMMIT but in vaine- hegot the dusty corner shown.

U.S. President Donald Trump criticized sharply CNN "for fake news, wasting time, wasting my time,

they all are scum – CNN, NBC, New York Times". And Trump repeated the word "SCUM" several times.
His press conference lasted exactly 45 minutes.
75% of this time Trump spent focusing on Iran, Israel and the Middle East conflict.
This is not the topic of my book and I will close it on this point.
Emil Tzolov , hallmark of speed and objectivity.

26. JUNE 2025

The NATO Summit in The Hague ended with acceptance of Volodymyr Zelenskyy's proposal to establish a new court for criminal prosecution on Russia for alleged atrocities and war crimes committed by Russia during its war on Ukraine.
Probably the court will act in The Hague.
Very much alike to the earlier Bosnia Tribunal in The Hague.
However this Tribunal failed to prosecute the notorious DutchBath for the Srebrenica massacre in 1995 where 8,000 Bosnian men and boys were slaughtered.
Every replication will mean an end of the story.

German foreign minister Wadephul visited unhindered the Ukrainian Capital Kyyv.
He was not shown together the Ukrainian ruler Volodymyr Zelenskyy.
In his speech he promised full German support to Ukraine and tried to intimidate both Russia and Vladimir Putin.
With him were representatives of the German arms industry to sign different agreements but they were unwilling "because they cannot plan the support to Ukraine".
Germany cannot deliver any F-16 fighter jets because it has none. Wadepfuhl intends to start joint ventures with Ukraine on the ground of mutual weaponry constructing with Ukraine.
Ukraine stepped back from the anti-personnel land mines treaty – the so called "Ottawa treaty 1997". Ukraine is the most heavily mined country in the World.

British prime minister sir Keir Starmer stroke a deal with U.S. President Donald Trump for 1.4 billion liter ethanol British import from the U.S.= 1,400,000,000 to ease situation Britain is currently in. Donald Trump has no "Sir" title. Business all over the globe !

*

20. JANUARY 2025

Donald Trump entered the White House as the 47th President of the United States of America.

Russia stopped gas delivery to neighboring Moldova to push social & economic turmoil there.
A cool strategic calculation. Ukraine proposed hypocritically Ukrainian coal as a compensation.
There was a mounting pressure on Donald Trump "to end the war in Ukraine".

Andriy Yermak – the Ukrainian Army chief of staff gave an extensive interview to Euronews in
which former NATO secretary general Jens Stoltenberg said bluntly:"The Bucharest agreement is nothing more than piece of paper !". Quite a conclusion ! And Mark Rutte – the current Nato Scry. General?
The Russian troops conquered the town of Vasilka- another important gain which enhance
Russian control on Donbas. At the same time President Zelenskyy visited a memorial in neighboring
Poland as shown on television.
The EU defense industry program sounds very much like Cold War Two: I personally
coined this term.
As usual Russian marine shadow fleet damaged yet another under sea transmission cable in the
Baltic sea- a good NATO reason to increase its marine presence there.
And again as frequently as usual Dutch police use narcotics to harm their victims short memory-
esp. before their court trials; so they cannot testify before their Courts. Actually Press Court Trials
designed esp. for the Press to silence up . A century long improved practice…

Danish Prime Minister Frederickson visited Germany to pledge German support in the raging
Greenland-USA scandal, while Coca-Cola was accused of contaminating its Coca-Cola
products – mostly Coca-Cola & Fanta – mainly in its Coca-Cola factory in Belgium.
Coca-Cola apologized and withdrew its Coca-Cola products from the markets.
Donald Trump was greeted by President Ronald Reagan at 1987 White House reception.
Ronald Reagan Presidential Library.
Ronald Reagan Presidential Library.
40,Presidential Drive, Simi Valley, CA 93065
In a speech, Reagan referred to the Soviet Union as an "evil empire" and as "the focus of evil in the modern world".
In 1983 Reagan ordered the U.S.invasion of Grenada.

Trump's peace proposal for the war in Ukraine, in which he sets three conditions, is being talked about this week.
The aim is to reach a final peace by May 9, a symbolic date for Europe and Russia. The first of these conditions
concerns Ukraine's NATO membership, with one of the most important conditions being that the country gives up
its ambition to join the Atlantic Treaty, an explicit demand from Russia.

Ukrainian drones said to have hit Russian Luckoil fuel depots in the Volgorod region – quite a distance !
As to the plane crash over Washington, D.C. President Trump accused the Biden administration "of hiring
inappropriate staff with **intellectual, epileptic and psychiatric deviations".**

FEBRUARY 2025

Russian rockets destroyed the city of Poltawa in geographical center of Ukraine. Kiiv confirmed the use of long rockets with 250 kg explosive against targets deep inside Russia. Ukrainian forces attacked strongly and destroyed significantly the Russian city of Sucha, Kursk region. Ukraine dropped down the recruitment age for men in the Ukrainian army from 25 to 18 years of age.
The German minimal salary amounted up to 1,300 euro net monthly.

Mark Rutte agitated again for higher expenditure of all NATO countries.
French Minister President Emanuel Makrone agreed and added "the European weaponry must be produced and used inside Europe itself". EU-Council President Antonio Costas fully agreed with him.
The Swedish Stated prosecutor admitted "the undersea optical cable rupture was not an act of sabotage" and let the captured ship free to continue its journey across the Baltic sea.
Donald Tump agreed to shut down the USAID, many of its officials set on a leave.
An Ukrainian war lord was accused to have helped Russia with his battalion in action and was executed by fire squad.
On the defense top in Brussels became clear that European Nato members have 372 types of different weaponry while for the United States this figure is on 32 (ARD)

U.S. President Donald Trump launched up his Gaza peace plan which I support fully.
He applied also for the Nobel Peace Price what I support truly too. No more details: facts!

Russia and Ukraine exchanged 150 prisoners of war from each side. The deal was brokered by the United Arab Emirates (UAE). Prisoners' swap is a rare form of cooperation between Russian and Ukraine.
Russia launched up a new space ship for military purposes to supervise. Poland increased its military budget to 4.7% of its GDP.
Massive shootings both in Belgium & Sweden with 11 people at least shot dead. Than followed by another shooting in Örebro, Sweden, West of Capital Stockholm leaving 11 people dead. As a matter of surprise Russia was not accused of the shooting: not yet.

The three former Soviet republics of Latwia, Lithuania & Estonia cut off their contacts from the Russian electricity grid. For the festival of it EU-Commission She President Ursula van der Leyen paid an week end visit to them and their Capitals. The decision came at the back ground of the overall European energy crisis for which we all pay double price. A kind of mental suicide we Europeans have to pay for. No single word on the crises from Germany – Germany is convicted of ablaze of its own election campaign. Quite a show!
This are the www.patriots.eu. Lavishly financed by the European Parliament. As Geerd Wilders put it "The Scholz-Macrone era is over. We step in! They are history!"

Ukraine hit the Russian city Rostov-on-Don by 76 drones.
Ukrainian troops increased their attacks against the Russian city of Kursk.
The German Commando point confirmed " in Schwesing bei Husum are Ukrainian soldiers trained on how to use Patriot anti-missiles defense systems", said ZDF. So it is a core of a war against Russia.

The European Investment bank President Nadia Calvino transferred 1 billion euro to miscellaneous Ukrainian banks for recovery already before the war ends – if – for reconstruction. So is there a war there or no war? With such free bank transfers!? It reads 1,000,000,000 euro as a lump sum ! We here in Europe are scavengers exploring the street containers for garbage food and suddenly 1,000,000,000 euro! So Ukrainian banks operate rather freely to accept the European Investment Bank donation of 1,000,000,000 euro to several Ukrainian banks simultaneously. Calvino posed for a joint photo with Volodymyr Zelenskyy like a real whore. This all well ahead of the European top in Munich, Germany later in February 2025. The U.S.A. was represented by U.S. Vice President Vance. The U.S. Defense Secretary
Pate Hegseth stated bluntly "Ukraine must retreat from the occupied territories and the European states must send peace
keeping forces in"; thus not American troops – no single U.S. ranger! In a whole an hour phone talk with Vladimir Putin
U.S. President Donald Trump reassuered him "No U.S. troops in Ukraine, no Ukraine in the 2014 border": A bitter pill for Ukraine , a triumph for Russia". ZDF & Euronews avoided any comment.
Kremlin spokesman Dmitryy Peskow stated "Russia will never swap the seized territories in Eastern Ukraine for the Ukrainian-seized Kursk regions. The Russian demands to Ukraine are:
1. No NATO membership
2. No EU membership.
3. Both sides found the phone talk important & decisive, "a historic shift"etc.
The phone call was said to be lasting 75 minutes incl. its translation times, BBC said,
"Trump is a great friend of Putin and he said again pleasant words to Putin in order to please him",stated the British Ambassador to Washington, Mr. Daniel Wittenburg : (Damian McGinnes??)
Car – hit attack in Munich one day only the annual Security Conference there ; as usual BBC reported first well ahead of the German ZDF- German native television
As usual police was unable stop the kamikaze attacker despite heavy police presence at the venue.

Already before the annual Munich conference Volodymyr Zelenskyy disagreed with the
American plan and criticized sharply Putin and his decisions in order to prolong the war; betting much on the annual Munich security conference the day after, attending in person. U.S. Defense Scry. stated "no Russian aggression against Ukraine took place during Donald Trump Presidency!" marking a diplomatic end of the war as BBC put it. British prime minister Keir Starmer phoned up president Zelenskyy to reassure him "no talks about Ukraine without Ukraine". The talks were scheduled to take place in Saudi Arabia.
Russia had even not put any delegation member to the Munich Security Conference while Volodymyr Zelenskyy ordered a barbaric drone attack attack on the Russian Chernobyl nuclear reactor exposing all of Europe at a nuclear disaster. Neither Russia nor Germany responded in words to the barbaric Ukrainian nuclear attack. BBC did. So who is exposing Europe at nuclear danger – Russia or Ukraine ?! EU-Commission President lost no single word onto.
As a fact Ukrainian drones bombarded barbaricaly the Russian nuclear reactor of Chernobyl increasing radiation level. Chernobyl is exactly 135 km northern from the Ukrainian capital Kyyv, very close to the Belorussian border.
In a television interview Volodymyr Zelenskyy looked very pale & bled (bledolik) demanding the increase of the Ukrainian Army from 82 to 100 brigades. Rather unrealistic. The news as it is. Europe must show relevance.
The media cut short Zelenskyy notion parroting Dmitry Kuleba – the former Ukrainian foreign minister
As to Russia it did not sent even a delegation to the Munich security conference.
As to Russia it established a new Russian navy base in Port Sudan.

So President Zelenskyy warned the West that "Russia doesnot want peace" and urged Europe to "form its own defense army".

The second half of the week Donald Trump spent in talks with Indian President Narandra Modi discussing with him topics of bilateral interest; thus not global problems.
The mutual trade balance of both countries amounts to $29 billion – 29,000,000,000 U.S. dollars .
With Donald Trump as a new U.S. the world got full of new news- both national & international.

The Munich Security Conference was chaired by a German diplomat.
The Munich car attack – bad advertising to the Munich EU-security conference the day after.

No condemnation of Russia so far. U.S. foreign minister Marco Rubio put it bluntly :" Ukrainian mineral resources in exchange of peace" . Wolodymyr Zelenskyy followed him at the conference in Saudi Arabia where the U.S. were represented by Marco Rubio but Europe was n o t represented there whatsoever. Zelenskyy was absent from the Paris conference though he lied "No talks on Ukraine without Ukraine!"And suddenly he was absent ! At the conference in Saudi Arabia the U.S. was represented by its Secretary of State Marco Rubio and Russia – by its Foreign Minister Sergey Lavrov. Both Ukraine and the European Union were not represented at the peace talks because Kremlin doubts in their legitimacy. Zelenskyy in fact visited Turkey and the Paris peace conference didn't even take place, such
a dissonance in Europe. Above all Donald Trump stated "Ukraine had had 3 years to end the war but president Zelenskyy
di not wanted this. Now the infrastructure is destroyed at 100% after 3 years of war. I will give Ukraine almost all the land they want but the regime in Kiiv is ilegimate – it is a martial law!" The discussion continued online. The peace talks in Saudi Arabia lasted only one day and ended with a speech of the Russian foreign minister Sergey Lavrov to the Russian
Duma (the Russian Parliament) in which he said "The Atlantic Alliance is bankrupt". Developing strategic ties with China he said "Xi Jin Ping is invited to Moscow military parade for the Victory Day 09th May 2025."
Sergey Lavrov reminded also "The Baltic states & Ukraine had collaborated with Nazi Germany millions upon millions
of time during the World War Two." He invited also Indonesia to join the BRICS-group.
President Zelenskyy lied bluntly "he had chosen not to attend the peace talks in Saudi Arabia because of complications" This is a blunt lie – neither Ukraine nor the European Union were admitted to the peace talks in Saudi Arabia" .
And Zelenskyy lied "This was his choice".
The White House sent a special envoy to Kiiv – General Keith Kellogg- to consulate Zelenskyy.
But Zelenskyy accused Donald Trump "of living in a space of disinformation " and "helping Putin to leave his international isolation in which he was trapped due to the Ukrainian war". "Zelenskyy popularity sank down to 4%", so D. Trump. Trump dubbed Zelenskyy as "a dictator without election who spilled $350 billion US Dollars in a 3-year war"- $350,000,000,000 United states dollars. Zelenskyy him declared unconditional joint of NATO if Russia breaks the
truce, so some Dutch media. Letland introduced German as a compulsory school language instead of Russian. Russian was compulsory school language for 75 years.

French President Emanuel Macrone started his U. S. visit with Donald Trump teaching "How can you be strong to China when you show weakness to Russia??!"Rather demagogue !
British prime minister sir Keir Starmer visit to Washington largely & lavishly advertised by British media despite the fact he has nothing to get neither from the U.S.A. nor from President Donald Trump personally. Wait & see!
In a rare press conference in Kyiv Volodymyr Zelenskyy stated "he will give up his Presidency in exchange for

Ukrainian NATO membership!" Zelenskyy demanded also bigger European & NATO guarantees for Ukraine. Difficult to believe!
The news as it is : Emil Tzolov

World leaders met in an international summit in Kyiv to express solidarity , to express support to Ukraine. As they traveled & met with no hinder in Ukraine the question rose : Is there war or all is only show?!
Trains run smoothly abandon of electricity, televisions run smoothly, even **AN UKRAINECAST**
was established – so it war in Ukraine or there is none ??
The show in Kyiv was a Canadian one is not clear who represented the U.S.A. - the biggest Ukrainian supporter during Joe Biden administration. Above all a petrol bomb exploded at the Russian consulate in the French port Marseille. Russian authorities demanded an explanation of the terrorist attack. French president Emanuel Makrone flew to Washington to agitate Donald Trump for more American aid to Ukraine. his visit coincided with British prime minister Keir Starmer visit to Washington too; so who first ?!
According to other reports Keir Starmer attended the world leaders' summit in Kyiv.

On a ceremony in Moscow President Vladimir Putin handed in awards & orders to "soldiers who have fought for Russia and Russian glory for 10 generations ahead". The number of the Russian soldiers killed in Ukraine amounted to 350,000. 800,000 others were wounded, said Euronews.

At the 3rd anniversary of the Russian-Ukrainian war Ukrainian president Volodymyr Zelenskyy gave freely Press conference in Capital Kyiv – untouched by the "war" – and even tried to speak some English hunting his own aims & purposes. Canadian prime minister Justine Trudeau praised him and admitted "Canada will continue to train on its ground Ukrainian soldiers and other Ukrainian military staff": the news without make-up ! Canada has its own high-level optical forces, so Zelenskyy. "The war is changing into technological war fare!". Upon the question of his opinion on Donald Trump Zelenskyy hesitated… And amid ironical laughs Zelenskyy admitted only "good" in overall laughter . My personal opinion on the summit is Ukraine is supported only by Canada & Spain in 17 minutes exposure; all other countries submitted only 7 minute press time at all. Among their questions was "why Ukraine changed its mind on the war?". The elucidation lasted 4 minutes at all.
An EU-diplomat dubbed the whole summit as "rather cakaphonic" and placed 4 further main questions Zelenskyy failed to answer. Instead he flung into "Soviet era weapon manufacture ever since!" So what Zelenskyy demand?
A 2045 future weaponry developed by the West for Ukraine and only for Ukraine ?! Zelenskyy replied:"Ukrainian weaponry production – artillery shells, drones even rockets & missiles ! " Quite a question Zelensky failed to respond at all. All pushed back into second place the German Parliament election which was "undemocratic" according to the German AfD leader Alice Weidel . AfD means :'Alternative for Deutschland", a translator's remark.
The Zelenskyy so called "Press conference in Kyiv" lasted over 3 hours mirrored by the media in over 8 hours'stretch.
The European Commission President Ursula von der Leyen brought 3.5 billion euro present to Ukraine at the summit: say & write 3,500,000,000 euro cadeau plus expensive flight tickets for all European delegates .
3,500,000,000 euro. The Ukrainian refugees to Western Europe outnumbered 6.6 million:
6,600,000 Ukrainian refugees! The news as it is by Emil Tzolov. No pen name in GOOGLE.com

After the German Parliamentary election Chancellor Friedrich Merz will reign with the German SPD but without ex-Chancellor Olaf Scholz – from the SPD too.
Germany was said to be the biggest export nation in the World (CNN)
 A highly unusual e-mail to the White House led me to 2 conclusions;
1. The White House has an e-mail address
2. The White House e-mail address is well known but unknown to me ! To whom ??

French prime minister's Emanuel Makrone visit to Washington degenerated into raw with U.S. President

Donald Trump. Full scandal, to name it cautiously. Macrone claimed falsely "France has paid 60% of all Western helps to Ukraine which includes EU & U S A . A sheer lie !
At a Press conference Russian foreign minister Sergey Lavrov stated "Russia is ready for peace talks with Ukraine but they were boycotted by dirty treacherous Ukrainian tricks & deceptions".

After the Washington mission of Emanuel Macrone failed president Volodymyr Zelenskyy decided to fly personally to Washington and promoted to Donald Trump the so called "row materials deal"- deposits of rare metals & minerals in exchange of American long-term help to Ukraine. The Ukrainian vast mineral resources deposits comprise lithium, titanium and graphite among others all kept in the Russian conquered zone. All fit to the U.S. military, space & defense industry needs , as CNN put it bluntly.

His visit coincided with the visit of the British prime minister Keir Starmer to Washington. So easy to fly to America – hop on , hop off ! Hop on - Kyiv ! Hop off – Washington !
Seemingly no sign of war at all. Earlier Zelenskyy had rejected similar American proposals "because of security guarantees lack". Currently the American support to Ukraine amounts to $350 billion. Say & write $350,000,000,000. American help to Ukraine up till now while Europe gave only $100 billions.
U.S. President Donald Trump had already denounced Zelenskyy as a "dictator" several times up till now but Zelenskyy remained unimpressed. Currently Donald Trump's agenda is overburdened by law suits so he really has little time for Zelenskyy and his skills as an actor by which he began his political career.
If the contract is not finalized by Zelenskyy his Washington trip makes no sense, Washington said bluntly .
Donald Trump named the Ukrainian $500 billion dept "a mire bag, not sharing humanitarian values but Ukrainian mineral resources: Lithium, Vanadium, Zirconium, Graphite etc. which Russia possibly owes too. So an empty bag of Ukrainian proposals !
Well before Zelenskyy Washington visit U.S. President Donald Trump gave an extensive Press conference which I recorded and which is affordable in copy upon request. He said "We buried $350 billion in Ukraine and we have no chance to get them back while Europe demanded back its meager $100 billion to Ukraine" Trump said also "Artificial Intelligence is very much energy consumptive so we have to double our energy production no matter how".

Further Trump said "we help Canada with $200 billion annually but the give back to us only 4%. Canada relies only entirely on U.S. aid that's why Canada must become the 51st state of the Unioted States of America."
"The U.S.A. GIVES THE BEST MILITARY EQUIPMENT TO UKRAINE: AMERICA HAS THE BEST MILITARY EQUIPMENT IN THE WORLD AND WE GIVE TO UKRAINE!"
"Ukraine gave very much victims in this war – over 1 million sodiers plus 2 million civilians President Joe Biden failed to prevent this war it never shouldn't happen".
No single word lost on Ukrainian NATO membership.
No single word on American military guaranty to Ukraine.
As to Keir Starmer he was just heading to Washington and
couldn't attend Trump's press conference but he will somewhen learn about it.
"CBS put a question to Camala (Harris) but she failed to answer it. ".

In his visit to Washington,D.C. British Prime Minister Keir Starmer named President Trump "a good friend" and solicitated for more American help to Ukraine. Donald Trump responded to "as non-senses" and refused to give any guaranty to Ukraine. He came back very soon empty handed. Russian President Vladimir Putin said "Russia has nothing against the Ukrainian-US – deal" So Donald Trump exempted !

In his Washington visit president Zelenskyy agreed to give Ukrainian minerals to the U.S.A. The revenues will flow into a joint U.S.- Ukrainian funds but the U.S. rejected again any guaranty to Ukraine.

The 5th visit Zelenskyy to the White House brought nothing and degenerated even into a quarrel. Trump accused Zelenskyy
"that he risks World war three". The mineral subsoil resources deal was not signed and the talks turned into "verbal spat":
Trump accused Zelenskyy of been not serious about peace "and have not the cards to dictate". As CNN put it "full chaos
and shouting match in the lovely Oval Office!"
Further Trump accused Zelenskyy of "gambling with his people and gambling with World War Three".
Zelenskyy was ordered to leave the White House; he flew to London to meet Keyr Starmer over the week end.
Many European leaders criticized sharply Donald Trump but Hungarian prime minister Victor Orban stood with him and even praised him. An emergency meeting of European leaders was scheduled for Sunday in the United Kingdom , Zelenskyy will attend "because the U.S. are not a reliable partner any more"…
Russia got very satisfied of the quarrel spat…

NATO secretary General Mark Rutte – a native Dutch in fact – commented onto by repeating the words "javelin , javelin, javelin…." President Trump reiterated his concept of $350 billion help Ukraine should be thankful for because "Ukraine is running off soldiers!"
As to Zelenskyy himself he landed in London at 11:00 Saturday while the EU-emergency top
was scheduled for Sunday afternoon, said Malcolm Riffkind – former British defense minister in a BBC interview.
Zelenskyy repeated his slanders to America. Keir Starmer didn't tweet at all unlike many European leaders- who actually ? Germany has no acting government after the German election chaos ?!
In fact weather is a massive part of flying.
What Zelenskyy wanted was support & publicity; he got both in London after he failed in Washington,so
Sahra Fick – BBC Russian team- even deepened the shouting match. Quite a spectacle.
In his visit to Downing street President Donald Trump was mentioned with no single word.
Macrone said: "There is one aggressor-Russia; there is one victim-Ukraine. We will support Ukraine for as long as it takes".
On Sunday Zelenskyy arranged a meeting with British King Charles to get reported yet again.
Turkey was invited to the talks too, "because it has the second largest NATO Army" (BBC).

Karl Bildt-former Swedish prime minister looking very much alike Keir Starmer-
stated to the BBC "this war cannot end without (military) pressure on Russia. He dubbed the EU peace efforts as "amateurish". Such a well trained hypocrisy !
BBC commentator Rob Watson in his 60ies mirrored heavily gesticulating with his hands & arms, as I saw it.
and president Zelenskyy came home empty-handed sleeping one night in London AA.

Polish prime minister was shown to hink towards the meeting-yes, hinking; so ill.
NATO Scry. General Mark Rutte arrived at14:10. Zelenskyy is expected to get additional 2 billion British Pounds of aid to continue the war, BBC said. As a matter of fact the summit was held at Lancaster House in London with the slogan :"Secure our future!".
Chancellor Olaf Scholz arrived at 14:30 despite the fact he will be acting German Chancellor for 3 further weeks only after this summit. Hid sly his face from the cameras.

The UK, France & Ukraine combined their efforts to present a Sunday peace plan by phone to U.S. President Donald Trump after he "kicked out Volodymyr Zelenskyy from the White House". This is the shortest summary I could produce on what has happened on the EU-emergency conference in London.

The Sunday emergency London summit ended without signing any documents.

The very next day President Donald Trump paused all U.S. military aid " to push Ukraine to the negotiating table". Keir Starmer countered hypocritically :"I want people to be proud on where they live, we fund 1.5 billion pounds to build thriving high streets, parks, youth clubs, libraries and cultural venues. Supporting local growth, breathing life back into your neighborhood… " So poetical ! According to Donald Trump "a humiliated prime minister". All European media emphasized on the word "pausing" carefully avoiding other words such as "stopping" & "freezing". The advisor to Volodymyr Zelenskyy Igor Novikov summarized it in one word: "We fight for our lives; we have no other choice!". Is this true ?
Donald Trump accused the Biden administration of spilling $350 billion of military aid to Ukraine plus U.S. military intelligence data spying on Russia, so he decided to "pause further U.S. aid". So poetical. Well bearing in mind the U.S. satellites from the space – the so called **STAR LINKS** – provided by multi billionair Ellon Musk free of charge. **The STAR LINKS can be only partly compensated by France & Luxemburg.**

Zelenskyy dubbed the Friday White House spat "regrettable" but failed to apologize, saying "Ukraine is ready to sign any mineral& security agreement with the U.S. " and insisted again on territorial guaranties.
J.D. Vance said , the minerals deal is better deterrent of Putin than troops from some random country. In a BBC interview former Swedish prime minister Karl Bildt named it " for Zelenskyy this was a stab in the back"
but declined to comment on Keir Starmer saying "he said what he'd said",and closed down the interview.

Zelenskyy continued to re-affirm "that Ukraine will not its weaponry without American & European security guaranty.

U.S. President Donald Trump spent 100 minutes time to address the Congress.
BBC News spent 100 minutes on a British raper aged 28. The news as it is !

In an officious fax to the White House Zelenskyy praised again Donald Trump and apologized for his recent Oval Office failure. The News as it is. Emil
Donald Trump promoted a black U.S. teenager into a CIA-agent already from his childhood on wards. Trump vowed also to "crack on the unelected burocrates". America - the country of the unlimited possibilities. The news as it is. EMIL.

After Washington paused the American intelligence help to Ukraine president Zelenskyy became softer and apologize in written to U.S. President Donald Trump.
French President Emanuel Macrone planed a second visit to Washington together with Keir Starmer and Volodymyr Zelenskyy to put U.S. President under pressure. Instead he attended a second emergency top on defense of European leaders in Brussels- again with Zelenskyy participation. Macrone warned Russia for French nuclear capability in order to make it "softer in the peace talks". He insisted "Russia must give up." He proposed joint European peace keeping troops to Ukraine. Russian foreign minister Sergey Lavrov replied "we will consider this as direct NATO involvement". The Russian peace demand is neutral Ukraine without NATO membership. The Ukrainian peace plan is one million men strong Ukrainian army – 1,000,000 – supported , trained and equipped by Western Europe. Rather unmodest plan. He plans also a visit to Mohammed ben Salman – the Crown Prince of Saudi Arabia – after his visit to the conference in Brussels, Belgium. Light spirited on visits.
"Ukraine has to negotiate peace with Russia because they have no choice.
Russia has to negotiate peace because they have no choice too: in a different way- only I know why",
said Donald Trump.

Yesterday is over. It is already today. I spent my time to pray to both God & Buddha to bless you & our relations. That's all. Emil, The Netherlands. The time now is
President Donald Trump established a new strategic national crypto reserve in bit coins his own Family has

assets in. The news as it is: Emil. However my own advice is not to risk to lay down assets in crypto.

Russia fired rockets to Kharkiv & Krivij Rijg and hit hotels there sheltering European civil servants there. In fact they were Western military advisors to Ukraine with crocodile tears onto.

At the Brussels top Ursula von der Leyen spoke English and even kissed Zelenskyy on his cheeks; Olaf Scholz by contrast delivered his speech in his native German. The negotiations took place behind closed doors. The leading voice was of British prime minister Keir Starmer who obviously pulled the strings.
Moscow expelled 2 further senior British diplomats for alleged spying.
Canada elected Mark Carney for a new prime minister to knot his tongue as he did; former bank director like Ernesto Che GevuEara. Che Guevara – a Cuban National Bank Director- was killed 1967 in Bolivia as a Father of 5 Orphans: Aleida, Hilda, Cella, Camillo….and one more

Mark Carney is the new Canadian prime minister to knot his tongue as he did; former bank director like Ernesto Che GevuEara. Che Guevara – a Cuban National Bank Director- was killed 1967 in Bolivia as a Father of 5 Orphans: Aleida, Hilda, Cella, Camillo….+ 1 . The news as it is : Emil, hall mark of truth.
In America every thing can happen.
* * *

Once upon my times while I was in the Army I read secretly Che Que Vara diary published in Berlin.
I hid this document secretly risking my life – or my time?? I understood: 1. He was a medical doctor to remedy social disease of society. 2. He was very ill despite his lung disease . 3) Nevertheless Guevara partisaned his mirror never betraying a friend. 4.) Finally he was betrayed & executed by the CIA – Central Investigating Agency of the U.S.A. in 1967. 5). Such a glory full partisan to die! I follow ! I have 20 years more to fight. The News as it is: Emil Tzolov, Hall Mark of truth.
*

The peace talks in Saudi Arabia led to the conclusion that the United States is an unreliable ally. United Europe must face the Russian aggression alone.
During the peace talks in Saudi Arabia became clear the real figure of the frozen Russian assets aboard: they are 358 billion euro yielding 32 million euro of interest. Many European countries proposed confiscation of the Russian assets in order to compensate the inflation havoc but France and Belgium vetoed this proposal sofar.
President Putin visited the newly liberated Kursk region for talks with President Trump special envoy Steve Witkoff. Both sides agreed for a 30 days truce. Basically Putin agreed to peace but showed some reservations most of all he rejected NATO-membership to Ukraine:"Too dangerous to agree to", he said. His words were: "Yes,but no!" And the list of the NO's comprised 30 positions. "The peace will be enduring only if war root causes are addressed. Ukraine does not mean peace but uses the pauses for further mobilization & weaponry] replenishment". Further Russian demand was to the complete surrender of the whole Ukrainian army and a future disband it- not simple giving up the occupied Russian territories but surrender. So president Zelenskyy accused Vladimir Putin "of sabotaging the peace talks!". British prime minister Keir Starmer accused too Vladimir Putin "of not taking seriously the peace talks". He accused Putin of "trying to delay the peace" despite the fact Putin met in Moscow the U.S. special envoy Steve Witkoff. BBC did not commented on this meeting at al: So far ! Far & fair. As to the Ukrainian troops' pull back from the occupied Russian areas BBC admitted "the Ukrainians pull back but this is retrieval not an encirclement as Russia claims!".
U.S. President Donald Trump was speaking at a joint Press conference with the NATO- Secretary General Mark Rutte in the Oval Office in Washington,D.C. in which they rejected the British position.
As to Canada Trump said "we don't need them, they need us however!". So bluntly ! All the world was frantically working during the week end by video links : Canada, the U.S.A. , Britain, France , Ukraine , Russia etc.
No week end in view at all.
The Captain of the Russian cargo ship which collided with an oil tanker appeared to Hull Magistrate Court;

Mr. Vladimir Motin was accused of negligence and man slaughter and will remain in custody till 14th April when he will be charged by the London Old Baily. Aah these Russians – collide with tankers and spill oil all over the world, BBC exclaimed !
Above all a fire broke out in a discotheque in the small town of Koçani- 59 young people died, 150 injured. President Zelenskyy extended his condolence to the victims' families! What else? The news as it is. Zelenskyy was invited to the G7 top in Canada in June 2025. Trade war between Canada & the U.S.A.- Canadian prime minister Mark Carney visited in one day France, Great Britain and a Press Conference in one single day..
It got known the size of the Russian Army – 1.5 million soldiers, while the Finnish army is staggering 900,000 soldiers under compulsory conscription and the biggest artillery in Europe.

In the phone talk with Donald Trump Russia insisted on security guarantees which means no Western weapon deliveries to Ukraine, recognition of the Russian territorial gains and stepping back to Russia of the Zaporizhija nuclear reactor which is actually a Russian one. It is the biggest in Europe. The Finnish president Cai-Göran-Alexander-Stubb -born on the 1st of April 1968 commented rather flamboyantly on the phone talk "Russia cannot decide neither on the NATO nor on the EU- membership of Ukraine!" .

On the phone Vl. Putin promised not to bombard neither Ukrainian power plants
nor Ukrainian energy infrastructure; on tv Ukrainian capital Kyiv was shown lavishly lit up by electric lamps. Unbelievable! Whom to trust ?On the phone indicated by Euronews I got no contact at all….
After an ample maze of news it became known that Vl.Putin rejected Donald
Trump's conditions on truce; "A vast humiliation to the American President", commented BBC. Euronews took exactly the opposite position. The only thing true was that EU-officials were not admitted to mingle in the phone talk; immediately afterwards V.Zelenskyy flew unrestrained to Helsinki for talks with the
Finnish president. From Finland Zelenskyy phoned up the U.S. President Donald Trump; on the conversation substance was not reported. A few words were spent on this meeting with a difficult balance. Russia however managed to destroy the power plant supplying the Ukrainian railways with electricity . Donald Trump commented "the phone call was useful" while German defense minister Boris Pistorius said exactly the opposite:"Number Zero" and "Putin plays a play!"; he advised Europe to take measures to arm Ukraine even further despite the fact his mandate expires on Easter. The EU-defense commissioner Cobillius urged Europe "to arm itself even stronger". The same position took the EU-Commission President Ursula von der Leyen in her 7 point "strategy paper".

Further peace talks were scheduled for 4 days later on again in Saudi Arabia; the U.S. delegation was lead by the U.S. Secretary of State Marco Rubio and the U.S. special envoy Steve Witkof. The U.S. stopped funding Radio Free Europe (=RFE, where I worked earlier) currently located in the Czech Republic.
French president Emanuel Macrone visited Berlin for talks with Friedrich Merz; he is however not a German Chancellor yet. Germany decided to keep its military budget to 1% of its GDP; only to compare with the Polish military budget of 5.8% of it GDP. Poland and the three Baltic states signed a treaty for canceling the anti-personal land mines ban already signed by 160 UN member states. Russia has not signed the treaty yet.

Still in Finland president Zelenskyy
As a matter of fact more details emerged on the phone call Zelenskyy placed to U.S. President Donald Trump-still hiding in lavish Finland with its 900,000 soldiers strong army - where he flew in unrestrained already at the begin this week: Zelenskyy proposed to the U.S.A. to take control of all Ukrainian power plants, all of the energy sector. All for the Ukrainian power plants' security.
This came from Finland where Zelenskyy is hiding after his White House spat attack back in February 2025.
It is not clear if Zelenskyy's Washington deal includes also the Zaporizhjie nuclear power plant which is actually Russian property liberated from Ukrainian occupation back in 2022. EPP Chairman Manfred Weber
praised the deal. "It will secure European safety-all over Europe", he lied to the media: "There is no cease

fire, this is the reality", he stressed. European Commission Foreign Chief Kaja Kallas promised 5 million more artillery shells to Ukraine: this means 13,699 shells daily! 5,000,000:365=13,699 shells daily. "The stronger Ukraine is on the battle field the stronger it will be at the negotiating table!" she emphasized with her usual stress exercising her nasty awful English: her initial proposal was 40 billion euro but finally the EU top in Brussels approved only 5 billion; not clear where the 5 billion euro will come from. 5,000,000,000 euro.

After his Finland visit president Zelenskyy flew to the Norway's capital Oslo to advertise again his failed policy. Germany awarded Ukraine with 3 billion euro new military aid; till 2028 it will grant further 8 billion euro aid. 5,000,000,000 +3,000,000,000 +8,000,000,000 = 16,000,000,000 euro.
U.S. President Donald Trump awarded Boeing with a new F-47 fighter jet contract.
Heathrow shut down because of power cut; the airport is said to consume more electricity than the whole of neighboring Capital London. Massive German Neo Nazis demonstrations in both Dresden and Capital Berlin. The news as it is . Emil, hallmark of objectivity.

During the peace talks in Saudi Arabia both the Russian and the Ukrainian delegations were lodged in one and the same hotel – The Ritz Carlton Hotel in Riyadh.; thus not Azizi in Borj. As a matter of fact the seize fire lasted only 30 hours but the both sides agreed not to attack their energy facilities but no one kept his promises. By hitting Russian energy hubs and oil depots the Ukrainians over smarted their enemy slowing down the Russian advance temp and increasing the Russian victims to 1,000 soldiers each day so the Russians were not pleased to talk about this. They were interested in keeping their Black Sea lanes open which is not very easy and to destroy more Ukrainian Black Sea port facilities in order to block Ukrainian exports. The main issue was stopping military actions both on the ground and in the air.
Both sides finally agreed on safe Black Sea navigation.

The talks were more on technical issues thus not on diplomatic ones , each delegation of 25 men strong.
At the same time Kaya Kallas visited Israel to polish her bumpy English.
All the same NATO Secretary General visited Poland and warned Russia not to attack Poland: "If you attack Poland the NATO reaction will be devastating" , ZDF 26-03-25 , 17:10. His warning was probably in English which he masters.

Neither the Germans nor the Dutch reported with no single word on the WH CHAT scandal.
Instead MAYBRIT – ILNER reports on Turkey. Aman van Waan ! Tulsi Gabbard – National Intelligence Director - couldn't recall any details of the scandal. However „The Atlantic" weekly magazine reported on those facts. What it leaked out is that its Editor Jeffrey Goldberg is a devoted democrat.

Volodymyr Zelenskyy again in Paris. How many times ?? Obviously president Macron of France used the turmoil to smuggle through his ideas into the European Union . Both Donald Trump and Mark Rubio were at this time in Washington, D.C. Germany was represented by Olaf Scholz who's mandate as a Chancellor expires on the 20th April 2025.
Super fidels ! At the same time the Eifel Tower in Paris was lavishly illuminated with blue and yellow lamps – the colors of the Ukrainian national flag in flamboyant gesture of solidarity. It became not clear however if NATO Secretary Genal Mark Rutte was present at the Paris meeting. I could not see him on the group photo. The British prime minister Keir Starmer said "Vladimir Putin plays plays as usual , Ukraine is on his play book". Starmer pushed for further sanctions against Russia. It
became known the current size of the Ukrainian army – one million soldiers – 1,000,000 while the peace keeping troops from 7 European countries would number ca. 20,000 soldiers. Only to compare – the German unemployment army hit staggering three million men & women – 3,000,000. The peace keepers will be named rather poetically "Reassurance forces" . It became like a slogan ! A catch word! They called themselves "Coalition of the willing".

Logically there must be "Coalition of the Non-willing" too: who will prevail and when ?? Meanwhile it got known that the number of European prisoners has drastically rozen – 1.5 million prisoners = 1,500,000. This only to compare facts.

At the same time Vladimir Putin was at the international top of the Arctic countries; he looked tired and older. He looks
how to come out from his international isolation. However he turned out to be smarter and more inventive than his Western
counterparts and proposed UN- mandate for Ukraine after the war ended.
His Ukrainian future vision is semi-independent territory under UN mandate.
Putin put also "it is a deep blunder to class Trump's Greenland ambitions "as a preposterous talk"" , said Yahoo;
The Trump administration sees Greenland's vast mineral ressources as vital for U.S. interests.
Putin took seriously Trump's efforts to claim Greenland for the U.S. The hint is clear-everybody can make what one wants into his back yard. Obviously Vl. Putin is active on several fronts simultaneously ..
Germany delayed again the chancellor nomination for the begin of May; it transferred its political chaos into neighboring France where Marine Lepen was forbidden to run for the presidential election .

APRIL 2025

German foreign minister Annalena Baerbock visited Kyiv for her 11th time; not clear for what.
Her mandate expires on 20th April – Easter. At the same time Russia was said to have launched a new barrage of drone attacks on Kharkiv but little was reported onto. Ukraine retaliated by hitting 2 Russian energy plants .
April began with the political beheading of the political actor Marine Le Pen by a conservative officious court inspired by president Emmanuel Macrone . He too has little time to stay in when the 2027 elections will sweep him away . Le Pen has only one scenario – to get acquitted.
The new Ukrainian foreign minister Andrej Sybiha took position to please the West. Both he and V.Zelenskyy started to plead for peace after 3 years rejecting it or at least impose Ukrainian conditions. So preposterous !

Democrat Corry Walker held the longest speech in the U.S. Congress history – 25:04 hours .
Poland started placing anti-personal land mines along its border with Russia in order to prevent eventual Russian invasion. The land mines are internationally banned by the Ottawa treaty. At the same time pop star Elton John continued to perform concerts in his native London at the age of 78. British style has been always exuberant !

Germany delay its Chancellor election for May 2025. The coalition treaty between the ruling parties CDU & SPD amounted to 144 pages of text in German. It is essential who'll be the Chancellor of Exchequer. Chancellor Olaf Scholz loiters. The CSU signed the coalition treaty first , CDU & SPD loiter on and on. Former German Chancellor Gerhardt Schröder went to a German court demanding more bureau space for his friends & satraps. Schröder is an advisor to a Russian oil company with 10,000 EUR monthly salary above his Chancellor rent.

The defense ministers of the Coalition of the Willing came together to discuss how to help Ukraine which is obviously losing to the Russian spring offensive. The Coalition of the Willings is no official entity but has over 2 million soldiers Europe wide under its command. John Healey – British defense minister- threatened Russia with further 4.5 billion pounds military aid to Ukraine in order to intimidate Vl.Putin. Only-he has not that money.
As for a joke a mistaken British embryo was implanted to mistaken British mother;
in Britain every mistake can happen ! Including a royal divorce or suspicious royal car crash death.

U.S. President Donald Trump commented on the high rise of U.S. import tariffs with the words :"I did it because some one has to do it!" Extraordinary Ukrainian prime minister on duty Denys Shmihal beat off all his peace proposals with the words "we are not a buffer zone". I fully sympathize with him. What about Keir Starmer ? He was involved in the heroic sinking of the Russian battle ship "Moskva" some 2 years earlier .When he has any dirty talk he refuses to go to the toilette. Ex German Chancellor Gerhardt Schröder failed with his pecuniary court trial.
As a consultant at a Russian oil company he gets 10,000 EUR monthly over his Chancellor pension.
The U.S. special envoy for Ukraine Steve Witkoff met Russian President Vladimir Putin in St. Petersburg to discuss for the 3rd time the Ukrainian war. At the same time in Germany deliberated the Coaltition of the Willing, the Ramstein Group
and the Ukrainian Contact Group. EU financial ministers' gathering in Warsaw. The last one can close the door.

All four came to nothing. Iran used the turmoil "to enrich uranium for a civil use" reaching enrichment level of 60% (BBC).

12. April 2025 in a mass British turmoil I predict current Labor Government will collapse and British prime minister Sir Keir Starmer will be ousted soon.

Ukrainian military site **MILITARNYI. Com** reported on a hit of Russian air crafts hangar in Tyotkino, Kursk region. So seemingly Ukraine too does not stick to any seize fire just as the Russians. Reportedly – and not for the first time Russia launched 97 drones into Ukraine; 57 were "intercepted". And the rest ? ? NATO Secretary General Mark Rutte visited the Odessa region in Ukraine but reported no irregularities.
German Chancellor-Candidate Friedrich Merz agreed with further German Taurus-MARSH rocket launchers delivery to Ukraine despite the objection they could be used for bombardment of the Russian Crimea bridge.
His Father is said to be former German Nazi.
Greece decided to buy 16 further Taurus-Marsh missiles "in order to defend itself against any aggression". It is not clear how many Western rockets Ukraine had engulfed from the West so far; no numbers were released yet. It is well known Greece is a NATO member and doesn't bother too much of its security. The news as it is.

Ailing feeble former U.S. president Joe Biden in his 80ies refilled his time by criticizing Donald Trump and his first 87 days in office, accusing him of "damage and misadministration". It is not clear who stood behind Biden but his remarks are unproper and wicked. The media stressed on the importance of his short speech and repeated it many times like parrots having something entirely else in their minds ! An U.S. federal judge indicted Donald Trump of "contempt of the court" and introduced legal steps into accusing him formally. If so Trump might face legal procedure.

The European Central Bank – ECB- sank the leading interest down to 2.5% making thus credits cheaper.
Who'll benefit from this is not clear – at least to me.
The U.S.A. stroke a deal with Ukraine for use of its mineral wealth. A special fund will be created supervised by both Washington and Kyiv. U.S. secretary of State Marko Rubio elucidated no further details but it leaked of importance is a graphite mine in central Ukraine . The U.S.A. will trade it in return for its military aid to Ukraine. U.S. vice president J.D.Vance visited Italy to discus … the Ukrainian war. He praised the Italian ceack down on migration. Italian prime minister Giorgia Meloni invited U.S. President Donald Trump for talks in Italy. Her invitation was accepted. Vance looked fat and fleshy while Trump – 40 years older – lashed Democratic Senator van Hollen for mingling into his Presidential duties. He rendered a sleazy account of his visit to an El Salvador prison.
It leaked also China delivered weaponry to Russia to fight in Ukraine; President Zelenskyy was infuriated and vowed "retribution next week!". In turn President Putin ordered 36-hours Easter seize-fire.
The German government placed submarine construction order for 6 billion EUR to a Kiel shipyard.

Two Russian cosmonauts and an American astronaut returned for Easter to the Earth after their joint 200 days' trip to outer Space. A paragon of peaceful coexistence! On the 20th April -Sunday-tennis player Alexander Zwerev hit his 28th birthday – the same day as Adolf Hitler! U.S.vice-president J.D.Vance used up the Easter vacation to visit the Vatican in a Sunday trip and to get blessed by Pope Francis. The very next day the Pope died aged 88; Vance learned the news in his aircraft bound for a state visit to India.

On 19. March 2025 Russia downed a French fighter jet over the Baltic Sea; the French armed forces joint staff reported on the incident only after Easter. Obviously they awaited a resurrection?!
It got known Egypt armed its air forces with Russian MIG-29 fighter jets – thus not French Mirage.

President Zelenskyy planed a peace talk with the U.S.A., the U.K and France for Wednesday after Easter. Russian President Vladimir Putin said "he had opportunity to speak many times to Pope Francis" and "he was an extraordinary person." U.S. President Donald Trump expressed his willing to attend to Pope Francis funeral scheduled for end of April 2025. Volodymyr Zelenskyy will attend too , after he was granted the charity to speak with the Pope earlier by phone. This became public only now and is not included in my earlier books. Former U.S. President Joe Biden will attend too in order to agitate world leaders against acting U.S. President Donald Trump.

After blessed by Pope Francis U.S. vice president J.D. Vance – not Cyrus Vance - arrived in India and signed a trade contract with worth $500 billion – it reads $500,000,000,000 . Rather impressive Pope bless. Vance visit lasted 4 whole days. He demanded bigger access for U.S. companies to the rich Indian market. In my view this will lead to inflation rise. The international pressure on the U.S. dollar rose from 25% to 40% ; calculation method unknown.

U.S. defense secretary Hegseth was accused for a second Pentagon security chat leak.
He denied all accusations massively supported by President Donald Trump :"It's an old story, try to find out something new", both said to the media.

The Russian attacks on Ukraine hold on. Führer Zelenskyy rejects for 5zillion times the Moscow peace proposals. Accepting them it will bring peace and prosperity to the whole of Ukraine. This can be achieved in surrendering of 50 miles disputed land on which lives practically no one . In a practical blunder president Zelenskyy dooms his people to 3-4 further years. For a peace he has nothing to offer – only cemeteries and ruins. Never the less he rams obstinately his anti-Russian no negotiation dogma gambling with world war 3 as U.S. President Donald Trump stated recently to the World.

Russia intensified its midnight missiles attacks on capital Kyiv using the absence of president Zelenskyy. Donald Trump accused him of being an obstacle to peace. Zelenskyy used his trip to South Africa to meet with president Cyril Ramaphosa. No details of their talks leaked yet. Trump remarked "if Zelenskyy does not make peace now he might lose the whole country in three years". He accused Zelenskyy of over confidence and arrogance in his approach". Zelenskyy fell back to a remark of former U.S. Secretary of State Mike Pompeo in which he said "the Crimea is Ukrainian". Trumps remark were muzzled by the media for more details. So Zelenskyy fired back on Trump's claim "he prolonged the war" and "he had nothing to boast about!" . Trump said negotiations with Ukraine are more difficult than with Russia. Zelenskyy prolongs the war un necessary by refusing to cede territory to Russia. Trump's peace plan foresees abandon of the Donetsk, Pokrovsk , Zaporizhie and Crimea regions and rejects Ukrainians NATO membership; the Zaporzhizhie nuclear power plant steps over to American control while Zelenskyy peace plan is unrealistic and obstinate. It's time for Zelenskyy to get the table. The Mayor of Kiyv-former box sportsman Vitalyy Klichko- agreed with territorial concessions to Russia:"It is not fair, it is painful but for the moment we have to compromise temporarily".
Polish President Andrzej Duda also summoned Ukraine to the negotiation table and ask for a compromise. British prime
minister Keir Statrmer said approximately the same delivering a speech on board aircraft carrier "H.M.Prince of Wales".
Russia intensified its strikes on Dnipropetrovsk, Poltava, Kherson, Odessa, Sumi, Cherkasy, Pavlohrad and on Capital Kiyv. Hypocritically V.Zelenskyy said "he has no mandate to give up Crimea". Such a spectacle !

In Torgau-Germany- festivities took place to mark the 80th anniversary of the unification of Russian and American troops
to mark the end of World War Two and the defeat of the National Socialism. The Russian Ambassador Neçaev was not

invited but he came as a private person. However he was forbidden to take the floor and to say few words on the event. Such a vitriolic malice !!

According to Donald Trump each side of the war loses 5,000 young soldiers weekly in the battles; he said this has to stop.
In the middle of the negotiating preparations a car bomb assassinated a senior Russian general Yaroslav Moscalik while
driving his Volkswagen Golf 25 km East of Moscow in Malashikha . Another Russian general – Igor Kirillov – was already killed- again by a car bomb some time earlier again in Moscow- December 2024. So it looks like Moscow is not a safe area for generals. General Yaroslav Moskalik was deputy Chief of staff of the Russian army. Thus in charge in many military operations against Ukraine and many other secrete Russian military details. Now his "secrete" was blown . Moskalik was said to have led the Crimea annexation in 2014. Formally the news of his assassination was brought in by Svetlana Petrenko – a spokes woman of the Russian Army. It became clear the Ukrainian peace rejection consists of 3 points:
1.No country has to dispute the Ukrainian peace
2.No Ukrainian territory can be negotiated
3.No foreign country can forbid any future Ukrainian treaty or alliance
Obvious any territory dispute to Russia is still a taboo zone for Kyiv.

POPE FRANCIS' FUNERAL IN ROME

The preparations for Pope Francis funeral in Italy began with the start of Air Force NR.1- Donald Trump took off bound to Rome at 15:00 CET from the Washington Ronald Reagan air port.
Former U.S. President Joe Biden followed with a separate air craft to agitate against him at the out skirts of the official funeral ceremony. Rome is preparing its self with high police presence, sniffer dogs to sniff explosives and snipers and sharp shooters on the rooftops.

Euronews kept busy with the assassination of Russian General Yaroslav Moskalik till 28th-29th of April 2025 by repeating steadily the General was assassinated by detonation of remote control road side bomb in Malashikha near Moscow; according to the decorations seen he was not a "simple General": General Yaroslav Moskalik was deputy Chief of staff of the Russian army . Obviously in possession of many military secretes; now the secretes were blown up. CBS News' Holly Williams reported extensively on the scheme as "Vladimir Putin began a high-stakes meeting of his cabinet". All the world acts on a stage ! From Ural to Alaska !

Massive electricity failure all over both Spain & Portugal. German energy experts – such as Markus Rövekamp and others-
failed to explain the blackout for 55 million people (ZDF) : in Madrid, Barcelona, Sevilla, Lisboa, Porto etc. Air traffic,
trains, phone connections, water supplies – all collapsed !

The day after
power was restored to only 2.5 million people.
And we shed crocodile tears for Ukraine!

CNN accused unfounded "Donald Trump of being unpopular in his 1st term even more unpopular in his 2nd term". Something I don't agree with: all the world cannot overturn Donald Trump I am full fan of ! As CNN John King - seemingly younger than President Trump – concluded wisely " One hundred days and yet not wiser!". Reflection.

MAY 2025

May began with no German Government at all.
President Donald Trump marked his 100 days in office with growing unpopularity – ca. 40% of the opinion polls.
South Korean Intelligence said 600 North Korean soldiers were killed fighting for Russia in the war on Ukraine.
This cannot be verified independently, said BBC News but illustrates the globalization of the conflict.

The United States has signed the craved Mineral Agreement with Ukraine .
Scott Bessent – U.S. Treasury Secretary – signed the deal from the American side while Ukrainian deputy prime minister Yulia Svyrydenko-39- flew specially to Washington for the signature . It is not a peace deal, not a security guaranty , it is pure economic agreement but it will make Vladimir Putin to rethink his calculations. The deal signed is a very bad news for Moscow. U.S. top diplomat Marco Rubio welcomed the treaty and named it a milestone of the Ukrainian security and
prosperity. Ukraine posses only 5% of the global resources of rare minerals and they are in the occupied eastern provinces but obviously the U.S.A. is satisfied of the deal. The BBC named it "positive noises" while British prime minister Sir Keir
Starmer assessed it as "historic milestone to boost Ukrainian economy and security"; "wider frame work to come", said Ukrainian president Volodymyr Zelenskyy.
Both countries will share the profits of the deal and it will encourage further U.S. investments in Ukraine.
It is a business deal not a peace deal, the Ukrainian debts to the U.S.A. remain unpaid.

U.S. National Security Advisor Mike Waltz
left his post for a sheer havoc & tragedy for the ruling party both in Washington and Kyiv.
Donald Trump commented sarcastically "You may change even your religion " in a nasty foggy political Washington weather. Waltz began new job as an U.S. ambassador to the U.N. Marko Rubio became nationalsecurity a\ advisor parallel with his engagement as a Secretary of state.
Russian President Vladimir Putin did not comment on all these changes.

According to my own prognosis Marco Rubio will be the next successor of Donald Trump as a president of the U.S.A. Already now he attacks strongly the German Government as "sheer dictatorship". With right or without we have to wait.
President Vladimir Putin declared 3 days truce for the festivities of the 80 th Jubileum of Nazi Germany defeat in 1945.
Volodymyr dubbed this "a sheer cynicism". In the World War Two Ukraine was an ally to Nazi Germany and used to print Ukrainian banknotes with a Hitler swastica. The international public kept full silence.

At Victory Day President Donald Trump announced his decision to re-open the notorious Alcatras prison;
It was closed in the 1960ies. Donald Trump expressed also "his deep sympathy with Holliwood and imposed 100% charge for foreign film customers because "they steel our films!""

No American reports on VE Day.

80 years earlier – in 1945 – Sir Winston Churchill said "We celebrate our victory in Europe; we cannot celebrate everywhere yet!" Tea party followed after the parade in London; the Ukrainian detachments marched in result. Both Ukrainian troops and Ukrainian president Volodymyr Zelenskyy attended the parade in London.
The Czech prime minister Pëtr Pavel promise 1.8 millions artillery shells as a help to Ukraine. This is not necessary to them to march in London "war parades" which lasted 4 days. Ahead of the victory parade in Moscow Ukraine bombarded
the Russian Capital airport to prevent foreign dignitaries to attend the parade. .

A slogan rose up :"Don't seek Russian help to save
Greenland!", so Euronews.

After six months brake Germany established new government with Friedrich Merz as a German Chancellor and Frei as a financial minister. Nevertheless Germany continues suffering under its recession. Annalena Baerbock and her Green party are slightly represented in the German Bundestag but not in the German Cabinet. And this is the end of the six months long German political crisis. Boris Pistorius continues his mandate as a German defense minister.
Very soon he is likely to have to intervene.

Only one hitch: in the German Bundestag election Chancellor CDU candidate Friedrich Merz failed to achieve majority. According art. 63 (2) of the German constitution (=Grundgesetzt) he failed. So he was elected in the 2nd round.
All politicians world wide are shocked ! It is for the first time in the German political history ! The German political chaos deepens. A sheer triumph for the German far-right AfD. Euronews reported instead on Rumanian election till 14:00.
As a result France and Poland lost enthusiasm to meet Friedrich Merz as German Chancellor. He started his first day of
office with a Paris visit to discuss with French President Emanuel Macron the French-German nuclear arms cooperation.
ZDF-correspondent Diana Zimmerman reported extensively onto.

Because of Donald Trump's austerity measures on education, development and research 350 top scientists threatened to leave the U.S.A. bound to Europe. European President Ursula von der Leyen welcomed them with a short speech . Donald
Trump did not commented. In an exclusive BBC interview former president Joe Biden criticized sharply Donald Trump
and his current international policy; it became not clear what Biden-aged 88 – wanted to say. He accused Trump of "confiscation not peace, freedom & democracy which are our U.S. values". He accused Trump pushing Ukraine to retreat some land to Russia. No single word on the mineral treaty signed both by Ukraine and U.S.A. recently.
U.S. Defense Secretary Pete Hegseth single-handedly halted U.S. military aid to Ukraine in the early days of the Trump administration. "It's incomprehensible," a senior Ukrainian lawmaker told Newsweek. U.S. arms shipments to Ukraine were briefly halted in early February, Reuters reported. The news agency reported Tuesday that Hegseth's office had issued a verbal order to halt 11 flights carrying weapons and supplies to Ukraine shortly after the Trump administration took office.
Ramzan Kadirov-48 years old Russian forces activist retired his position for health reasons.

After a Washington meeting British prime minister Sir Keir Starmer -Labor, 62 years old-convinced the U.S. to reduce the American tariffs to 10 percent, British steel and British aluminium to 0%. Donald Trump named this "a historic deal" and it is really a such one.

The American President insisted a 30-days cease fire instead the Russian proposal of 3 days only to celebrate the 80th anniversary of the Russian victory in the World War II. The celebration ended with a huge military parade in the Red Square in Moscow with world leaders from 27 countries including the Chinese President Xi Jin Ping and others. So Vladimir Putin demonstrated once again he was not isolated internationally. Ukrainian president Volodymyr Zelenskyy named the parade "a full scale cynicism" while Putin cited Sir Winston Churchill phrase "talking jaw to jaw is better than war!"

The EU-foreign ministers met together for a conference in Lemberg, Western Ukraine. They followed the Zelenskyy proposal to establish an international war crime tribunal for Russian war crimes in Ukraine. The Ukrainian name of Lemberg is Lwiw, the Russian name is Lvov. No extra security measures were taken because Lemberg is not in the war zone.

4 European prime ministers visited Kyiv to show support to V. Zelenskyy :prime ministers of France, Britain, Germany & Poland resp. Emmanuel Macrone, Keir Starmer , Friedrich Merz and Donald Tusk. So it is visible there is no war at least in Kyiv they demonstrated Dutch courage to visit it unlimited: They put an ultimatum to Putin – either to accept the Western proposal or to face even tougher sanctions. The Kremlin spokes man Dmitryy Peskow said : "There are no communication channels to the West, how to accept or reject their plan ?! Very clear logic – even for Keir Starmer.

Ukraine has disposed an alleged Hungarian spy network in Ukraine; the Hungarian authorities named this "an Ukrainian propaganda trick". Hungary has a small Hungarian minority living in Ukraine.

All of the sudden President Putin proposed direct peace talks with Ukraine in Istanbul for 15.May Thursday . Both sides make clear distinction between seize fire and truce. The Europeans are not united esp. because of the U.S. reservations, said ZDF. Zelenskyy repeted several times:"I will wait for Putin on Thursday, 15th May, Turkey". However the chances for this diplomacy are slim.

Kremlin replied sour :"This is not the kind of speech to speak with Russia !" Well ahead of the peace talks in Turkey Poland ordered Moscow to close the Russian consulate in Capital Warsaw. Only the consulate in Poznan remained open. Quite an anti-Russian symphony ! Cardinal Robert Francis Prevost – bishop of Chicago- was elected as new 267th Pope under the name POPE LEO XII. Donald Trump welcomed his election 15 minutes before I did so. As a matter of fact his Vice-President J.D.

Vance is a catholic too – he converted to Catholicism in 2019. The Pope urged an end of the Ukrainian war in his inauguration speech. After the Mess the Pope met Ukrainian leader Zelenskyy for an enlarged talk. The ZDF dubbed mistakenly Friedrich Merz as an U.S. vice-president (18-05-2025, 19:08). Merz instead of Vance. My sharp ear hearing!

The deal U.S. President Donald Trump stroke with Saudi Crown Prince Mohamed Ben Salman was for 160 Boeing air crafts for $600 billion – $600,000,000,000. The Crown Prince didn't even thank him for the deal "because it was a private non U.S. one". Boeing employs some million workers world wide. (BBC News, ZDF in addition).

Mathew Watwaker-a NATO spokes man demanded 5% defense contribution to all its members deducted from all their country GDP. A bit overdone. Overdone dear Sirs.

In Constanz German special forces arrested 3 Ukrainian saboteurs set to attack German infrastructure .

Chancellor Friedrich Merz addressed the German Bundestag in non-sence 58 minutes speech for which I recall noth. German ZDF-TV canceled its 17:00 news broadcast habit. More to follow to their call off. Some Elsinor tragedy - probably. No Shakespear involved . The news as it is.

Ford on strike at its German branch in Collogne.

Kremlin sent **Vladimir Medinsky** to Istanbul to negotiate the peace plan with Ukrainian president Volodymyr Zelenskyy.
Medinsky is a Russian editor of a book on the Ukrainian war. He led the Russian delegation back in March 2022. He is an ideologist of Russian full scale invasion into Ukraine.
 At the end of the week UK defense minister John Healey met his German counterpart Boris Pistorius to discuss further 2 million rounds heavy caliber ammunition delivery to Ukraine. Both criticized sharply Vladimir Putin and his approach
to the peace talks. Robert Brieger – EU military Committee Chair man promised too more ammunition to Ukraine. "with the aim to double the number compared to the previous year", he said to Euronews.
Both President Zelenskyy and President Putin did not come to the peace talks.
"The Russian delegation missed any decision makers", said snubbing Zelenskyy, himself on a visit in Albania – ca. 1,000 km away from Istanbul, dubbed by CNN as "theater like pathetic clown". Finally they decided a prisoners of war swap – a 1,000 prisoners from each side – and a continuation of the talks in June. **Vladimir Medinsky** seems to be a rather skilled negotiator after all!

One day later Kremlin spokes man Dmitryy Peskov asked who will sign eventual agreements from Ukrainian side?! Zelenskyy President mandate expired already in May 2024 - "so he is out of legitimacy", said Peskov. The conflict roots were not been touched by any side, said BBC correspondent John Inwood.

The head of the Ukrainian catholic church handed in to Pope Leo XIV a list of **momentous** Ukrainian prisoners of war and asked for their release. The late Pope Frances had had several times intervened for Ukrainian prisoners' release.
Former U.S. President Joe Biden diagnosed with cancer on score 9 of the Gleason scale. President Donald Trump extended
his condolence and sympathy to him and wished him speedy recovery (CBS). At the same time Amazon announced "Russians are survivors because they have one extra chromosome". Which could be true. True legend !

The long expected trunk call between Donald Trump & Vladimir Putin brought nothing despite of its duration of 2 hours -
translation time included- Putin simply did not disarray from his vacation at the Black Sea resort of Sochi with a subtropical scent. We have to wait for another phone call. President Zelenskyy failed to comment onto. The news as it is.
According to the CNN Putin was unmoved. After the phone call he visited the Kursk nuclear power plant so it is unbelievable that he mad the phone call in the Black Sea resort of Sochi. Zelenskyy turned off the Russian claims saying "He is obliged by constitution to defend the Ukrainian people "and "The prolonged negotiations only help Putin to buy time ". Which all might be true.

In a wealthy Madrid suburb Ukrainian secret service shot dead pro-Russian politician Andrij Portnov while driving his children to school; he was aid to the former pro-Russian president Victor Yanukovich.

The Polish Parliament condemned both Russia and Belorussia for encouraging illegal migrants to stream to Poland asking for asylum and thus destabilizing both Poland and Europe. There is quarrel between Poland and Germany: Germany sends back the migrants to Poland but Poland rejects to accept them, so they stranded. In the full time both German TV channels – ARD & ZDF failed to report on the strifle , they kept busy with Peepy Long Stocking – a Scandinavian saga 80 years ago. Little reported on the current event Germany

sent its 45 tank brigade of 5,000 soldiers to Lithuanian capital Vilnus – Rudnikai to strengthen German presence there; Vilnus is close to the Russian border and some 1,000 km away from Germany. German Chancellor Friedrich

Merz blessed the event in a television show-up. As a matter of reality the current soldiers number is only 400 men. Obviously Germany is not flush with cash yet nor any time soon. Ukraine rejected bluntly the Russian plan of demilitarized buffer zone in the disputed areas between Russia and Ukraine and claimed again the conquered narrow patch in the Kursk region. So hypocritical !

U.S.President Donald Trump announced $175 billion strategic defense system plan in Space called "Golden Dome."The Congress Budget Commission evaluated his program at $570 billion; it will speed up the arm racing at the venue of Space. Trump is set to accomplish his plan by the end of his term.
Further on his administration threatened the European Union to get charged by 50% tariffs on its exports to the United States. Instead to negotiate those charges the EU prefers to get involved in the Ukrainian war on the losing side. Such a short-sighted policy ! Such short-sighted politicians from 26 countries ! Too much interrogation marks !

Boris Bondarev, an expert in international relations and foreign policy and a former Russian diplomat, stated in a "Moscow Times "article that Russia's goal is to "exhaust both Ukrainian society and Western countries, and especially Europe, in order to end military support for Kiev."
Immediately after the start of the large-scale Russian invasion, Poland proved to be Ukraine's best friend of all its neighbors. Unlike many Western leaders, the Polish leadership did not urge Ukrainians to surrender, but believed that it was possible to stop Russia.

In a television interview CDU-political spokes man Armin Lasched guaranteed that Israeli Prime Minister Benjamin Netanyahoo will be not arrested upon his entry in Germany despite the International Arrest Warrent against him issued by the International Criminal Court ICC which accused him of massive genocide in Gaza. Armin Laschet assured him "he will be not arrested in Germany despite the arrest warrant against him . What about Vladimir Putin ? He too is accused by the ICC for genocide.
As to Armin Lasched – body weight 120 kg – he is spokesman of the CDU – Parliamentary fraction in the German Bundestag. 120 kg body weight equal to 265 pounds, an overwhelming politician

U.S. President Donald Trump-with no neck tie- wrote on X:"Putin is insane! Absolutely crazy! I knew him for a long time and I got along with him but now not any more because he sends rockets and kills people so I don't like him at all "and he threatened Putin with further sanctions. Kremlin countered with the words "the U.S. President is rather overloaded emotionally !" It looks very much like Cold War _ 2.
Diesel scandal at Volkswagen car factory in Wolfsburg,Germany.
Volkswagen Boss Martin Winterkorn jailed for 4 years. At the same time the British Monarch King Charles visited Canada to open the session of the Canadian Parliament in a gesture of show of solidarity with the Canadian people; he demonstrated support against the U.S. plans and ambitions to turn Canada into 51st
U.S. state.
French president Emmanuel Macrone toured Vietnam, Indonesia and Singapore to promise broad French support to them and intensifying their foreign trade with France. The three countries suffer from the heavy American trade tariffs which Washington imposed on them in May 2025.

The Western allies lifted all restrictions on Ukraine to use of long-range missiles against Russia, said the new German Chancellor Friedrich Merz. Now Ukraine has permit to attack any military target deep inside Russia such as fuel stores and ammunition depots and thus to defend itself against Russian attacks beating them off in advance. The Western allies are France, Germany, UK and U.S.A., said Merz. He visited Finland and praised its bravery against potential Russian aggression. The scope of the TAURUS-MARSH rockets is 500 km (313 miles) and the permit of their use is escalation of the war. The former German Chancellor Olaf Scholz had opposed such a permit to the Ukraine. The Russian foreign minister Sergey Lavrov was not surprised at all:" We know of this permit

already long long time ago", he said. With knowledge or without it the war escalation is a war escalation. So simple. Already the very next day Ukrainian president Volodymyr Zelenskyy arrived in Berlin for talks with the German Chancellor Friedrich Merz . Merz looked a little bit perplexed. Zelenskyy looked furious and "wanted to bury Russia", as he said. He was received with military salutes and brass music. Merz agreed with the Ukrainian demand to hit with German missiles Russian targets deep inside Russia – something which we know already and which is escalation of the war. Friedrich Merz promised German help to Ukraine to facilitate its own missiles production and to thrust them against Russia. Merz stressed "infantry wins battles logistic wins wars". BBC said for him "he is very ambitious!"
Merz stressed on cooperation with the Ukraine on the field of military, industry, agriculture,
and also "Putin speaks the language of peace, he speaks the language of aggression". Merz thanked Zelensky for coming to Berlin while Zelensky thanked the journalists for coming to the news conference.
"We have to pressure Russia for a seize fire and Germany must increase its military supply to Ukraine" while Merz rejected discussing publically details. Both stressed the importance of the frozen Russian assets amounting to 50 billion euro. Zelensky insisted on Ukrainian participation in the NATO summit in June "Standing out of the summit means victory of Russia but not over Ukraine but over Nato" while Merz concluded "we have invested sufficiently in diplomacy". Zelensky accused Putin of delaying the peace negotiations . Merz promised again German aid of 5 billion EUR = 5,000,000,000 and additional military equipment
German help for joint military production of long range weapons both in Germany and inside in Ukraine while Zelensky expressed his hope for further seizure of Russian assets abroad. Moscow named this a sheer new provocation. For a first time Zelenskyy was dressed in a suit but without neck tie.

A short summary to close this chapter : Germany promised to Ukraine full military, industrial, logistical, humanitarian and other support because Chancellor Friedrich Merz is an adventurer. Germany is the second - largest supporter to Ukraine after the U.S.A. esp. these 5,000,000,000 EUR granted to Ukraine today.
Both sides showed no nuance of disagreement; they rejected the Russian proposal of buffer zone around Kursk, Bryansk, Belgorod & Sumi regions which Zelensky rejected with the words "we must make this war most painful to Russia". In the nuances of the reception the figure of the German unemployment became known – 3.9 million; 3,900,000. And in Ukraine – even more.

According to Zelensky Russia had allegedly amassed 50,000 troops along the Ukrainian border (which border?) and prepares them for a huge summer offensive. Which might be true.

In a televised interview the Russian foreign minister Sergey Lavrov set the peace talks in Istanbul for 2nd of June 2025 which is Monday. Literary Lavrov said in "Stambyul". He stressed on the root cause of the conflict which should be removed. The Russian delegation will be led again by **Vladimir Medinsky** – a prolific Russian writer. Meanwhile Jacques Baud published his book "How West Lead Ukraine to Defeat " .
In the meantime Turkish foreign minister Fidan visited Moscow and spoke with both Vladimir Putin and Sergey Lavrov. The Kremlin speaker Dmitrij Peskov declared "with the treaties forged with Ukraine Germany and the West entered direct war with Russia".
U.S. President Donald Trump set 14-days dead lock for Vladimir Putin to start the peace talks . Putin obviously is keeping his time limit. An Ukrainian drone killed the Mayor of Stavropol in the disputed regions. 10,000 Russian troops entered the town of Tzetzevka. The Russian pre-condition for the peace talks in Istanbul is full stop of the Western weaponry to Ukraine.

The European Parliament discussed in Brussels the vote withdrawal of Hungary. The discussion started in 2018 because Hungary frequently misused its right of veto to block important European decisions regarding the Ukrainian war and "it leads Europe by the nose by vetoing it".

JUNE 2025

The month of June began with a railway bridge and Russian passenger train blown up by Ukraine in the Bryansk and in Kursk regions leaving 70 people dead. Neither Ukraine nor Russia claimed responsibility. Ukrainian ballistic missiles hit 4 strategic Russian air fields 1,000 – 4,000 km away from the front line one of them in Olenya, Murmansk, Irkutsk, , Ivanovo and Ryazan - destroying 41 fighter bombers parked on the tarmac before they even managed to take
off; this is was said to be one third of the strategic bombers Russia has on stock. The preparations for this attack had lasted 18 months . The harm amounted to $7 billion - $7,000,000,000 and The NewsWeek dubbed it "The Russian Pearl Harbor." The strategic bomb jets were capable of carrying nuclear explosives.
The speculations rose that these audacious attacks were launched from inside Russia after been smuggled there in proximity. A great humiliation for Russia one day before the Russian-Ukrainian peace talks in Istanbul. Nato secretary general Mark Rutte rejected any American involvement. He warned "that very soon Europe will be not able to defend itself against any new Russian aggression ".

In an ample press conference in Glasgow British prime minister Sir Keir Starmer said "if we want to deter a war we must prepare for a war". The UK is up to furnish 12 new attack submarines, six new ammunition factories and raise its defense budget up to 2.5% of its GDP. It sounds good but the construction of one of these submarine can takes 10 years.
"Nothing works unless we all work together! We deliver peace through strength". And he revealed his defence plan: "We never work alone. We work through our strategic strength: we praise Nato great again! The UK is steadfast ally to Ukraine".
Parallel to the peace talks in Istanbul a conference of Baltic and North-European prime ministers took place in Lithuania with participation of the Ukrainian head Volodymyr Zelenskyy. In his speech he condemned Russia in many ways and asked for more military and industrial aid to Ukraine. He plans 15 billion pounds aid to Ukraine; Lithuanian defense minister Da Vile Sakaliene accused Kremlin "of mocking at the United States of America" obviously aiming to escalate the conflict to international level.
The Istanbul peace talks brought nothing – Russia rejected all Ukrainian demands, esp. unconditional cease fire and return of the abducted Ukrainian children back home. Neither President Putin nor President Zelenskyy attended the talks. Both delegations exchanged documents through the Turkish side. The Russian demand was its claim on the regions of Donetsk, Cherson, Zaporizhiya and Luhansk-regions Russia unlawfully occupied but never fully controlled . Both sides remained deeply divided on key issues.

Britain released a new weapon factory – a "clear message to Russia", said British defense minister John Healey. EU foreign policy head and vice – president of the European Commission Kaja Kallas warned of growing relations of Russia and China:"The global security ties are extremely worried of such relations", she rattled .
U.S. Secretary of State Marko Rubio accused the German regime of tyranny in view of its treatment of the AfD party. Russia started suspicious maneuvers in the Baltic Sea – Poland protested in vain.The new Polish
President Karol Nawrocky is against Ukrainian membership in Nato. As president he is supreme commander

of the Polish armed forces.

It became clear that Russia posses tactical nuclear weapons and the West – not. A sheer cross road .

Former German foreign minister Annalena Baerbock became president of the U.N.O. General Assembly for one year despite strong Russian objection. A largely ceremonial post , she'll get inaugurated on 09.September 2025.

The Nato defence ministers convened in Brussels ; U.S. defence secretary Pete Hegseth advocated again for 5% of GDP for all member states. They all discussed the option of 5% of the overall budget to be spent on reliable defence .

In Washington, D.C. President Trump received German Chancellor Friedrich Merz and praised him for his good English, for the high German defence spending and Merz commitment to resolve the Ukrainian crisis; finally Merz is 8 cm taller than Donald Trump. It became known that Donald Trump's grandfather Friedrich was born in Germany-Kreis Bad Dürkheim somewhere in Rheinland-Pfalz

Both leaders plan war and war escalation. The media spilled superlatives all over the carpets. Unlike me.

ZDF Washington correspondent Ulf Schmiese confused several times the names of the both leaders-unlike me.

Both leaders avoided the tariff issue-unlike me-the tariffs on German steel and German aluminum.

The discussions took place in a friendly and warm atmosphere.

Multi Billionair Elon Musk suggested "Donald Trump must step down and be replaced by his Vice-President J.D.Vance!". He accused Trump of ingratitude .So what is Merz doing in Washington and in the White House ??

Merz is the 4th European leader to visit Washington after Macrone, Melony and Zelenskyy.

The conversation lasted 40 minutes, afterwards Merz headed back for Germany. No Press-conference.

Merz only said "we have to push on Putin stronger, stronger, stronger to make him stop this war.

We are entirely with Ukraine!" It got known however that one day before his visit Donald Trump had had a phone call with Vladimir Putin. **Nothing and yet again nothing was reported on this phone conversation between the two state men.** Both have to meet again in ten days at the G7 top in Canada.

Trump designated the U.S. relations to Germany as "tip-top".

Meanwhile Ukraine attacked four Russian fuel reservoirs and set them afire.

And again meanwhile Russia offered political asylum to Elon Musk – Donald Trump's top man & top advisor, reported the Russian State Media TASS.

For the prisoners' of war exchange the Ukrainian side simply did not appear at the meeting point:

such Ukrainian demagogy! The Russian Army liberated the city of Dnepropetrovsk – the utmost West of the Donetsk region. The Ukrainian army denied such a happening as "propaganda". It dismissed the Russian numbers as "propaganda"esp.the firing of 500 Russian on Ukrainian target. Only there is one hitch – such Ukrainian targets seem to be endless. How could the Russians hit every day new targets? And new targets? And new targets? And new, a new, anew?! Ukrainian President Wolodymyr Zelenskyy named the situation "very difficult" but elucidated no details. So we have to consume his 1,001 night stories and clap applause to his narrative. The news was brought to public by CNN Berlin correspondent Frederik Pleitgen.

Nato Secretary General Mark Rutte – former Dutch prime minister – warned that "Russia will attack Nato within 5 years with missiles 5 times faster than the sound; there is no east or west , there is only one Nato; the European capitals are only few minutes away from the Russian hit", he said to Euronews during his visit to London. He urged the Nato countries to increase their defence spending to 3.5% of their GDP or to face a Russian aggression. His host Sir Keir Starmer agreed fully with him. Mark Rutte named this a "Quantum Leap".

It sounds like the Chinese "Great Leap " in the Mao Tse Dung's times. Nothing is new. No new inventions.

The U.S. Health Secretary Robert J. Kennedy Junior fired 17 of his team because of sloppy work. Could happen !

In the aftermath of the rebellion in Los Angeles U.S. Defence Secretary Hegseth said "he and Trump can send U.S. troops everywhere in the U.S.A." And beyond, I would say!

Vice-President J.D. Vance said "the blood feud between Trump and Elon Musk is not going for the good of Musk".

And this is the end of the Story ! Nothing new: already 1977 Judas Priest released a song called "Dissident Agressor"! So simple !
In the Berlin Willi-Brandt House German SPD Chairman Rolf Heinrich Mützelich advocated for "talks with Moscow to avoid any armed confrontation". The party top and the German SPD defence minister Boris Pistorius ridiculed him instead to take any constructive discussion: the political chaos in Germany continues even after the resignation of Chancellor Olaf Scholz in May 2025.
Rolf Heinrich Mützelich himself – aged 65 - is rather controversial but pragmatic, a critic of Volodymyr Zelenskyy.

Dr. Bittner-SPD- German jurist and author- wrote on 08.August 2022- from a machine translation:
"The political situation is appalling and the persecution of dissenters in connection with the Ukraine war is taking the form of unbridled fascism. It is unacceptable that state terrorism is being carried out here under the eyes of the world public. The
persecution of critics and opposition figures by Ukrainian government organizations must be stopped immediately. The federal government (of Germany) is called upon to lodge a protest with the Zelenskyy government against the discrimination against
German nationals in Ukraine… and to stop all aid for Ukraine. The list of the CCD must be deleted immediately."
CCD means Common Core of Data database maintained by the National Center for Education Statistics NCES.

German defence minister Boris Pistorius came for the weekend to Kiyv. He declared "the full German support to Ukraine."
Pistorius pointed out "the new German government is sticking with Ukraine and even it will increase its support to Ukraine "es koste was es wolle": "Whatsoever the cost might be!"" . The President of the European Union Ursula von der Leyen also expressed support for Ukraine :"Es koste was es woll!" She too is a German. Her German is better than mines:
because she is a native German. Finally Boris Pistorius promised 900 billion euro help to Ukraine mostly in the form of
joint missiles & drones production in Ukraine, reported finally the German ARD (First German Television). No videos shown; obvious secretes available.

The very next day Zelenskyy hosted a conference in the eastern Ukrainian city of Odessa with the leaders of Eastern European Nato countries. They condemned Russian invasive politic and decided to stand together against Kremlin At the same time
German Chancellor Friedrich Merz hosted Danish prime minister Metta Frederiksen, greeted her with a military honors and military orchestra and discussed with her the Ukrainian war reiterating aid to Ukraine and firm policy against Russia. The top
of their agenda was the war in Ukraine and the European security. No further details were released for their joint meeting.
The Odessa conference was absolutely redundant in the face of the fact G7 top in Alberta, Canada and Nato top in the Netherlands are impending in June 2025.

100 prominent members of the left wing of the German SPD-party published a manifesto against the stationing in Germany of U.S. medium-range missiles and stressed upon diplomatic talks with Moscow not a military confrontation with Russia. They criticized the current German policy of confrontation against Russia. They criticized the planed defence spending increase of 5%
The manifesto illustrates the deep division within their own party SPD, reigning now in coalition with Christian-Democratic Union CDU of Chancellor Friedrich Merz.
At the same time Russian President Vladimir Putin gave a command to strengthen the Russian army to face the growing European coalition seeking confrontation with Russia.

In a talk show Euronews revealed the number of Ukrainian refugees in Europe – 4.3 million= 4,300,000 refugees.
The British budget deficit rose to 100 billions pound – double as much as its defence spending, said British member of Parliament Mel Stride in an Euronews interview.
On 15. June 2025 President Trump marked his 79th birth day with an imposing military parade in Washington, D.C. 6,000 soldiers and 128 army tanks took part in the parade. The very same day Trump flew to Alberta, Canadia to attend the 3-days G7 top in Alberta; a venue for bilateral talks rather than show of unity.
Ukrainian president Volodymyr Zelenskyy too attended the top in his intrusive style in the Canadian Rocky Mountains despite the fact that his native Ukraine is n o t among the leading 7 industrial nations of the world. He lodged in the luxurious Hotel in **Kananaskis. U.S. President Donald Trump said "we wouldn't be here if President Putin attended too"** His talks with German Chancellor Friedrich Merz – a hard-liner were scheduled already for the first day. Their talk lasted exactly 20 minutes.
The Middle East war shifted the center of the talks far way from Ukraine focus so that Trump
left the G7 top prematurely , so new sanctions on Russia couldn't be discussed and president Zelenskyy could not speak with Trump; he spoke with the Nato Secretary General Mark Rutte who also attend the G7 top.
Zelenskyy demanded more military help, more political pressure on Russia and more military heavy armor against it. "We are not looking at a cease fire – we're looking for a better than a cease fire" said Trump to journalists accompanying him backwards on board of his air craft; thus not his helicopter. Aboard Air_Force_1 Trump gave a short Press conference and stated "Macrone always does it the wrong way!" Said bluntly Trump simply refused to sign the G7 final document.

The reason for leaving prematurely the summit Donald Trump handed over to his spokeswoman **Karoline Leavitte**.to explain the details which led him to his decision. Anyway Trump re-assured the G7 he would attend the Nato summit in The Netherlands . But the fact is clear – the G7 got G-6 and Volodymyr Zelenskyy has to come in vain let alone to go back home with some profit. " In fact Trump left the summit because he wanted to celebrate his birthday in a closer circle and because he is skeptical of more sanctions on Russia as they will hurt the U.S.A. too", put it the BBC reporter on the G7 summit James Landale. Practically " Trump deserted the summit." "Obviously President Trump had lost his taste for diplomacy", commented the BBC impartially. The G7 ended without signing any treaty, any declaration, any joint statement on Russia's invasion in Ukraine and this was a bitter disappointment for Volodymys Zelenskyy, as BBC commented.
And this the end of Part 3 of my book. Above all Russia set a new peace condition to Ukraine- to destroy all the weaponry it got from the West and iused it on the battle field. As to Donald Trump he simply fired his intelligence director (Suzi Gabor ??)

In Bulgaria police arrested 3 Ukrainians for kidnapping a minor person and asking a ransom for his life, so ABV.bg.
Russian President Vladimir Putin declared his readiness for peace talks with Ukraine. Ukraine its self
agreed to allow Ukrainian citizens to have double citizenship to motivate their coming back to Ukraine after the war. It is the first time in Ukrainian history for such a decision fluctuating in the centuries past.
The Israeli defence minister Israel Katz compared Iranian Ayatollah Ali Homeini with Adolf Hitler and denied him the right to exist , saying bluntly "He is a modern days Adolf Hitler".
Spanish Prime Minister Pedro Sanches refused the NATO bid of 5% defense spending of its GDP.
As an over touristed Fatherland he blew alarm whistle of overcrowded home land .
A classic paragon of discrepancy inside of NATO itself.

The Russian summer offensive continued.
Only than European media implied there was such a military campaign.

In the eve of NATO top in The Hague German Chancellor Friedrich Merz delivered detailed "Government explanation " to the German Bundestag – the German Parliament.

He promised "political security both in inland and abroad" ; he criticized the current Iranian regime, the Hamaz and the Hezbollah and flattered both Israel and the United States of America.
He praised also the foreign ministers both of France and Great Britain.
Further in his speech Merz praised Kiyv and its peace proposals towards Russia.
He accused Russia of intimidation of the entire European and American space.
He praised the Baltic Brigade 45 and its establishment by German advice and help .
He criticized both German and EU bureaucracy and promised its decline, degradation & limitation.
Only at the end Merz addressed the German economy and its growth provided by the industrious German people. His speech duration was 33 minutes. The left wing of the coalition SPD insisted on negotiation with Russia but in vain. Merz exclaimed The German Bundeswehr must stay the largest army of Europe whatsoever it may mean!"
AfD Chief Tino Cruppala contradicted to Merz in many aspects and nuances.
He said "we're not informed sufficiently on the nuances – only at the final point when bills come!"
According to him "one German tank cost as much as one German school".
He used the words "meine verehrte Damen und Herren "instead of the usual standard words "Meine geehrte Damen und Herren". It happened ! AfD politicians shown laughing happily during his speech.

The German ZDF showed B'90 leader Anton Hofreiter sleeping during the German Bundestag debate.
From all I concluded German Chancellor Friedrich Merz did not attend the NATO–Summit in The Hague where I used to report from.

NATO summit in The Hague where president Zelenskyy delivered a speech. Afterwords Zelenskyy was invited to a lavish NATO -dinner in The Hague where many streets were blocked or banned for traffic.

.. Summary .
The NATO member countries agreed with the American demand to raise their military spending to 5% of their GDP. Only Spain disagreed and made exception. It makes $700 billion.

NATO Secretary General Mark Rutte – a Dutch man just like me – was very officious to Trump and even named him at one point "DADDY" because he is only 51 and Trump 75. On the NATO photo Dutch King Wilhelm Alexander posed at Trump's right side and the Turkish Prime minister Recep Tayyp Erdogan on his left side.
So this NATO summit was nick-named THE TRUMP SUMMIT.
 At the Press Conference -impacted by some journalist questions – Trump promised 12 more F-35 fighter jets for Great Britain and more U.S. Patriot-launcher to Ukraine. His talks with the Ukrainian Minister-President Volodymyr Zelenskyy took place behind closed doors. We'll never learn what the two men discussed and how their discussion ended but Ukrainian NATO-membership was excluded. 25 minutes after the Press Conference Trump took off home from a military airfield near The Hague thus not the Amsterdam International Airport of Schiphol. Never before I have seen so strong massive police presence in The Hague as today.
Not even at Bill Clinton Sofia visit in the 1999ies. Only now the World understood what the "Coalition of the Willing" means and I will not comment on it. Abe tazi Kaya Kalas e mnogo gadna be ! Ebati Liglata! Ligla w progress! .
Zelenskyy himself had breeded vast hidden ambitions to address again the TRUMP SUMMIT but in vaine- hegot the dusty corner shown.

U.S. President Donald Trump criticized sharply CNN "for fake news, wasting time, wasting my time, they all are scum – CNN, NBC, New York Times". And Trump repeated the word "SCUM" several times.

His press conference lasted exactly 45 minutes.
75% of this time Trump spent focusing on Iran, Israel and the Middle East conflict.
This is not the topic of my book and I will close it on this point.
Emil Tzolov , hallmark of speed and objectivity.

26. JUNE 2025

The NATO Summit in The Hague ended with acceptance of Volodymyr Zelenskyy's proposal to establish a new court for criminal prosecution on Russia for alleged atrocities and war crimes committed by Russia during its war on Ukraine.
Probably the court will act in The Hague.
Very much alike to the earlier Bosnia Tribunal in The Hague.
However this Tribunal failed to prosecute the notorious DutchBath for the Srebrenica massacre in 1995 where 8,000 Bosnian men and boys were slaughtered.
Every replication will mean an end of the story.

German foreign minister Wadephul visited unhindered the Ukrainian Capital Kyyv.
He was not shown together the Ukrainian ruler Volodymyr Zelenskyy.
In his speech he promised full German support to Ukraine and tried to intimidate both Russia and Vladimir Putin.
With him were representatives of the German arms industry to sign different agreements but they were unwilling "because they cannot plan the support to Ukraine".
Germany cannot deliver any F-16 fighter jets because it has none. Wadepfuhl intends to start joint ventures with Ukraine on the ground of mutual weaponry constructing with Ukraine.
Ukraine stepped back from the anti-personnel land mines treaty – the so called "Ottawa treaty 1997". Ukraine is the most heavily mined country in the World.

British prime minister sir Keir Starmer stroke a deal with U.S. President Donald Trump for 1.4 billion liter ethanol British import from the U.S.= 1,400,000,000 to ease situation Britain is currently in. Donald Trump has no "Sir" title. Business all over the globe !

JULY 2025

Denmark started its presidency over the EU for the next 6 month.
The Danish prime minister Mette Frederiksen promised full support for Ukraine
and its membership in the European Union. On the ceremony Frederikson stepped in
into office were present the European Commission President Ursula von der Leyen ,
the President of the European Council Antonius Costas and of course Volodymyr Zelenskyy- can something happen
without him!? "Ukraine belongs to the European
Family and NATO ",Mette reassured Zelenskyy.The news as it is. "Maximum pressure
must be put on Hungary to lift its veto on the Ukrainian EU – membership" added
Mette Frederiksen.

According to EU- statistics for the month of June Russia has launched 5,432 drones on
Ukrainian targets, said ZDF. Ukraine wheat was largely accepted from Brussels and a
special price mechanism was set for Ukrainian products inside of the EU. It was named
"new trade deal". Technical details of the deal still have to be agreed upon. Angry Polish
and French farmers protested against the cheap Ukrainian agrar products imports into the
EU but in vain.
The German arm producer Rhein-Metal started the production of details and accessories
for the F-15 fighter jets. The German arm industry employs ca. 284,000 skilled workers
in different locations scattered across the country, said the ZDF.

Euronews aired Russian on air commands on how to down a passangers Azal plane broadcasted on the
3rd & 33rd minute each hour. The command in Russian indicated direction, speed, altitude, azimuth and
heading– all in ciphers & details. The first missile missed its target that's why the fire was repeated.
This is only the begin of a great great news. Th news never sleeps.
So does Emil. A fluent Russian speaker.
French president Emmanuel Macrone placed a phone call with the Russian President Vladimir Putin.
In the phone call which lasted 2 hours – 120 minutes – he insisted on Russia peace talks to stop
its war on Ukraine. Putin insisted the peace plan must include the current Russian territorial gains and
"the new territorial reality". Putin dubbed the talk "sustainable".

At the same time the U.S.A. reduced its delivery of ammunition and shells to Ukraine "because of inland
shortage". Extra concerened are the "Patriot" anti-aircraft missiles shipments. The move came despite earlier
U.S. promises for weapon and ammunition shipments to Ukraine. The news brought satisfaction to Moscow.

 German Chancellor Friedrich Merz received in Capital Berlin the Chinese leader Xi Jin Ping and asked him
 "to agitate his friend Putin to stop the war in Ukraine!" This was a flink manoever to deflect German public
 opinion from brocken pre-election promise about price of domestic electricity . The news as it is. There are 17

million poor people in Germany, living under the poverty line, said the German ARD. At the same time German interior minister Alexander Dobrindt entered direct talks with the terror regime of the Taleban. Nothing- but really nothing – on these talks was reported. Obviously Dobrindt mission has failed.

U.S. President Donald Trump placed one hour phone talk with the Russian President Vladimir Putin. Putin insisted on annexation of 4 Ukrainian regions and ban for Ukrainian NATO membership. Trump was reported "dissapointed" from the phone call.
Russia became the first country in the World to recognize officially the Taliban regime in Afghanistan. Already back to 2022 Russia started to export gas, oil and wheat to Afghanistan. President Zelensky made a phone call to President Donald Trump and named the phone call "constructive"and "fruitfull"; he implied something in the sense "make a lasting peace through strength".

Russia closed several of its airports "because safety concerns of imminent threat of Ukrainian terror attacks", obviously after careful intelligence collection. Mette Frederickson – now European President for
6 months - stressed bluntly on European security and defence increase in a long long speech.

All of the sudden Russia started to hit Ukrainian targets as far to the West as the border town of
Luzk – close to the Polish border. The Russian KINZHAL rockets overwhelmed the Ukranian defence consisting of British fabricated **Patriot-, GMLRS & Hellfire- Rockets** fabricated by the British producer BAE in the town of **Warton-Lancashire, UK** where also the Eurofighter jets **Typhoon** *are produced.*
*There is surplus of redundant British BAE – Systems capacities as the last customer was **Qatar in 2017,***
reported AP (=Assossiated Press). The Russian strategy is to overwhelm , to overburden, to overstretch the Ukrainian defence capability until it runs short of ammunition and by making them defenseless
to riddle the Ukrainian targets without any punishment. So simple !! At the same time president Zelensky visited again Rom and the Vatican for new talks with Pope Leo XIV. Obviously earlier talks born no fruits.
An Europen court found formally Russia guilty of downing the Malaysian aircraft MH17 back in 2014. All 298 passengers on board died inclusive Dutch professor working actively on a new HIV-medicine. The formal procedure was launched by 2 countries only: The Netherlands and Ukraine.
EU-President Ursula von der Leyen survived the non-confidence vote in European Parliament with 360 votes "against",18 abstained and only 175 votes "for" missing thus the majority required of two thirds. Her position as EU-President however was strongly weakened and Zelenskyy's position too, said Alberto Alemanno – professor of law – in an interview for "Euronews".
U.S. Secretary of state Marko Rubio said to Russian foreign minister Sergey Lavrov "he is frustrated over Putin's reluctance to force peace in Ukraine". My personal perception is that Putin has his internal idea, intention or ambition which he's not in a hurry to display to the World; peace negotiations are always difficult and they drag into the lengthy until the common sense of the both parties is reached last not least because they speak frequently different languages and arbitary must be set on.
Both leaders spoke at the ASEAN – top in Kuala Lumpur and remained both undevicive and futile.
Donald Trump threatened Russia with new sanctions but also this did not achieve the result expacted.
The recovery conference of the European leaders was directed by Olena Zelenskyy – wife of Volodymyr Zelenskyy- and brought no results, said ZDF.
Dutch bureaucrats use to censor frequently the ZDF and other TV channels by blocking them;
the latest example was the switching off a documentary film on the tennis legend Boris Backer.

Finally U.S. President Donald Trump changed his mind and agreed to deliver air defense rockets including the "Patriot-Surface" missiles systems which Ukraine needed badly. More details still to
come. President Donald Trump forbade Ukraine to attack Russian oil containers and oil depots.
Slowly the first portions of American military aid started again to flow in to Ukraine but they are not sufficient.

The "Patriot" missiles launchers are crucially needed because Ukraine cannot defend itself in one day only Russia fired 1,800 missiles , drones and ballistic rockets also on Western Ukraine too. The "Patriot" U.S. delivery to Ukraine will start via Nato and the Europeans have to pay for it: "The U.S. doesn't have them and we have to manufacture them, but the Europeans have to pay for these missiles".
In a television interview Donald Trump promised to do so and added:
"I don't like Putin at all-he talks nice by phone to the people in the morning and bombs them in the night with smart bombs! I don't like him at all because I am disappointed in him" and "I don't trust anyone".
Trump had planed a visit to Britain in September 2025.
Joahim Bitterlik- former German ambassador to Nato- doubted there will be peace in Ukraine any time soon. He founds the 50-days ultimatum is exaggerated. However German defence minister Boris Pistorius flew to Washington to arrange the delivery details with the U.S. defence secretary Pete Hegseth. Finally change, finally break through ! The proposed 100% tariffs on Russia aims to make Putin to re-consider his position.

Trump offered to Europe to pay for the "Patriot"- Systems delivery "because this is an European problem and Ukraine is an European country". The "Patriots"will be sent to Ukraine via European Nato countries. He discussed the details with Nato Secretary General Mark Rutte – a former Dutch Prime minister.
Trump made "a special report on EU" which includes the following points: 1). An ultimatum with 50 days dead lock for President Putin to end the war. 2).Intimidation to the Russian allies China , India and Brazil to charge them with 100% tariffs if they continue to support Russia. The ZDF Washington correspondent Elmar Thevessen elucidated his threats as unrealistic. The U.S.A. will deliver the weapons to the European countries who pay for that and than transfer the weaponry to Ukraine. Three NATO countries agreed to deliver "Patriot" missiles from their own stock piles – Germany 2 systems, Norway – 1 system and Denmark one too. The price of each "Patriot-Surface missiles " is $ 100,000 each. They can strike both ballistic and cruise missiles and even low flying drones and exactly their capability makes them so unique .
Besides the sharp abrupt change of mind of President Donald referring whether or not to deliver U.S. weaponry to Ukraine two more Nato countries – Danmark and The Netherlands – decided to deliver several of their own "Patriot"-missiles launchers to Ukraine.
President Zelenskyy remained very satisfied by the deal and spilled over with a flood of thanks to Donald Trump. In a prolonged phone call he praised lavishly the U.S. President and admired his commitment to bring peace in Europe.
The President of the European Commission Mrs. Ursula von der Leyen announced the EU-budget of **2 trillion** euro for the period 2028-2034. From this money Ukraine will get 100 billion euro, said the Euronews. This means **200,000,000,000 euro**: "This is the budget as the reality of today and the challenges of tomorrow" she said on television.

Mean while it became known that Russia keeps on producing weaponry four times more ammunition and armors than all Nato member countries : 4 million artillery shells in 2023 and 4.4 million shells in 2024 planing to produce 7 million artillery shells for 2025 .
In summary Nato countries lag behind with production of 4 times less artillery shells than Russia- 1.2 million shells in 2024 planing 3 million shells for 2025-obviously lagging behind. That's why Nato Secretary General Mark Rutte-former Dutch prime minister- advised all Nato countries to produce more and more and not to lag behind.

His message came after German Chancellor Friedrich Merz visited
London for talks with British Prime Minister Sir Keir Starmer . Both leaders signed a treaty on mutual trade and security with means cooperation on the industrial and military fields which is the first British-German treaty ever. Entering the history as the Kensington treaty it is a stark warning against Russia and encounters the U.S. slogan "America first". The most significant point of the treaty which will enter in

history as Kensington treaty is that an aggression on either country will be treated as aggression on both countries. This implies in full Russian aggression. The assistance duty of the historic Kensington friendship treaty serves as a repellent to any Russian aggression. The message to Kremlin is clear: "we are strong despite the Brexit!" Nation have no friends – only interests.
The approach of the two countries will also assist the reconstruction of postwar Ukraine.

The treaty comprises 27 inner proud pages and includes British access to German e-gates what soever this will mean. The German investment in the UK amounts to 200 million pounds, said Sir Keir Starmer.

Former Russian President Dmitriy Medvedev officially tried to intimidate the West "with pre-emptive Russian strike on the West"; his post now is deputy chief of the Russian Security council. However Ukraine attacked Moscow with drones and caused a fire in one of the Moscow's suburbs. (Euronews).

A fire broke broke out in a Moscow suburb after Ukraine launched drone strikes on the Russian Capital. In over 80 Polish cities and towns manifestations broke out against the refugees' flood from neighboring Ukraine. One of the speakers fell back to the legendary Polish king Jan III Sobiecky:
"The history must repeat", he said to the mobs. (Euronews).

In a ZDF-interview German President Frank-Walter Steinmeier advocated the military conscription in Germany: "It was abolished back in 2011 but now all political & military factors have changed", he said to the camera. The 5% share of the Nato-country budget of their GDP's is already achieved, he added. The second half of his interview was focused on the hot Iran-Israel conflict.
At the same time Slovakian president Robert Fico allerted the EU because Russia stopped the gas supply to his country. Fico blocked the 18 points EU-sanctions package against Russia.
The U.S. special envoy Keith Kellogg visited Kiyv for talks and remained there for a whole week.
That are the facts !

AUGUST 2025

German Chancellor Friedrich Merz visited France for talks with the French President Emanuel Macron. They agreed on many items how to reduce their US-dependency.
The unemployment rate in Germany hit the 3 million mark.
The coffee and tomato prices rose by 24 %.
The U.S. President introduced $ 15,000 entry fee for foreigners willing to enter the U.S.A. Trump abolished also the Secrete Service Protection of Camilla Harris- a Democrat candidate for U.S. president. It leaked former Democrat U.S. President Joe Biden had prolonged illegally her Secrete Service Protection till July 2026.
Trump sent also 2 nuclear submarines to patrol the north Atlantic and the Baltikum.
He sent his special envoy for Ukraine Steve Witkoff to Moscow to hand in a new ultimatum to Russian President Vladimir Putin.
On the 80th anniversary of the nuclear masacre of Hiroshima he uttered no single word.
High ranking Nato activist Ivo Daalder put it bluntly :**"Trump will not risk war with Russia to protect Ukraine!"**
Trump himself re - iterated "better if Putin meets Zelenskyy without me "
while Russian foreign minister Sergey Lavrov stressed " security talks without Russia lead to nowhere".
The EU- Foreign Affairs Officer reprimanded Putin for gambling of time .
Chancellor Merz received Canadian prime minister Mark Karney in Berlin.
Both statesmen declared they stand firmly behind Ukraine.

The German television ZDF reflected on Putin , who "continue to draw his fantasies further and further" The U.S.A. will not sent soldiers to Ukraine, while both France and Great Britain are willing : For Germany it will be a full debacle at the back stage of the fact the German Bundeswehr lacks already now 150,000 soldiers to bridge it own domestic defence gap. However German East block Officer Wagner – Green B'90- praised Chancellor Merz for his enthusiasm for Ukraine. Without Germany would collapse already tomorrow, he stated. At the same time Russian President Vladimir Putin visited China in 5 days' discussion with top Chinese activists. "A red carpet for Putin", he said with admiration. However there were no security guarantees for Ukraine yet, though the European Union berries the main weight of the Ukrainian war. For how long?
There is already full chaos inside Germany – political, economic, financial, personel, financial and military ! At the same time Ukraine started working on security concept after the war.

Germany arrested 4 Ukrainian saboteurs for blowing up the Nord Stream pipeline to Europe : Ukrainians, not Russians. 7 others Ukrainian saboteurs are still at large. These

ones already arrested were captured in the Italian sea resort of Rimini while leisure at the sun and swimming in the Adriatic Sea for pleasure while their fellows alleged are being fighting against Russia. Difficult to believe. Moreover in the Lisbon funicular crash most of the victims were exactly Ukrainian nationals lavishly visiting beforehand a plenty of other European leisure centers.

Russian President Vladimir Putin declared bluntly "Any foreign troops both national and international are unacceptable for Russia. Foreign troops cannot provide peace in Ukraine". "President Zelenskyy is invited to Moscow for talks not for capitulation", he said to BBC Moscow correspondent Steve Rosenberg and repeated this on the world economic forum in Vladivostok : "Any foreign troops in Ukraine will be a legitimate target for Russia"
EU foreign and defense ministers met in Copenhagen to discuss joint European forces in Ukraine. No details leaked. Only that they agreed on a new sanction packet on Russia – the 19th since the war begin. Ukrainian president Volodymyr Zelenskyy was not admitted to the conference. Instead he will travel all over Europe to arrange new security for Ukraine. Nobody trust him at all ! In a Sunday interview German Chancellor Merz stressed "Ukraine cannot capitulate! Otherways next is the next country-thus Poland – and next – Germany". Merzdemonstrates remarkable industry-he worked all summer long without any summer vacation.
Russia concentrated troops to capture the strategic East Ukrainian town of Pokrovsk.
Since the begin of the war each side lost one million soldiers – both killed and wounded.

The Swiss government granted security and immunity to the Russian president Putin.
He will attend an international conference there in September 2025.
On the last August Sunday the Shanghai organization including several national leaders congregated in China for talks on mutual interests, among them Russian President Putin, Turkish President Erdogan,Indian President Modi and Chinese leader Xi Jin Pin.
The Western media reported little or even nothing on this conference.
It was said that Chinese President Xi Jin Pin criticized the West and compared its policy with the cold war. President Modi reassured Putin that India stays with Russia in difficult times. The white doves are tired ! Above this Russia introduced censorship on internet connections, mobile phones, SMS's etc. with 50 euro penalty.

SEPTEMBER AND OCTOBER 2025

Jens Spahn and A.Miersch- SPD-respectively CDU-fraction chiefs in the German Bundestag- arrived in Kiiv to show solidarity with the Ukrainian ruler Volodymyr Zelenskyy.
Among numerous topics they discussed the use of the frozen Russian assets which amount to 600 billion euro. Russian President Vladimir Vl. Putin was said to have set again unacceptable peace conditions to Ukraine . Though with some caution Western media stopped to praise president Zelenskyy and the Ukrainian army because they have no success and no territory gains anymore.
The Chief of the European Commission Ursula von der Leyen proposed 10,000 peace keeping troops in Ukraine. This will be discussed later on in Paris, said ZDF Brussels reporter Andreas Stamm.
Speaking during the summit in China, Putin continued to defend his decision to invade Ukraine, once again blaming the West for the war. Afterwards Russia and China signed multiple treaties of mutual interest.
Following the Alaska meeting, US Special envoy Steve Witkoff said Putin had agreed to security guarantees for Ukraine as part of a potential future peace deal, though Moscow has yet to confirm this.
At the military parade in Beijing China displayed its whole arsenal of weaponry including ballistic missiles, hypersonic rockets, unmanned underwater drones etc. and the three world leaders posed for a joint photo – President Putin of Russia, Indian President Narandra Modi , Chinese President Xi Jin Pin and North Korea leader Kim. Kim described his obligation to Russia as fraternal duty. As a matter of fact Vladimir Putin escorted President Kim to his car- a sheer gesture of curtsy .
 President Trump called this a conspiracy against the United States. Literary he wrote in Twitter : "Dear Xi! Dear Vladimir! My congratulations while you conspire together against the U.S.A. "
Thus no single word on sanctions against Russia.
In Washington Trump met Polish president Karol Nawrocki and re-assured him of the full US support in case of Russian invasion. The USA has already 10,000
soldiers in Poland but is willing and able to increase this number.
The BBC concluded wisely the war in Ukraine has shifted from military to diplomatic activity, which is basically true but a little bit too late. An earlier conclusion may have saved million of lives.
It seems like BBC trades the situation.

Coalition of the willing convened in Paris to discuss the Ukrainian war. President Zelenskyy was sitting between President Macrone and Sir Keir Starmer. German Chancellor Friedrich Merz attended the meeting by video link .
Russia replied it didn't accept any European troops in Ukraine nor Ukrainian membership in Nato.
 Donald Trump called them by phone and advised Europe to use pressure on Russia by not not buying Russian oil. He promised he'll advise India to do the same. French President Emanuel Macrone declared 16,000 French volunteers are ready and waiting for deploy in Ukraine. That's !

In which language ?? Above this Ukraine sets seize fire as precondition for any peace talks.
As a matter of fact the Coalition of the Willing achieved nothing – at the very same day Sir Keir Starmer flew back to London to settle a scandal of his Cabinet, president Macron of France muttered a 10 minutes interview, and Ukrainian President Volodymyr stated nothing at all .
Despite this Germany strives militarization turning a blind eye to its own problems and its own budget deficit of 82 billion EUR. Above this the German army- The Bundeswehr – lacks 150,000 soldiers even if it will deploy women into the army. The situation in France and Britain too is not different – the all miss resources in term of personnel, equipment, supply, financial source etc. but we will learn all this after the war ends. Currently the German Bundeswehr counts for 182,000 soldiers, the German defence minister intends to raise up this number to 250,000 soldiers including women too. Both protests and obstructions to the compulsory conscription in Germany rise.

Deep political chaos in France where the budget deficit rose to 44 billion EUR compared with neighboring Germany with 28 billion EUR. The inflation rate in France hit 5.8% while in Germany it is 2.38%. At the same time 30 sheep walked into a pub in Yorkshire, England; hahaha! This was only the prelude to Germany where a sabotage action left capital Berlin without electricity

 no trams, no S-bahns, no metro, no refrigerators, no lifts, no escalators:
in one word a party of sabotage acts to punish Germany for its weapon exports towards Ukraine.
Worse is still to come ! Hahaha !

U.S. President Donald Trump renamed the U.S. defence ministry into U.S. secretary of war. Doubtless a sheer saber rattling !
On a weekend Russian Cruize missiles hit the main governmental building in the Ukrainian capital Kyiv. It is the first time Russia hits Ukrainian governmental building in the course of the whole war.
However it was Sunday so that there were no officials in the building; a kind of barbaric mercy !
President Zelenskyy condemned the bombardment which was vile and barbaric and vowed retaliation.
It is the first time ever Russia bombards government buildings and government facilities.
Volodymyr Zelenskyy accused Vladimir Putin of testing the world.
Kremlin spokes man Dmitriy Peskov dismissed his words as a libel.
U.S. President Donald Trump promised a bitter end to the conflict.

German firm APX Robotics developed , envoyed and endorsed sophisticated hardware
mostly for military usage and displayed for public enjoy in a London exhibition. In its products Artificial **Intelligence (AI)** was largely disposed. The Rhein Metal with thanks , others with both machine and submachine guns. As Lord Byron said once upon the times : "Its blatant age of new inventions of killing
bodies and wracking souls; Both propagated with the best intentions" . Some when in the 1800ies.

Russian drones entered Polish skies on its eastern border and were properly shot down.
Polish President Donald Tusk demanded care according article 4 of Nato.
In this case Russia used GERBERA- drones with extra fuel tanks to enable a bigger reach West.
In a telephone call with Donald Trump became clear
Nato Secretary General Mark Rutte took a very sly neutral position.
Earlier he served as Dutch prime minister. So now The Netherlands scrambled F-35 jet fighters to dispatch the Polish border. *However Nato Secretary General Mark Rutte – former Dutch Prime Minister in ruined kingdom – admonished Russian President Vladimir Vladimirovich Putin to stop his attacks because it seems frantically for Nato too expensive to down any Russian drone – 7-8 Nato missiles for each cheap Russian Gerbera drone downed (ZDF) .*

Former German foreign minister Annalena Baerbock started her new work as speaker of U.N. General Assemble . Her nickname in Germany was "Annalänchen" – a little bit childish.
German Military University – in Munich.
Russia and Belorussia started a joint military manouvre under the name "ZAPAD" (WEST).
To display fragile power to the WEST. Both countries have joint west borders with Ukraine.
So the Western anxiety is big Russia may transfer troops 2022-style more over the West may be outnumbered with 10,000 Russian troops taking. The sore points are two
 Other sources number the figure of 31,000 soldiers- something rather unrealistic !
"Future unmanned"is the slogan of the London missiles exhibition. The fear is ubiquitous !
Russia may outnumber the expensive Western defence missiles by cheap Iranian Shahet drones.
The other Achilles heel of the story is the Russian enclave of Kaliningrad – it prones 65 km along the Polish border which means the Nato border. Both fears may be true; may be not at all.

Russia is suspected to use the manouvre corridor for launching invasion to its neighbors.
10,000 Russian soldiers are reported to have taken part into the manouvre .
Otherwise reports claim 31,000 – the eyes of fear are big !
Poland claimed 40,000 soldiers as counter troops

Ukraine spokes persons declared as to the Russian provocation on Poland "NATO is crazy helpless". At the same time Russia decreased the credit rate down to 17% in order to boost economic growth. So who is really crazy ?? **Western media were as crazy as to accuse Putin as if he intends frantic war with Japan. As crazy as I find no words to comment.**

The Utah Governor accused Russia tries to encouraging violence in the USA after the assassination of Kirk ". This is quite possible : why not to use the flamboyant opportunity. The death of Charly Kirk generated a sheer waterfall, an avalanche of public grief about it. Obviously he was very close friend to President Trump.
Iran appealed for an Islamic NATO establishment. This the bitter fruit of the US-foreign policy. President Donald Trump attended a huge military royal parade at the Windsor Castle. Former U.S. President Barack O'bama commented viciously on this event "the assassination of Charlie Kirk threw the USA into a b tremendous political crises". The news as it is ….
 Garry O'Donehugh did not read his report, he talked to the cameras !
BBC News tumbled to praised Sir Keir Starmer & his policy
while the moderator mixed up U.S. politics and baby-boom in one pot only.
A sheer oil garbage of lies I kept to remain clean.

In demonstrations & meetings France denounced the 8 years old rule of Emanuel Macron.
A new choice is actually not available. Many French men demonstrated openly against massive French debts . France is once again deeply indebted.

Donald Trump's blitz visit ended with $300 billion U.S. investments into Great Britain.
Both sides could not reach any agreement both on Ukraine and Israel.
President Zelenskyy allowed young Ukrainian men to travel abroad with the clear aim to overwhelm the West with a new wave of Ukrainian refugees, expats and migrants to make the West bow to the failed Ukrainian cause. The number of the Ukrainian refugees in Germany surpassed the one million hallmark, reported the ZDF . And it will climbed up any further.

At U.S. President Donald Trump visited London for one day for talks with the royal family and

British Prime minister Sir Keir Starmer. He agreed to invest in Britain $300 billion and abolish the tax on British steel and aluminium . Keir Starmer – nick name the Yorkshire- got very pleased and satisfied. Slowly he gains altitude into the American relationship.
At the Windsor Castle military parade former U.S. president Barack Obama – Democrat commented viciously "Charlie Kirk death plunged the U.S.A. into a deep political crises". Obama was President 12 years earlier but continued to spat President Trump regularly – this the 3rd time in a year of malicious remarks against Donald Trump : something is brothing and roaring in the U.S.A.
The news as it is !

A massive Russian cybernetic attack destroyed three big European air ports schedule: London, Berlin & Brussels . with failed procedure of both check-in passengers and their baggage so that they had to manual check-in operations. They distincted clearly between hacker attacks and hack-in attacks and break-in attention.
 Moscow denied any responsibility as if in a schedule flights.

 A raw broke out over Russian fighter jets disturbing Nato airspace over Estonia. EU-Vice President Kaja Kallas – who is native Estonian just like me – accused them of ringing the alarm. Kremlin refused any responsibility claiming the jets were on a regular mission just as many times as before. As a matter of fact Estonia scrambled 4 Italian fighter jets located there to respond to the Russian "attack". It became known in a core of truth that the Russian jets flew over the Bay of Finland thus not over Estonia. However Estonia demanded a special Nato meeting according to article 4 of the Nato statute. Allegedly the Russian fighter jets were said to have been flying at unbelievable 150 meter height.
Earlier Poland boasted to have downed an unprecedented number of Russian drones over its skies and insisted "the Russian planes should have been shot down" while Sweden distributed happening's videos. Yet again Polish government informed urgently Russia that "Every Russian equipment over Polish skies will be downed no matter of being there in a delusion, miscalculated or deliberately over supreme Polish sovereign .
Several British charities dropped off royal connections over the Epstein Royal (sexual) UK scandal. More to come in Part III of my book. Altogether the Brits dug in into a very deep long-rage scandal. Russia attacked up new the Ukrainian city of Kharkiv close to the common border. 280,000 households remained again without gas & electricity shortly before winter step-in. In its part of of the happening Ukraine hit and destroyed a Russian fuel refinery depot deep inside Russia in the Saratow region.

Both Russia and the United States agreed to meet each other in 2-weeks time some place in Hungary to discuss the war and promote peace finally.

The Nato is vulnerable but n o t the Nato members, stated Nato Scry, Mark Rutte in an unevitable bad English. What I remember of him he liked to save his post as a Dutch Prime Minister even after 2 years after his resignation as a Dutch Prime Minister. Maybe the King helped him to ??
His native country of origin is The Kingdom of The Netherlands : an absolute monarchy
In many parts of the Dutch society deadly police shots appeared to the The Sun shines all over Holland - both North and South Holland. It's time for heaven, time for sin - let's start !! The clubs open already at 18:00 .

Germany rang its alarm bells after unidentified drones were spotted over both German and Polish skies. German defence minister Boris Pistorius – Boris just like the German tennis legend Boris Becker- declined to deal with the matter, because Germany is not at war yet.
He transferred the matter to the German police , but German interior minister Alexander Dobrindt

decline any comment.

Germany presented its new budget plan – 9 months after the year actually began.
It comprised 520 billion EUR 174 billions of which old debts as ZDF stated
For the year 2025 Germany was the venue of 200,000 bankruptcy – mostly small or middle enterprises.
With 3-4 workers it counts 800,000 new unemployed to the staggering XXXXXXXXXXXXX

All debts are very easy to plan but difficult to pay back.

No American leader said nothing about the latest Nato invasions by Russian drones & air planes.
German Defence Minister Boris Pistorius summoned to tranquility and Nato all in all
warned in for caution not escalation. In a rare speech Nato Secretary General Mark Rutte even
sounded not so very much enthusiastic. Danish prime minister Mette Fredericson condemned clearly
the Russian air forces intrusion into Denmark as a "provocation and intimidation". What else have
Denmark to serve back to the Russian intrusion ?? Otherwise many Western media pronounced
wrongfully the name of the big German city of Hamburg as "Hum Bugg". Could happen but why to us ?

U.S. President Donald Trump reversed yet again his Ukraine policy: in New York he urged Ukrainian
President Volodymyr Zelenskyy "he can received back his territorial already "and "Russia is a paper
tiger!" Kremlin spokesman Dmitryy Peskov countered "Russia is not a tiger but a bear". Followed
by lavish Dutch compliments : Mark Rutte looked all over his own pictures as nervous ?!
Volodymyr Zelenskyy replyed "Ukraine conspired peace and freedom all over Europe. "
Which might turn it free?! Rather free beyond 3.5 years of war with Russia which turned out a
spike all against Russia, nothing for Russia , despite U.S. demands to Russia. Could happen -
not rare into Russia in its recent history – Russia had had nothing else of all its invaders than
encounter them starting into The Great Nordic Russian invasion in the 1800ies.
Thus freedom of replica, freedom recess of all current History ?
Why not ?
White not at all??
Europe is rich – Europe can afford sniff a bad dog Russia ?? Why not ?? As long as Putin is in
we cannot expect anything progressive, no single deal into peace. Despite of all our short visioned
fouled down European politicians : without them we would have satisfied Europe without war?!
We failed.
All Europe failed and now Ukraine failed: Zelenskyy claimed his shadowed roll to please Europe :
and he failed to please Europe 3.5 years long of war against Russia:
The International Olympic Committee decided to lift its own decisions of ban imposed earlier on both
Russians and Belorussians sportsmen and sports women.
At the same time Ukrainian President Volodymyr Zelenskyy claimed reconnaisent drones
from Hungary flew in for several minutes into Ukrainian air space.

Police broke up ring trafficking Kenyans to fight for Russia in Ukraine. They were trafficking under
false job promises.
In the NRW German election lost the SPD to the CD for the first time in last 80 years.
NRW – Nord Rhein Westfallen – is the biggest German state with 18 million population -
thus more than the Netherlands .
Running afraid of all Russian (cyber) attacks Denmark and Scandinavia cut off all its commercial
flights in order to avoid any single Russian drones attacks adding additional havoc to the whole EU-
mess. Danish Prime Minister Mette Fredericson failed to comments on Danish (cyber) attacks

restrictions. Could happen !!

At Nato difference proximity in Warsaw 2,500 international visitors attended to denounce Russia: Polish star chaser Donald Tusk attended limping on his own right knee. The European foreign ministers came together in Copenhagen to form manifest their support to Ukraine.
If they fail the post-war aid to Ukraine will be suck in from the frozen Russian bank assets equal to 200 billion euro. Meanwhile the Chief of the IAEA Raphael Grossi visited Ukraine and expressed great concern about the state of the Russian nuclear power plant in Zaporzhizhia.
Ukrainian President Zelenskyy shuttles frantically to introduce insane crazy politics of the West to benefit everything to Ukraine in terms of help to Ukraine where it does not remarks. More ??

Rather confess nor apologize for the current EU polish campaign . It will stop very soon with all of our grievences.

Words 6,144 spilled on right now on Ukraine disaster. Even now 6,144 words had spent all the West helps Ukraine – far less than current data . Ukraine is visible weak.
The German car producers' top with German Chancellor Friedrich Merz all clear and unclear tools became introduced and glorified on the all over German glorification to spouse down the current German unemployment The current German unemployment rate hit the 3,000,000 mark.

Poland refused to extradite to Germany the North Stream Pipe Line saboteur 2022 Volodymyr Zhuravlev "because his deed was a military one and not a German one", so Poland which manufactured and glorified all anti-Russian sabotages both home and abroad.
On his Washington talks with President Trump Zelenskyy failed to receive American Tomahawk missiles by which he intended to hit targets deep inside Russia. The price of a single Tomahawk is $200 million and their range is 2,500 km. Nevertheless Trump described the talks in Washington as "cardiac" and America needs the Tomahawks too for its selfdefence". In fact Donald Trump demanded from Zelenskyy "All the parties must get frozen their current frontiers, their boundaries". So President Zelenskyy had to fly back to his native Ukraine empty handed : no destructive American made Tomahawk missiles were granted to Ukraine in order not to escalate the war any further in the grave yard of Europe Zelenskyy push up to inseminate to all of Europe".
President Trump has planned visits to Indonesia, Malaysia and Japan; so probably he will have no time for the planned top with Vladimir Putin in Hungary this week. The planing collapsed and ended with freezing of the U.S. assets of both major Russian oil suppliers Rosneft and Lukoil. U.S. President Donald Trump literally said "we have to tighten the screws of the Russian economy" and "Putin has to come to the tango". After his lavish luxusary and expensive visits to London, Paris and Brussels Ukrainian president with an expired mandate Volodymyr Zelenskyy commented "Ukraine will cede no territory to Russia", aiming the age of 73 years old ailing Russian President Vladimir Vladimirovich Putin.
Obviously the stakes are high of who will inherit him and his property estimated of $200 billion.
Donald Trump postponed his meeting with Putin for December 2025 : "Hopefully Putin will dance to the tango", he said literary.
The EU failed to grant Ukraine 140 billion EUR state loan to combat the Russian aggression.
President Zelenskyy reckoned this not enough . Speaking at EU top in Brussels he demanded much more from Russia whose assets are frozen in Belgian banks.
He stated, "This will help Ukraine produce weaponry faster and cheaper to defend itself against the Russian aggression". In his speech Zelenskyy also criticized sharply China "because it has no interest in the Ukrainian victory on Russia".

In the middle of his speech Zelenskyy lost the chain of his thoughts and started stuttering.
Finally he managed to uttered "Our plan does not begin with a cease fire but with our will to implement the
the frozen Russian assets for production inside Ukraine of drones, missiles and electronic jamming gadgets
which will be quicker, cheaper and faster".
The President of the European Commission Ursula von der Leyen dubbed this hypocritically "a reparation loan".
Afterwards Zelenskyy flew from Brussels to London for talks with both the British Prime Minister Sir
Keir Starmer
and the British King Charles III. All three decided to insist on more U.S. long-range U.S. missiles for Ukraine.
Now it became clear "Zelenskyy is gambling with World War Three" .
as President Donald Trump rebuked Zelensky already in February 2025 during his Washington visit.
However Zelensky was received by the Guard of Honour to display London support for Kiyv.

Parallel to Zelensky London visit German minister Reiche flew to Kyyv for talks with somebody who replaced him:
1st German Television ARD described Zelensky as "crippled,tired and warn off"
At a public rally Hungarian President Victor Orban denounced sharply the "Coalition of the Willings: they want
to send people in the war, to let people die in the war and they called it poetically, inimitably and with elegance
"Coalition of the Willing"", said Orban to a massive Budapest manifestation. He asked his supporters to choose
between him and peace or choose his opposition rival ……………..
and war: we all are threatened and intimidated by war in the heart of Europe.

The Lithuanian President Gitanas Nauseda protested sharply – also in Brussels – against the violation by Russian air
crafts of the Lithuanian airspace.
In the North Ukraine town of Ovruch a suicide bomber detonated his bomb at the local railway station killing himself
and 3 Ukrainian policemen. The kamikaze bomber died later on in ambulance; his reasons and his motivation
remained unknown, said Euronews used up as used as to use.
Reiche. And Reiche again: this is the name of the German female minister which repeatedly springs at the news.
German ZDF reporter in Kiiv is currently cut off. ZDF means Zweites Deutsches Fernsehen – Second German
Television.

Joint training manoeuvres of the German police forces and German army – the Bundeswehr- ended with
several wounded soldiers respectively policemen. German Chancellor Friedrich Merz took no stand on
the victims and avoided all comments.
Finally the Russian position became known because it leaked, infiltrated through in the media:
Kremlin insists upon exit of the Baltic countries from both Nato and the European Union
and the exit of Poland from Nato.
It took three years of war until this position got known because it infiltrated to transparency
through in the media despite of both the muzzle and the sly censorship .
President Zelensky made several sebaceous trips both to Washington and other places of the world see-saw
move but he kept hiding in swamps the Russian position which is crystal clear. It seems President Trump
had right in saying "Zelensky gambles with world war three".

The commander of the sabotage team on the North Stream pipe line blowing was extradited to Germany,
his name was said to be ………………

Russia started bombing capital Kyiv with brand bombs, the city was engulfed by massive fires.
Russian oil giant Rosneft introduced new reorganisations in its structures and branches.
At Donald Trump Japan visit both the Emperor and the Prime Minister SanaeTakaichi
proposed him to be granted with the Nobel peace price

and presented Washington with 250 cherry trees.
Trump said "The new golden age of the bilateral relations is currently happening "
He granted $500 billion to boost the Japanese investment in the U.S.A.
He reduced also the U.S. tariffs on Japan down to 15%.
His next stop was South Korea which Trump visited a f t e r Japan.
There he met also the Chinese President Xi Jin Pin.
President Vladimir Putin advertised a new brand of nuclear powered cruise missiles which Russia had successfully tested . Donald Trump remained unimpressed by his intimidation. He advised Putin "to bring peace into Ukraine instead of testing new missiles". While making his statement Putin was dressed in a khaki coloured military fatigues.
In another interview Putin - dressed in different clothes – stated "Russia had tested successfully another nuclear powered torpedo "Posseidon "". It can not be intercepted and when it is close to the coast line it can provoke powerful radioactive tsunami. This was the second Russian nuclear test within a week. As an aftermath of Putin's ample statement Donald Trump announced U.S.A. will renew its own nuclear tests the latest one of which was in 1992.
*

NOVEMBER 2025

JULY 2025

Denmark started its presidency over the EU for the next 6 month.
The Danish prime minister Mette Frederiksen promised full support for Ukraine
and its membership in the European Union. On the ceremony Frederikson stepped in
into office were present the European Commission President Ursula von der Leyen ,
the President of the European Council Antonius Costas and of course Volodymyr Zelenskyy- can something happen
without him!? "Ukraine belongs to the European
Family and NATO ",Mette reassured Zelenskyy.The news as it is. "Maximum pressure
must be put on Hungary to lift its veto on the Ukrainian EU – membership" added
Mette Frederiksen.

According to EU- statistics for the month of June Russia has launched 5,432 drones on
Ukrainian targets, said ZDF. Ukraine wheat was largely accepted from Brussels and a
special price mechanism was set for Ukrainian products inside of the EU. It was named
"new trade deal". Technical details of the deal still have to be agreed upon. Angry Polish
and French farmers protested against the cheap Ukrainian agrar products imports into the
EU but in vain.
The German arm producer Rhein-Metal started the production of details and accessories
for the F-15 fighter jets. The German arm industry employs ca. 284,000 skilled workers
in different locations scattered across the country, said the ZDF.

Euronews aired Russian on air commands on how to down a passangers Azal plane broadcasted on the
3rd & 33rd minute each hour. The command in Russian indicated direction, speed, altitude, azimuth and
heading– all in ciphers & details. The first missile missed its target that's why the fire was repeated.
This is only the begin of a great great news. Th news never sleeps.
So does Emil. A fluent Russian speaker.
French president Emmanuel Macrone placed a phone call with the Russian President Vladimir Putin.
In the phone call which lasted 2 hours – 120 minutes – he insisted on Russia peace talks to stop
its war on Ukraine. Putin insisted the peace plan must include the current Russian territorial gains and
"the new territorial reality". Putin dubbed the talk "sustainable".

At the same time the U.S.A. reduced its delivery of ammunition and shells to Ukraine "because of inland
shortage". Extra concerened are the "Patriot" anti-aircraft missiles shipments. The move came despite earlier
U.S. promises for weapon and ammunition shipments to Ukraine. The news brought satisfaction to Moscow.

German Chancellor Friedrich Merz received in Capital Berlin the Chinese leader Xi Jin Ping and asked him
 "to agitate his friend Putin to stop the war in Ukraine!" This was a flink manoever to deflect German public
opinion from brocken pre-election promise about price of domestic electricity . The news as it is. There are 17

million poor people in Germany, living under the poverty line, said the German ARD. At the same time German interior minister Alexander Dobrindt entered direct talks with the terror regime of the Taleban. Nothing- but really nothing – on these talks was reported. Obviously Dobrindt mission has failed.

U.S. President Donald Trump placed one hour phone talk with the Russian President Vladimir Putin. Putin insisted on annexation of 4 Ukrainian regions and ban for Ukrainian NATO membership. Trump was reported "dissappointed" from the phone call.
Russia became the first country in the World to recognize officially the Taliban regime in Afghanistan. Already back to 2022 Russia started to export gas, oil and wheat to Afghanistan. President Zelensky made a phone call to President Donald Trump and named the phone call "constructive"and "fruitfull"; he implied something in the sense "make a lasting peace through strength".

Russia closed several of its airports "because safety concerns of imminent threat of Ukrainian terror attacks", obviously after careful intelligence collection. Mette Frederickson – now European President for
6 months - stressed bluntly on European security and defence increase in a long long speech.

All of the sudden Russia started to hit Ukrainian targets as far to the West as the border town of
Luzk – close to the Polish border. The Russian KINZHAL rockets overwhelmed the Ukranian defence consisting of British fabricated **Patriot-, GMLRS & Hellfire- Rockets** fabricated by the British producer BAE in the town of **Warton-Lancashire, UK** where also the Eurofighter jets **Typhoon** *are produced.*
There is surplus of redundant British BAE – Systems capacities as the last customer was **Qatar in 2017,**
reported AP (=Asssossiated Press). The Russian strategy is to overwhelm , to overburden, to overstretch the Ukrainian defence capability until it runs short of ammunition and by making them defenseless
 to riddle the Ukrainian targets without any punishment. So simple !! At the same time president Zelensky visited again Rom and the Vatican for new talks with Pope Leo XIV. Obviously earlier talks born no fruits.
An Europen court found formally Russia guilty of downing the Malaysian aircraft MH17 back in 2014. All 298 passengers on board died inclusive Dutch professor working actively on a new HIV-medicine. The formal procedure was launched by 2 countries only: The Netherlands and Ukraine.
EU-President Ursula von der Leyen survived the non-confidence vote in European Parliament with 360 votes "against",18 abstained and only 175 votes "for" missing thus the majority required of two thirds. Her position as EU-President however was strongly weakened and Zelenskyy's position too, said Alberto Alemanno – professor of law – in an interview for "Euronews".
U.S. Secretary of state Marko Rubio said to Russian foreign minister Sergey Lavrov "he is frustrated over Putin's reluctance to force peace in Ukraine". My personal perception is that Putin has his internal idea, intention or ambition which he's not in a hurry to display to the World; peace negotiations are always difficult and they drag into the lengthy until the common sense of the both parties is reached last not least because they speak frequently different languages and arbitary must be set on.
Both leaders spoke at the ASEAN – top in Kuala Lumpur and remained both undevicive and futile.
Donald Trump threatened Russia with new sanctions but also this did not achieve the result expected.
The recovery conference of the European leaders was directed by Olena Zelenskyy – wife of Volodymyr Zelenskyy- and brought no results, said ZDF.
Dutch bureaucrats use to censor frequently the ZDF and other TV channels by blocking them;
 the latest example was the switching off a documentary film on the tennis legend Boris Backer.

Finally U.S. President Donald Trump changed his mind and agreed to deliver air defense rockets including the "Patriot-Surface" missiles systems which Ukraine needed badly. More details still to
 come. President Donald Trump forbade Ukraine to attack Russian oil containers and oil depots.
 Slowly the first portions of American military aid started again to flow in to Ukraine but they are not sufficient.

The "Patriot" missiles launchers are crucially needed because Ukraine cannot defend itself in one day only Russia fired 1,800 missiles , drones and ballistic rockets also on Western Ukraine too. The "Patriot" U.S. delivery to Ukraine will start via Nato and the Europeans have to pay for it: "The U.S. doesn't have them and we have to manufacture them, but the Europeans have to pay for these missiles".
In a television interview Donald Trump promised to do so and added:
"I don't like Putin at all-he talks nice by phone to the people in the morning and bombs them in the night with smart bombs! I don't like him at all because I am disappointed in him" and "I don't trust anyone".
Trump had planed a visit to Britain in September 2025.
Joahim Bitterlik- former German ambassador to Nato- doubted there will be peace in Ukraine any time soon. He founds the 50-days ultimatum is exaggerated. However German defence minister Boris Pistorius flew to Washington to arrange the delivery details with the U.S. defence secretary Pete Hegseth. Finally change, finally break through ! The proposed 100% tariffs on Russia aims to make Putin to re-consider his position.

Trump offered to Europe to pay for the "Patriot"- Systems delivery "because this is an European problem and Ukraine is an European country". The "Patriots"will be sent to Ukraine via European Nato countries. He discussed the details with Nato Secretary General Mark Rutte – a former Dutch Prime minister.
Trump made "a special report on EU" which includes the following points: 1). An ultimatum with 50 days dead lock for President Putin to end the war. 2).Intimidation to the Russian allies China , India and Brazil to charge them with 100% tariffs if they continue to support Russia. The ZDF Washington correspondent Elmar Thevessen elucidated his threats as unrealistic. The U.S.A. will deliver the weapons to the European countries who pay for that and than transfer the weaponry to Ukraine. Three NATO countries agreed to deliver "Patriot" missiles from their own stock piles – Germany 2 systems, Norway – 1 system and Denmark one too. The price of each "Patriot-Surface missiles " is $ 100,000 each. They can strike both ballistic and cruise missiles and even low flying drones and exactly their capability makes them so unique .
Besides the sharp abrupt change of mind of President Donald referring whether or not to deliver U.S. weaponry to Ukraine two more Nato countries – Danmark and The Netherlands – decided to deliver several of their own "Patriot"-missiles launchers to Ukraine.
President Zelenskyy remained very satisfied by the deal and spilled over with a flood of thanks to Donald Trump. In a prolonged phone call he praised lavishly the U.S. President and admired his commitment to bring peace in Europe.
The President of the European Commission Mrs. Ursula von der Leyen announced the EU-budget of **2 trillion** euro for the period 2028-2034. From this money Ukraine will get 100 billion euro, said the Euronews. This means **200,000,000,000 euro**: "This is the budget as the reality of today and the challenges of tomorrow" she said on television.

Mean while it became known that Russia keeps on producing weaponry four times more ammunition and armors than all Nato member countries : 4 million artillery shells in 2023 and 4.4 million shells in 2024 planing to produce 7 million artillery shells for 2025 .
In summary Nato countries lag behind with production of 4 times less artillery shells than Russia- 1.2 million shells in 2024 planing 3 million shells for 2025-obviously lagging behind. That's why Nato Secretary General Mark Rutte-former Dutch prime minister- advised all Nato countries to produce more and more and not to lag behind.

His message came after German Chancellor Friedrich Merz visited
London for talks with British Prime Minister Sir Keir Starmer . Both leaders signed a treaty on mutual trade and security with means cooperation on the industrial and military fields which is the first British-German treaty ever. Entering the history as the Kensington treaty it is a stark warning against Russia and encounters the U.S. slogan "America first". The most significant point of the treaty which will enter in

history as Kensington treaty is that an aggression on either country will be treated as aggression on both countries. This implies in full Russian aggression. The assistance duty of the historic Kensington friendship treaty serves as a repellent to any Russian aggression. The message to Kremlin is clear: "we are strong despite the Brexit!" Nation have no friends – only interests.
The approach of the two countries will also assist the reconstruction of postwar Ukraine.

The treaty comprises 27 inner proud pages and includes British access to German e-gates what soever this will mean. The German investment in the UK amounts to 200 million pounds, said Sir Keir Starmer.

Former Russian President Dmitriy Medvedev officially tried to intimidate the West "with pre-emptive Russian strike on the West"; his post now is deputy chief of the Russian Security council. However Ukraine attacked Moscow with drones and caused a fire in one of the Moscow's suburbs. (Euronews).

A fire broke broke out in a Moscow suburb after Ukraine launched drone strikes on the Russian Capital. In over 80 Polish cities and towns manifestations broke out against the refugees' flood from neighboring Ukraine. One of the speakers fell back to the legendary Polish king Jan III Sobiecky:
"The history must repeat", he said to the mobs. (Euronews).

In a ZDF-interview German President Frank-Walter Steinmeier advocated the military conscription in Germany: "It was abolished back in 2011 but now all political & military factors have changed", he said to the camera. The 5% share of the Nato-country budget of their GDP's is already achieved, he added. The second half of his interview was focused on the hot Iran-Israel conflict.
At the same time Slovakian president Robert Fico allerted the EU because Russia stopped the gas supply to his country. Fico blocked the 18 points EU-sanctions package against Russia.
The U.S. special envoy Keith Kellogg visited Kiyv for talks and remained there for a whole week.
That are the facts !

AUGUST 2025

German Chancellor Friedrich Merz visited France for talks with the French President Emanuel Macron. They agreed on many items how to reduce their US-dependency.
The unemployment rate in Germany hit the 3 million mark.
The coffee and tomato prices rose by 24 %.
The U.S. President introduced $ 15,000 entry fee for foreigners willing to enter the U.S.A. Trump abolished also the Secrete Service Protection of Camilla Harris- a Democrat candidate for U.S. president. It leaked former Democrat U.S. President Joe Biden had prolonged illegally her Secrete Service Protection till July 2026.
Trump sent also 2 nuclear submarines to patrol the north Atlantic and the Baltikum.
He sent his special envoy for Ukraine Steve Witkoff to Moscow to hand in a new ultimatum to Russian President Vladimir Putin.
On the 80th anniversary of the nuclear masacre of Hiroshima he uttered no single word.
High ranking Nato activist Ivo Daalder put it bluntly :"**Trump will not risk war with Russia to protect Ukraine!**"
Trump himself re - iterated "better if Putin meets Zelenskyy without me "
while Russian foreign minister Sergey Lavrov stressed " security talks without Russia lead to nowhere".
The EU- Foreign Affairs Officer reprimanded Putin for gambling of time .
Chancellor Merz received Canadian prime minister Mark Karney in Berlin.
Both statesmen declared they stand firmly behind Ukraine.

The German television ZDF reflected on Putin , who "continue to draw his fantasies further and further" The U.S.A. will not sent soldiers to Ukraine, while both France and Great Britain are willing : For Germany it will be a full debacle at the back stage of the fact the German Bundeswehr lacks already now 150,000 soldiers to bridge it own domestic defence gap. However German East block Officer Wagner – Green B'90- praised Chancellor Merz for his enthusiasm for Ukraine. Without Germany would collapse already tomorrow, he stated. At the same time Russian President Vladimir Putin visited China in 5 days' discussion with top Chinese activists. "A red carpet for Putin", he said with admiration. However there were no security guarantees for Ukraine yet, though the European Union berries the main weight of the Ukrainian war. For how long?
There is already full chaos inside Germany – political, economic, financial, personel, financial and militery ! At the same time Ukraine started working on security concept after the war.

Germany arrested 4 Ukrainian saboteurs for blowing up the Nord Stream pipeline to Europe : Ukrainians, not Russians. 7 others Ukrainian saboteurs are still at large. These

ones already arrested were captured in the Italian sea resort of Rimini while leisure at the sun and swimming in the Adriatic Sea for pleasure while their fellows alleged are being fighting against Russia. Difficult to believe. Moreover in the Lisbon funicular crash most of the victims were exactly Ukrainian nationals lavishly visiting beforehand a plenty of other European leisure centers.

Russian President Vladimir Putin declared bluntly "Any foreign troops both national and international are unacceptable for Russia. Foreign troops cannot provide peace in Ukraine". "President Zelenskyy is invited to Moscow for talks not for capitulation", he said to BBC Moscow correspondent Steve Rosenberg and repeated this on the world economic forum in Vladivostok : "Any foreign troops in Ukraine will be a legitimate target for Russia"
EU foreign and defense ministers met in Copenhagen to discuss joint European forces in Ukraine. No details leaked. Only that they agreed on a new sanction packet on Russia – the 19th since the war begin. Ukrainian president Volodymyr Zelenskyy was not admitted to the conference. Instead he will travel all over Europe to arrange new security for Ukraine. Nobody trust him at all ! In a Sunday interview German Chancellor Merz stressed "Ukraine cannot capitulate! Otherways next is the next country-thus Poland – and next – Germany". Merzdemonstrates remarkable industry-he worked all summer long without any summer vacation.
Russia concentrated troops to capture the strategic East Ukrainian town of Pokrovsk.
Since the begin of the war each side lost one million soldiers – both killed and wounded.

The Swiss government granted security and immunity to the Russian president Putin.
He will attend an international conference there in September 2025.
On the last August Sunday the Shanghai organization including several national leaders congregated in China for talks on mutual interests, among them Russian President Putin, Turkish President Erdogan,Indian President Modi and Chinese leader Xi Jin Pin.
The Western media reported little or even nothing on this conference.
It was said that Chinese President Xi Jin Pin criticized the West and compared its policy with the cold war. President Modi reassured Putin that India stays with Russia in difficult times. The white doves are tired ! Above this Russia introduced censorship on internet connections, mobile phones, SMS's etc. with 50 euro penalty.

SEPTEMBER AND OCTOBER 2025

Jens Spahn and A.Miersch- SPD-respectively CDU-fraction chiefs in the German Bundestag- arrived in Kiiv to show solidarity with the Ukrainian ruler Volodymyr Zelenskyy.
Among numerous topics they discussed the use of the frozen Russian assets which amount to 600 billion euro. Russian President Vladimir Vl. Putin was said to have set again unacceptable peace conditions to Ukraine . Though with some caution Western media stopped to praise president Zelenskyy and the Ukrainian army because they have no success and no territory gains anymore.
The Chief of the European Commission Ursula von der Leyen proposed 10,000 peace keeping troops in Ukraine. This will be discussed later on in Paris, said ZDF Brussels reporter Andreas Stamm.
Speaking during the summit in China, Putin continued to defend his decision to invade Ukraine, once again blaming the West for the war. Afterwards Russia and China signed multiple treaties of mutual interest.
Following the Alaska meeting, US Special envoy Steve Witkoff said Putin had agreed to security guarantees for Ukraine as part of a potential future peace deal, though Moscow has yet to confirm this.
At the military parade in Beijing China displayed its whole arsenal of weaponry including ballistic missiles, hypersonic rockets, unmanned underwater drones etc. and the three world leaders posed for a joint photo – President Putin of Russia, Indian President Narandra Modi , Chinese President Xi Jin Pin and North Korea leader Kim. Kim described his obligation to Russia as fraternal duty.
As a matter of fact Vladimir Putin escorted President Kim to his car- a sheer gesture of curtsy .
President Trump called this a conspiracy against the United States. Literary he wrote in Twitter :
"Dear Xi! Dear Vladimir! My congratulations while you conspire together against the U.S.A. "
Thus no single word on sanctions against Russia.
In Washington Trump met Polish president Karol Nawrocki and re-assured him of the full US support in case of Russian invasion. The USA has already 10,000
soldiers in Poland but is willing and able to increase this number.
The BBC concluded wisely the war in Ukraine has shifted from military to diplomatic activity, which is basically true but a little bit too late. An earlier conclusion may have saved million of lives.
It seems like BBC trades the situation.

Coalition of the willing convened in Paris to discuss the Ukrainian war. President Zelenskyy was sitting between President Macrone and Sir Keir Starmer. German Chancellor Friedrich Merz attended the meeting by video link .
Russia replied it didn't accept any European troops in Ukraine nor Ukrainian membership in Nato.
Donald Trump called them by phone and advised Europe to use pressure on Russia by not not buying Russian oil. He promised he'll advise India to do the same. French President Emanuel Macrone declared 16,000 French volunteers are ready and waiting for deploy in Ukraine. That's !

In which language ?? Above this Ukraine sets seize fire as precondition for any peace talks.
As a matter of fact the Coalition of the Willing achieved nothing – at the very same day Sir Keir Starmer flew back to London to settle a scandal of his Cabinet, president Macron of France muttered a 10 minutes interview, and Ukrainian President Volodymyr stated nothing at all .
Despite this Germany strives militarization turning a blind eye to its own problems and its own budget deficit of 82 billion EUR. Above this the German army- The Bundeswehr – lacks 150,000 soldiers even if it will deploy women into the army. The situation in France and Britain too is not different – the all miss resources in term of personnel, equipment, supply, financial source etc. but we will learn all this after the war ends. Currently the German Bundeswehr counts for 182,000 soldiers, the German defence minister intends to raise up this number to 250,000 soldiers including women too. Both protests and obstructions to the compulsory conscription in Germany rise.

Deep political chaos in France where the budget deficit rose to 44 billion EUR compared with neighboring Germany with 28 billion EUR. The inflation rate in France hit 5.8% while in Germany it is 2.38%. At the same time 30 sheep walked into a pub in Yorkshire, England; hahaha! This was only the prelude to Germany where a sabotage action left capital Berlin without electricity

no trams, no S-bahns, no metro, no refrigerators, no lifts, no escalators:
in one word a party of sabotage acts to punish Germany for its weapon exports towards Ukraine.
Worse is still to come ! Hahaha !

U.S. President Donald Trump renamed the U.S. defence ministry into U.S. secretary of war. Doubtless a sheer saber rattling !
On a weekend Russian Cruize missiles hit the main governmental building in the Ukrainian capital Kyiv. It is the first time Russia hits Ukrainian governmental building in the course of the whole war. However it was Sunday so that there were no officials in the building; a kind of barbaric mercy !
President Zelenskyy condemned the bombardment which was vile and barbaric and vowed retaliation.
It is the first time ever Russia bombards government buildings and government facilities.
Volodymyr Zelenskyy accused Vladimir Putin of testing the world.
Kremlin spokes man Dmitriy Peskov dismissed his words as a libel.
U.S. President Donald Trump promised a bitter end to the conflict.

German firm APX Robotics developed , envoyed and endorsed sophisticated hardware
mostly for military usage and displayed for public enjoy in a London exhibition. In its products Artificial **Intelligence (AI)** was largely disposed. The Rhein Metal with thanks , others with both machine and submachine guns. As Lord Byron said once upon the times : "Its blatant age of new inventions of killing
bodies and wracking souls; Both propagated with the best intentions" . Some when in the 1800ies.

Russian drones entered Polish skies on its eastern border and were properly shot down.
Polish President Donald Tusk demanded care according article 4 of Nato.
In this case Russia used GERBERA- drones with extra fuel tanks to enable a bigger reach West.
In a telephone call with Donald Trump became clear
Nato Secretary General Mark Rutte took a very sly neutral position.
Earlier he served as Dutch prime minister. So now The Netherlands scrambled F-35 jet fighters to dispatch the Polish border. *However Nato Secretary General Mark Rutte – former Dutch Prime Minister in ruined kingdom – admonished Russian President Vladimir Vladimirovich Putin to stop his attacks because it seems frantically for Nato too expensive to down any Russian drone – 7-8 Nato missiles for each cheap Russian Gerbera drone downed (ZDF) .*

Former German foreign minister Annalena Baerbock started her new work as speaker of U.N. General Assemble . Her nickname in Germany was "Annalänchen" – a little bit childish.
German Military University – in Munich.
Russia and Belorussia started a joint military manouvre under the name "ZAPAD" (WEST).
To display fragile power to the WEST. Both countries have joint west borders with Ukraine.
So the Western anxiety is big Russia may transfer troops 2022-style more over the West may be outnumbered with 10,000 Russian troops taking. The sore points are two
 Other sources number the figure of 31,000 soldiers- something rather unrealistic !
"Future unmanned"is the slogan of the London missiles exhibition. The fear is ubiquitous !
Russia may outnumber the expensive Western defence missiles by cheap Iranian Shahet drones.
The other Achilles heel of the story is the Russian enclave of Kaliningrad – it prones 65 km along the Polish border which means the Nato border. Both fears may be true; may be not at all.

Russia is suspected to use the manouvre corridor for launching invasion to its neighbors.
10,000 Russian soldiers are reported to have taken part into the manouvre .
Otherwise reports claim 31,000 – the eyes of fear are big !
Poland claimed 40,000 soldiers as counter troops

Ukraine spokes persons declared as to the Russian provocation on Poland "NATO is crazy helpless". At the same time Russia decreased the credit rate down to 17% in order to boost economic growth. So who is really crazy ?? **Western media were as crazy as to accuse Putin as if he intends frantic war with Japan. As crazy as I find no words to comment.**

The Utah Governor accused Russia tries to encouraging violence in the USA after the assassination of Kirk ". This is quite possible : why not to use the flamboyant opportunity. The death of Charly Kirk generated a sheer waterfall, an avalanche of public grief about it. Obviously he was very close friend to President Trump.
Iran appealed for an Islamic NATO establishment. This the bitter fruit of the US-foreign policy. President Donald Trump attended a huge military royal parade at the Windsor Castle. Former U.S. President Barack O'bama commented viciously on this event "the assassination of Charlie Kirk threw the USA into a b tremendous political crises". The news as it is ….
 Garry O'Donehugh did not read his report, he talked to the cameras !
BBC News tumbled to praised Sir Keir Starmer & his policy
while the moderator mixed up U.S. politics and baby-boom in one pot only.
A sheer oil garbage of lies I kept to remain clean.

In demonstrations & meetings France denounced the 8 years old rule of Emanuel Macron.
A new choice is actually not available. Many French men demonstrated openly against massive French debts . France is once again deeply indebted.

Donald Trump's blitz visit ended with $300 billion U.S. investments into Great Britain.
Both sides could not reach any agreement both on Ukraine and Israel.
President Zelenskyy allowed young Ukrainian men to travel abroad with the clear aim to overwhelm the West with a new wave of Ukrainian refugees, expats and migrants to make the West bow to the failed Ukrainian cause. The number of the Ukrainian refugees in Germany surpassed the one million hallmark, reported the ZDF . And it will climbed up any further.

At U.S. President Donald Trump visited London for one day for talks with the royal family and

British Prime minister Sir Keir Starmer. He agreed to invest in Britain $300 billion and abolish the tax on British steel and aluminium . Keir Starmer – nick name the Yorkshire- got very pleased and satisfied. Slowly he gains altitude into the American relationship.
At the Windsor Castle military parade former U.S. president Barack Obama – Democrat commented viciously "Charlie Kirk death plunged the U.S.A. into a deep political crises". Obama was President 12 years earlier but continued to spat President Trump regularly – this the 3rd time in a year of malicious remarks against Donald Trump : something is brothing and roaring in the U.S.A.
The news as it is !

A massive Russian cybernetic attack destroyed three big European air ports schedule: London, Berlin & Brussels . with failed procedure of both check-in passengers and their baggage so that they had to manual check-in operations. They distincted clearly between hacker attacks and hack-in attacks and break-in attention.
 Moscow denied any responsibility as if in a schedule flights.

 A raw broke out over Russian fighter jets disturbing Nato airspace over Estonia. EU-Vice President Kaja Kallas – who is native Estonian just like me – accused them of ringing the alarm. Kremlin refused any responsibility claiming the jets were on a regular mission just as many times as before. As a matter of fact Estonia scrambled 4 Italian fighter jets located there to respond to the Russian "attack". It became known in a core of truth that the Russian jets flew over the Bay of Finland thus not over Estonia. However Estonia demanded a special Nato meeting according to article 4 of the Nato statute. Allegedly the Russian fighter jets were said to have been flying at unbelievable 150 meter height.
Earlier Poland boasted to have downed an unprecedented number of Russian drones over its skies and insisted "the Russian planes should have been shot down" while Sweden distributed happening's videos. Yet again Polish government informed urgently Russia that "Every Russian equipment over Polish skies will be downed no matter of being there in a delusion, miscalculated or deliberately over supreme Polish sovereign .
Several British charities dropped off royal connections over the Epstein Royal (sexual) UK scandal. More to come in Part III of my book. Altogether the Brits dug in into a very deep long-rage scandal. Russia attacked up new the Ukrainian city of Kharkiv close to the common border. 280,000 households remained again without gas & electricity shortly before winter step-in. In its part of of the happening Ukraine hit and destroyed a Russian fuel refinery depot deep inside Russia in the Saratow region.

Both Russia and the United States agreed to meet each other in 2-weeks time some place in Hungary to discuss the war and promote peace finally.

The Nato is vulnerable but n o t the Nato members, stated Nato Scry, Mark Rutte in an unevitable bad English. What I remember of him he liked to save his post as a Dutch Prime Minister even after 2 years after his resignation as a Dutch Prime Minister. Maybe the King helped him to ??
His native country of origin is The Kingdom of The Netherlands : an absolute monarchy
In many parts of the Dutch society deadly police shots appeared to the The Sun shines all over Holland - both North and South Holland. It's time for heaven, time for sin - let's start !! The clubs open already at 18:00 .

Germany rang its alarm bells after unidentified drones were spotted over both German and Polish skies. German defence minister Boris Pistorius – Boris just like the German tennis legend Boris Becker- declined to deal with the matter, because Germany is not at war yet.
He transferred the matter to the German police , but German interior minister Alexander Dobrindt

decline any comment.

Germany presented its new budget plan – 9 months after the year actually began.
It comprised 520 billion EUR 174 billions of which old debts as ZDF stated
For the year 2025 Germany was the venue of 200,000 bankruptcy – mostly small or middle enterprises.
With 3-4 workers it counts 800,000 new unemployed to the staggering XXXXXXXXXXXXX

All debts are very easy to plan but difficult to pay back.

No American leader said nothing about the latest Nato invasions by Russian drones & air planes.
German Defence Minister Boris Pistorius summoned to tranquility and Nato all in all
warned in for caution not escalation. In a rare speech Nato Secretary General Mark Rutte even
sounded not so very much enthusiastic. Danish prime minister Mette Fredericson condemned clearly
the Russian air forces intrusion into Denmark as a "provocation and intimidation". What else have
Denmark to serve back to the Russian intrusion ?? Otherwise many Western media pronounced
wrongfully the name of the big German city of Hamburg as "Hum Bugg". Could happen but why to us ?

U.S. President Donald Trump reversed yet again his Ukraine policy: in New York he urged Ukrainian
President Volodymyr Zelenskyy "he can received back his territorial already "and "Russia is a paper
tiger!" Kremlin spokesman Dmitryy Peskov countered "Russia is not a tiger but a bear". Followed
by lavish Dutch compliments : Mark Rutte looked all over his own pictures as nervous ?!
Volodymyr Zelenskyy replyed "Ukraine conspired peace and freedom all over Europe. "
Which might turn it free?! Rather free beyond 3.5 years of war with Russia which turned out a
spike all against Russia, nothing for Russia , despite U.S. demands to Russia. Could happen -
not rare into Russia in its recent history – Russia had had nothing else of all its invaders than
encounter them starting into The Great Nordic Russian invasion in the 1800ies.
Thus freedom of replica, freedom recess of all current History ?
Why not ?
White not at all??
Europe is rich – Europe can afford sniff a bad dog Russia ?? Why not ?? As long as Putin is in
we cannot expect anything progressive, no single deal into peace. Despite of all our short visioned
fouled down European politicians : without them we would have satisfied Europe without war?!
We failed.
All Europe failed and now Ukraine failed: Zelenskyy claimed his shadowed roll to please Europe :
and he failed to please Europe 3.5 years long of war against Russia:
The International Olympic Committee decided to lift its own decisions of ban imposed earlier on both
Russians and Belorussians sportsmen and sports women.
At the same time Ukrainian President Volodymyr Zelenskyy claimed reconnaisent drones
from Hungary flew in for several minutes into Ukrainian air space.

Police broke up ring trafficking Kenyans to fight for Russia in Ukraine. They were trafficking under
false job promises.
In the NRW German election lost the SPD to the CD for the first time in last 80 years.
NRW – Nord Rhein Westfallen – is the biggest German state with 18 million population -
thus more than the Netherlands .
Running afraid of all Russian (cyber) attacks Denmark and Scandinavia cut off all its commercial
flights in order to avoid any single Russian drones attacks adding additional havoc to the whole EU-

mess. Danish Prime Minister Mette Fredericson failed to comments on Danish (cyber) attacks restrictions. Could happen !!

At Nato difference proximity in Warsaw 2,500 international visitors attended to denounce Russia: Polish star chaser Donald Tusk attended limping on his own right knee. The European foreign ministers came together in Copenhagen to form manifest their support to Ukraine.
If they fail the post-war aid to Ukraine will be suck in from the frozen Russian bank assets equal to 200 billion euro. Meanwhile the Chief of the IAEA Raphael Grossi visited Ukraine and expressed great concern about the state of the Russian nuclear power plant in Zaporzhizhia. Ukrainian President Zelenskyy shuttles frantically to introduce insane crazy politics of the West to benefit everything to Ukraine in terms of help to Ukraine where it does not remarks. More ??

Rather confess nor apologize for the current EU polish campaign . It will stop very soon with all of our grievances.

Words 6,144 spilled on right now on Ukraine disaster. Even now 6,144 words had spent all the West helps Ukraine – far less than current data . Ukraine is visible weak.
The German car producers' top with German Chancellor Friedrich Merz all clear and unclear tools became introduced and glorified on the all over German glorification to spouse down the current German unemployment The current German unemployment rate hit the 3,000,000 mark.

Poland refused to extradite to Germany the North Stream Pipe Line saboteur 2022 Volodymyr Zhuravlev "because his deed was a military one and not a German one", so Poland which manufactured and glorified all anti-Russian sabotages both home and abroad.
On his Washington talks with President Trump Zelenskyy failed to receive American Tomahawk missiles by which he intended to hit targets deep inside Russia. The price of a single Tomahawk is $200 million and their range is 2,500 km. Nevertheless Trump described the talks in Washington as "cardiac" and America needs the Tomahawks too for its selfdefence". In fact Donald Trump demanded from Zelenskyy "All the parties must get frozen their current frontiers, their boundaries". So President Zelenskyy had to fly back to his native Ukraine empty handed : no destructive American made Tomahawk missiles were granted to Ukraine in order not to escalate the war any further in the grave yard of Europe Zelenskyy push up to inseminate to all of Europe".
President Trump has planned visits to Indonesia, Malaysia and Japan; so probably he will have no time for the planned top with Vladimir Putin in Hungary this week. The planing collapsed and ended with freezing of the U.S. assets of both major Russian oil suppliers Rosneft and Lukoil. U.S. President Donald Trump literally said "we have to tighten the screws of the Russian economy" and "Putin has to come to the tango". After his lavish luxusary and expensive visits to London, Paris and Brussels Ukrainian president with an expired mandate Volodymyr Zelenskyy commented "Ukraine will cede no territory to Russia", aiming the age of 73 years old ailing Russian President Vladimir Vladimirovich Putin.
Obviously the stakes are high of who will inherit him and his property estimated of $200 billion.
Donald Trump postponed his meeting with Putin for December 2025 : "Hopefully Putin will dance to the tango", he said literary.
The EU failed to grant Ukraine 140 billion EUR state loan to combat the Russian aggression.
President Zelenskyy reckoned this not enough . Speaking at EU top in Brussels he demanded much more from Russia whose assets are frozen in Belgian banks.
He stated, "This will help Ukraine produce weaponry faster and cheaper to defend itself against the Russian aggression". In his speech Zelenskyy also criticized sharply China "because it has no interest in the Ukrainian victory on Russia".

In the middle of his speech Zelenskyy lost the chain of his thoughts and started stuttering.
Finally he managed to uttered "Our plan does not begin with a cease fire but with our will to implement the
the frozen Russian assets for production inside Ukraine of drones, missiles and electronic jamming gadgets
which will be quicker, cheaper and faster".
The President of the European Commission Ursula von der Leyen dubbed this hypocritically "a reparation loan".
Afterwards Zelenskyy flew from Brussels to London for talks with both the British Prime Minister Sir
 Keir Starmer
and the British King Charles III. All three decided to insist on more U.S. long-range U.S. missiles for Ukraine.
Now it became clear "Zelenskyy is gambling with World War Three" .
as President Donald Trump rebuked Zelensky already in February 2025 during his Washington visit.
However Zelensky was received by the Guard of Honour to display London support for Kiyv.

Parallel to Zelensky London visit German minister Reiche flew to Kyyv for talks with somebody who replaced him:
1st German Television ARD described Zelensky as "crippled,tired and warn off"
At a public rally Hungarian President Victor Orban denounced sharply the "Coalition of the Willings: they want
to send people in the war, to let people die in the war and they called it poetically, inimitably and with elegance
"Coalition of the Willing"", said Orban to a massive Budapest manifestation. He asked his supporters to choose
between him and peace or choose his opposition rival ……………..
and war: we all are threatened and intimidated by war in the heart of Europe.

The Lithuanian President Gitanas Nauseda protested sharply – also in Brussels – against the violation by Russian air
crafts of the Lithuanian airspace.
In the North Ukraine town of Ovruch a suicide bomber detonated his bomb at the local railway station killing himself
and 3 Ukrainian policemen. The kamikaze bomber died later on in ambulance; his reasons and his motivation
remained unknown, said Euronews used up as used as to use.
Reiche. And Reiche again: this is the name of the German female minister which repeatedly springs at the news.
German ZDF reporter in Kiiv is currently cut off. ZDF means Zweites Deutsches Fernsehen – Second German
Television.

Joint training manoeuvres of the German police forces and German army – the Bundeswehr- ended with
several wounded soldiers respectively policemen. German Chancellor Friedrich Merz took no stand on
the victims and avoided all comments.
Finally the Russian position became known because it leaked, infiltrated through in the media:
Kremlin insists upon exit of the Baltic countries from both Nato and the European Union
and the exit of Poland from Nato.
It took three years of war until this position got known because it infiltrated to transparency
through in the media despite of both the muzzle and the sly censorship .
President Zelensky made several sebaceous trips both to Washington and other places of the world see-saw
move but he kept hiding in swamps the Russian position which is crystal clear. It seems President Trump
had right in saying "Zelensky gambles with world war three".

The commander of the sabotage team on the North Stream pipe line blowing was extradited to Germany,
his name was said to be ……………..

Russia started bombing capital Kyiv with brand bombs, the city was engulfed by massive fires.
Russian oil giant Rosneft introduced new reorganisations in its structures and branches.
At Donald Trump Japan visit both the Emperor and the Prime Minister SanaeTakaichi
proposed him to be granted with the Nobel peace price

and presented Washington with 250 cherry trees.
Trump said "The new golden age of the bilateral relations is currently happening "
He granted $500 billion to boost the Japanese investment in the U.S.A.
He reduced also the U.S. tariffs on Japan down to 15%.
His next stop was South Korea which Trump visited a f t e r Japan.
There he met also the Chinese President Xi Jin Pin.
President Vladimir Putin advertised a new brand of nuclear powered cruise missiles which Russia had successfully tested . Donald Trump remained unimpressed by his intimidation. He advised Putin "to bring peace into Ukraine instead of testing new missiles". While making his statement Putin was dressed in a khaki coloured military fatigues.
In another interview Putin - dressed in different clothes – stated "Russia had tested successfully another nuclear powered torpedo "Posseidon "". It can not be intercepted and when it is close to the coast line it can provoke powerful radioactive tsunami. This was the second Russian nuclear test within a week. As an aftermath of Putin's ample statement Donald Trump announced U.S.A. will renew its own nuclear tests the latest one of which was in 1992.
*

NOVEMBER 2025

I will not exam the German parliamentary election on 23rd February because of the whole political chaos all over Germany…

JULY 2025

Denmark started its presidency over the EU for the next 6 month.
The Danish prime minister Mette Frederiksen promised full support for Ukraine
and its membership in the European Union. On the ceremony Frederikson stepped in
into office were present the European Commission President Ursula von der Leyen ,
the President of the European Council Antonius Costas and of course Volodymyr Zelenskyy- can something happen
without him!? "Ukraine belongs to the European
Family and NATO ",Mette reassured Zelenskyy.The news as it is. "Maximum pressure
must be put on Hungary to lift its veto on the Ukrainian EU – membership" added
Mette Frederiksen.

According to EU- statistics for the month of June Russia has launched 5,432 drones on
Ukrainian targets, said ZDF. Ukraine wheat was largely accepted from Brussels and a
special price mechanism was set for Ukrainian products inside of the EU. It was named
"new trade deal". Technical details of the deal still have to be agreed upon. Angry Polish
and French farmers protested against the cheap Ukrainian agrar products imports into the
EU but in vain.
The German arm producer Rhein-Metal started the production of details and accessories
for the F-15 fighter jets. The German arm industry employs ca. 284,000 skilled workers
in different locations scattered across the country, said the ZDF.

Euronews aired Russian on air commands on how to down a passangers Azal plane broadcasted on the
3rd & 33rd minute each hour. The command in Russian indicated direction, speed, altitude, azimuth and
heading– all in ciphers & details. The first missile missed its target that's why the fire was repeated.
This is only the begin of a great great news. Th news never sleeps.
So does Emil. A fluent Russian speaker.
French president Emmanuel Macrone placed a phone call with the Russian President Vladimir Putin.
In the phone call which lasted 2 hours – 120 minutes – he insisted on Russia peace talks to stop
its war on Ukraine. Putin insisted the peace plan must include the current Russian territorial gains and
"the new territorial reality". Putin dubbed the talk "sustainable".

At the same time the U.S.A. reduced its delivery of ammunition and shells to Ukraine "because of inland
shortage". Extra concerened are the "Patriot" anti-aircraft missiles shipments. The move came despite earlier
U.S. promises for weapon and ammunition shipments to Ukraine. The news brought satisfaction to Moscow.

 German Chancellor Friedrich Merz received in Capital Berlin the Chinese leader Xi Jin Ping and asked him
 "to agitate his friend Putin to stop the war in Ukraine!" This was a flink manoever to deflect German public
 opinion from brocken pre-election promise about price of domestic electricity . The news as it is. There are 17

million poor people in Germany, living under the poverty line, said the German ARD. At the same time German interior minister Alexander Dobrindt entered direct talks with the terror regime of the Taleban. Nothing- but really nothing – on these talks was reported. Obviously Dobrindt mission has failed.

U.S. President Donald Trump placed one hour phone talk with the Russian President Vladimir Putin. Putin insisted on annexation of 4 Ukrainian regions and ban for Ukrainian NATO membership. Trump was reported "dissappointed" from the phone call.
Russia became the first country in the World to recognize officially the Taliban regime in Afghanistan. Already back to 2022 Russia started to export gas, oil and wheat to Afghanistan. President Zelensky made a phone call to President Donald Trump and named the phone call "constructive"and "fruitfull"; he implied something in the sense "make a lasting peace through strength".

Russia closed several of its airports "because safety concerns of imminent threat of Ukrainian terror attacks", obviously after careful intelligence collection. Mette Frederickson – now European President for
6 months - stressed bluntly on European security and defence increase in a long long speech.

All of the sudden Russia started to hit Ukrainian targets as far to the West as the border town of
Luzk – close to the Polish border. The Russian KINZHAL rockets overwhelmed the Ukranian defence consisting of British fabricated **Patriot-, GMLRS & Hellfire- Rockets** fabricated by the British producer BAE in the town of **Warton-Lancashire, UK** where also the Eurofighter jets **Typhoon** *are produced.*
There is surplus of redundant British BAE – Systems capacities as the last customer was **Qatar in 2017,**
reported AP (=Assossiated Press). The Russian strategy is to overwhelm , to overburden, to overstretch the Ukrainian defence capability until it runs short of ammunition and by making them defenseless
 to riddle the Ukrainian targets without any punishment. So simple !! At the same time president Zelensky visited again Rom and the Vatican for new talks with Pope Leo XIV. Obviously earlier talks born no fruits.
An Europen court found formally Russia guilty of downing the Malaysian aircraft MH17 back in 2014. All 298 passengers on board died inclusive Dutch professor working actively on a new HIV-medicine. The formal procedure was launched by 2 countries only: The Netherlands and Ukraine.
EU-President Ursula von der Leyen survived the non-confidence vote in European Parliament with 360 votes "against",18 abstained and only 175 votes "for" missing thus the majority required of two thirds. Her position as EU-President however was strongly weakened and Zelenskyy's position too, said Alberto Alemanno – professor of law – in an interview for "Euronews".
U.S. Secretary of state Marko Rubio said to Russian foreign minister Sergey Lavrov "he is frustrated over Putin's reluctance to force peace in Ukraine". My personal perception is that Putin has his internal idea, intention or ambition which he's not in a hurry to display to the World; peace negotiations are always difficult and they drag into the lengthy until the common sense of the both parties is reached last not least because they speak frequently different languages and arbitary must be set on.
Both leaders spoke at the ASEAN – top in Kuala Lumpur and remained both undevicive and futile.
Donald Trump threatened Russia with new sanctions but also this did not achieve the result expected.
The recovery conference of the European leaders was directed by Olena Zelenskyy – wife of Volodymyr Zelenskyy- and brought no results, said ZDF.
Dutch bureaucrats use to censor frequently the ZDF and other TV channels by blocking them;
 the latest example was the switching off a documentary film on the tennis legend Boris Backer.

Finally U.S. President Donald Trump changed his mind and agreed to deliver air defense rockets
including the "Patriot-Surface" missiles systems which Ukraine needed badly. More details still to
 come. President Donald Trump forbade Ukraine to attack Russian oil containers and oil depots.
Slowly the first portions of American military aid started again to flow in to Ukraine but they are not sufficient.

The "Patriot" missiles launchers are crucially needed because Ukraine cannot defend itself in one day only Russia fired 1,800 missiles , drones and ballistic rockets also on Western Ukraine too. The "Patriot" U.S. delivery to Ukraine will start via Nato and the Europeans have to pay for it: "The U.S. doesn't have them and we have to manufacture them, but the Europeans have to pay for these missiles".
In a television interview Donald Trump promised to do so and added:
"I don't like Putin at all-he talks nice by phone to the people in the morning and bombs them in the night with smart bombs! I don't like him at all because I am disappointed in him" and "I don't trust anyone".
Trump had planed a visit to Britain in September 2025.
Joahim Bitterlik- former German ambassador to Nato- doubted there will be peace in Ukraine any time soon. He founds the 50-days ultimatum is exaggerated. However German defence minister Boris Pistorius flew to Washington to arrange the delivery details with the U.S. defence secretary Pete Hegseth. Finally change, finally break through ! The proposed 100% tariffs on Russia aims to make Putin to re-consider his position.

Trump offered to Europe to pay for the "Patriot"- Systems delivery "because this is an European problem and Ukraine is an European country". The "Patriots"will be sent to Ukraine via European Nato countries. He discussed the details with Nato Secretary General Mark Rutte – a former Dutch Prime minister.
Trump made "a special report on EU" which includes the following points: 1). An ultimatum with 50 days dead lock for President Putin to end the war. 2).Intimidation to the Russian allies China , India and Brazil to charge them with 100% tariffs if they continue to support Russia. The ZDF Washington correspondent Elmar Thevessen elucidated his threats as unrealistic. The U.S.A. will deliver the weapons to the European countries who pay for that and than transfer the weaponry to Ukraine. Three NATO countries agreed to deliver "Patriot" missiles from their own stock piles – Germany 2 systems, Norway – 1 system and Denmark one too. The price of each "Patriot-Surface missiles " is $ 100,000 each. They can strike both ballistic and cruise missiles and even low flying drones and exactly their capability makes them so unique .
Besides the sharp abrupt change of mind of President Donald referring whether or not to deliver U.S. weaponry to Ukraine two more Nato countries – Danmark and The Netherlands – decided to deliver several of their own "Patriot"-missiles launchers to Ukraine.
President Zelenskyy remained very satisfied by the deal and spilled over with a flood of thanks to Donald Trump. In a prolonged phone call he praised lavishly the U.S. President and admired his commitment to bring peace in Europe.
The President of the European Commission Mrs. Ursula von der Leyen announced the EU-budget of **2 trillion** euro for the period 2028-2034. From this money Ukraine will get 100 billion euro, said the Euronews. This means **200,000,000,000 euro**: "This is the budget as the reality of today and the challenges of tomorrow" she said on television.

Mean while it became known that Russia keeps on producing weaponry four times more ammunition and armors than all Nato member countries : 4 million artillery shells in 2023 and 4.4 million shells in 2024 planing to produce 7 million artillery shells for 2025 .
In summary Nato countries lag behind with production of 4 times less artillery shells than Russia- 1.2 million shells in 2024 planing 3 million shells for 2025-obviously lagging behind. That's why Nato Secretary General Mark Rutte-former Dutch prime minister- advised all Nato countries to produce more and more and not to lag behind.

His message came after German Chancellor Friedrich Merz visited
London for talks with British Prime Minister Sir Keir Starmer . Both leaders signed a treaty on mutual trade and security with means cooperation on the industrial and military fields which is the first British-German treaty ever. Entering the history as the Kensington treaty it is a stark warning against Russia and encounters the U.S. slogan "America first". The most significant point of the treaty which will enter in

history as Kensington treaty is that an aggression on either country will be treated as aggression on both countries. This implies in full Russian aggression. The assistance duty of the historic Kensington friendship treaty serves as a repellent to any Russian aggression. The message to Kremlin is clear:
"we are strong despite the Brexit!" Nation have no friends – only interests.
The approach of the two countries will also assist the reconstruction of postwar Ukraine.

The treaty comprises 27 inner proud pages and includes British access to German e-gates what soever this will mean. The German investment in the UK amounts to 200 million pounds, said Sir Keir Starmer.

Former Russian President Dmitriy Medvedev officially tried to intimidate the West "with pre-emptive Russian strike on the West"; his post now is deputy chief of the Russian Security council. However Ukraine attacked Moscow with drones and caused a fire in one of the Moscow's suburbs. (Euronews).

A fire broke broke out in a Moscow suburb after Ukraine launched drone strikes on the Russian Capital.
In over 80 Polish cities and towns manifestations broke out against the refugees' flood from neighboring Ukraine. One of the speakers fell back to the legendary Polish king Jan III Sobiecky:
 "The history must repeat", he said to the mobs. (Euronews).

In a ZDF-interview German President Frank-Walter Steinmeier advocated the military conscription in Germany:
"It was abolished back in 2011 but now all political & military factors have changed", he said to the camera.
The 5% share of the Nato-country budget of their GDP's is already achieved, he added. The second half of his interview was focused on the hot Iran-Israel conflict.
At the same time Slovakian president Robert Fico allerted the EU because Russia stopped the gas supply to his country. Fico blocked the 18 points EU-sanctions package against Russia.
The U.S. special envoy Keith Kellogg visited Kiyv for talks and remained there for a whole week.
That are the facts !

AUGUST 2025

German Chancellor Friedrich Merz visited France for talks with the French President Emanuel Macron. They agreed on many items how to reduce their US-dependency.
The unemployment rate in Germany hit the 3 million mark.
The coffee and tomato prices rose by 24 %.
The U.S. President introduced $ 15,000 entry fee for foreigners willing to enter the U.S.A. Trump abolished also the Secrete Service Protection of Camilla Harris- a Democrat candidate for U.S. president. It leaked former Democrat U.S. President Joe Biden had prolonged illegally her Secrete Service Protection till July 2026.
Trump sent also 2 nuclear submarines to patrol the north Atlantic and the Baltikum. He sent his special envoy for Ukraine Steve Witkoff to Moscow to hand in a new ultimatum to Russian President Vladimir Putin.
On the 80th anniversary of the nuclear masacre of Hiroshima he uttered no single word.
High ranking Nato activist Ivo Daalder put it bluntly :**"Trump will not risk war with Russia to protect Ukraine!"**
Trump himself re - iterated "better if Putin meets Zelenskyy without me "
while Russian foreign minister Sergey Lavrov stressed " security talks without Russia lead to nowhere".
The EU- Foreign Affairs Officer reprimanded Putin for gambling of time .
Chancellor Merz received Canadian prime minister Mark Karney in Berlin.
Both statesmen declared they stand firmly behind Ukraine.

The German television ZDF reflected on Putin , who "continue to draw his fantasies further and further" The U.S.A. will not sent soldiers to Ukraine, while both France and Great Britain are willing : For Germany it will be a full debacle at the back stage of the fact the German Bundeswehr lacks already now 150,000 soldiers to bridge it own domestic defence gap. However German East block Officer Wagner – Green B'90- praised Chancellor Merz for his enthusiasm for Ukraine. Without Germany would collapse already tomorrow, he stated. At the same time Russian President Vladimir Putin visited China in 5 days' discussion with top Chinese activists. "A red carpet for Putin", he said with admiration. However there were no security guarantees for Ukraine yet, though the European Union berries the main weight of the Ukrainian war. For how long?
There is already full chaos inside Germany – political, economic, financial, personel, financial and militery ! At the same time Ukraine started working on security concept after the war.

Germany arrested 4 Ukrainian saboteurs for blowing up the Nord Stream pipeline to Europe : Ukrainians, not Russians. 7 others Ukrainian saboteurs are still at large. These

ones already arrested were captured in the Italian sea resort of Rimini while leisure at the sun and swimming in the Adriatic Sea for pleasure while their fellows alleged are being fighting against Russia. Difficult to believe. Moreover in the Lisbon funicular crash most of the victims were exactly Ukrainian nationals lavishly visiting beforehand a plenty of other European leisure centers.

Russian President Vladimir Putin declared bluntly "Any foreign troops both national and international are unacceptable for Russia. Foreign troops cannot provide peace in Ukraine". "President Zelenskyy is invited to Moscow for talks not for capitulation", he said to BBC Moscow correspondent Steve Rosenberg and repeated this on the world economic forum in Vladivostok : "Any foreign troops in Ukraine will be a legitimate target for Russia"
EU foreign and defense ministers met in Copenhagen to discuss joint European forces in Ukraine. No details leaked. Only that they agreed on a new sanction packet on Russia – the 19th since the war begin. Ukrainian president Volodymyr Zelenskyy was not admitted to the conference. Instead he will travel all over Europe to arrange new security for Ukraine. Nobody trust him at all ! In a Sunday interview German Chancellor Merz stressed "Ukraine cannot capitulate! Otherways next is the next country-thus Poland – and next – Germany". Merzdemonstrates remarkable industry-he worked all summer long without any summer vacation. Russia concentrated troops to capture the strategic East Ukrainian town of Pokrovsk. Since the begin of the war each side lost one million soldiers – both killed and wounded.

The Swiss government granted security and immunity to the Russian president Putin.
He will attend an international conference there in September 2025.
On the last August Sunday the Shanghai organization including several national leaders congregated in China for talks on mutual interests, among them Russian President Putin, Turkish President Erdogan,Indian President Modi and Chinese leader Xi Jin Pin.
The Western media reported little or even nothing on this conference.
It was said that Chinese President Xi Jin Pin criticized the West and compared its policy with the cold war. President Modi reassured Putin that India stays with Russia in difficult times. The white doves are tired ! Above this Russia introduced censorship on internet connections, mobile phones, SMS's etc. with 50 euro penalty.

SEPTEMBER AND OCTOBER 2025

Jens Spahn and A.Miersch- SPD-respectively CDU-fraction chiefs in the German Bundestag- arrived in Kiiv to show solidarity with the Ukrainian ruler Volodymyr Zelenskyy.
Among numerous topics they discussed the use of the frozen Russian assets which amount to 600 billion euro. Russian President Vladimir Vl. Putin was said to have set again unacceptable peace conditions to Ukraine . Though with some caution Western media stopped to praise president Zelenskyy and the Ukrainian army because they have no success and no territory gains anymore.
The Chief of the European Commission Ursula von der Leyen proposed 10,000 peace keeping troops in Ukraine. This will be discussed later on in Paris, said ZDF Brussels reporter Andreas Stamm.
Speaking during the summit in China, Putin continued to defend his decision to invade Ukraine, once again blaming the West for the war. Afterwards Russia and China signed multiple treaties of mutual interest.
Following the Alaska meeting, US Special envoy Steve Witkoff said Putin had agreed to security guarantees for Ukraine as part of a potential future peace deal, though Moscow has yet to confirm this.
At the military parade in Beijing China displayed its whole arsenal of weaponry including ballistic missiles, hypersonic rockets, unmanned underwater drones etc. and the three world leaders posed for a joint photo – President Putin of Russia, Indian President Narandra Modi , Chinese President Xi Jin Pin and North Korea leader Kim. Kim described his obligation to Russia as fraternal duty.
As a matter of fact Vladimir Putin escorted President Kim to his car- a sheer gesture of curtsy .
President Trump called this a conspiracy against the United States. Literary he wrote in Twitter :
"Dear Xi! Dear Vladimir! My congratulations while you conspire together against the U.S.A. "
Thus no single word on sanctions against Russia.
In Washington Trump met Polish president Karol Nawrocki and re-assured him of the full US support in case of Russian invasion. The USA has already 10,000
soldiers in Poland but is willing and able to increase this number.
The BBC concluded wisely the war in Ukraine has shifted from military to diplomatic activity, which is basically true but a little bit too late. An earlier conclusion may have saved million of lives.
It seems like BBC trades the situation.

Coalition of the willing convened in Paris to discuss the Ukrainian war. President Zelenskyy was sitting between President Macrone and Sir Keir Starmer. German Chancellor Friedrich Merz attended the meeting by video link .
Russia replied it didn't accept any European troops in Ukraine nor Ukrainian membership in Nato.
Donald Trump called them by phone and advised Europe to use pressure on Russia by not not buying Russian oil. He promised he'll advise India to do the same. French President Emanuel Macrone declared 16,000 French volunteers are ready and waiting for deploy in Ukraine. That's !

In which language ?? Above this Ukraine sets seize fire as precondition for any peace talks.
As a matter of fact the Coalition of the Willing achieved nothing – at the very same day Sir Keir Starmer flew back to London to settle a scandal of his Cabinet, president Macron of France muttered a 10 minutes interview, and Ukrainian President Volodymyr stated nothing at all .
Despite this Germany strives militarization turning a blind eye to its own problems and its own budget deficit of 82 billion EUR. Above this the German army- The Bundeswehr – lacks 150,000 soldiers even if it will deploy women into the army. The situation in France and Britain too is not different – the all miss resources in term of personnel, equipment, supply, financial source etc. but we will learn all this after the war ends. Currently the German Bundeswehr counts for 182,000 soldiers, the German defence minister intends to raise up this number to 250,000 soldiers including women too. Both protests and obstructions to the compulsory conscription in Germany rise.

Deep political chaos in France where the budget deficit rose to 44 billion EUR compared with neighboring Germany with 28 billion EUR. The inflation rate in France hit 5.8% while in Germany it is 2.38%. At the same time 30 sheep walked into a pub in Yorkshire, England; hahaha! This was only the prelude to Germany where a sabotage action left capital Berlin without electricity

 no trams, no S-bahns, no metro, no refrigerators, no lifts, no escalators:
in one word a party of sabotage acts to punish Germany for its weapon exports towards Ukraine.
Worse is still to come ! Hahaha !

U.S. President Donald Trump renamed the U.S. defence ministry into U.S. secretary of war. Doubtless a sheer saber rattling !
On a weekend Russian Cruize missiles hit the main governmental building in the Ukrainian capital Kyiv. It is the first time Russia hits Ukrainian governmental building in the course of the whole war.
However it was Sunday so that there were no officials in the building; a kind of barbaric mercy !
President Zelenskyy condemned the bombardment which was vile and barbaric and vowed retaliation.
It is the first time ever Russia bombards government buildings and government facilities.
Volodymyr Zelenskyy accused Vladimir Putin of testing the world.
Kremlin spokes man Dmitriy Peskov dismissed his words as a libel.
U.S. President Donald Trump promised a bitter end to the conflict.

German firm APX Robotics developed , envoyed and endorsed sophisticated hardware
mostly for military usage and displayed for public enjoy in a London exhibition. In its products Artificial **Intelligence (AI)** was largely disposed. The Rhein Metal with thanks , others with both machine and submachine guns. As Lord Byron said once upon the times : "Its blatant age of new inventions of killing
bodies and wracking souls; Both propagated with the best intentions" . Some when in the 1800ies.

Russian drones entered Polish skies on its eastern border and were properly shot down.
Polish President Donald Tusk demanded care according article 4 of Nato.
In this case Russia used GERBERA- drones with extra fuel tanks to enable a bigger reach West.
In a telephone call with Donald Trump became clear
Nato Secretary General Mark Rutte took a very sly neutral position.
Earlier he served as Dutch prime minister. So now The Netherlands scrambled F-35 jet fighters to dispatch the Polish border. *However Nato Secretary General Mark Rutte – former Dutch Prime Minister in ruined kingdom – admonished Russian President Vladimir Vladimirovich Putin to stop his attacks because it seems frantically for Nato too expensive to down any Russian drone – 7-8 Nato missiles for each cheap Russian Gerbera drone downed (ZDF) .*

Former German foreign minister Annalena Baerbock started her new work as speaker of U.N. General Assemble . Her nickname in Germany was "Annalänchen" – a little bit childish.
German Military University – in Munich.
Russia and Belorussia started a joint military manouvre under the name "ZAPAD" (WEST).
To display fragile power to the WEST. Both countries have joint west borders with Ukraine.
So the Western anxiety is big Russia may transfer troops 2022-style more over the West may be outnumbered with 10,000 Russian troops taking. The sore points are two
 Other sources number the figure of 31,000 soldiers- something rather unrealistic !
"Future unmanned"is the slogan of the London missiles exhibition. The fear is ubiquitous !
Russia may outnumber the expensive Western defence missiles by cheap Iranian Shahet drones.
The other Achilles heel of the story is the Russian enclave of Kaliningrad – it prones 65 km along the Polish border which means the Nato border. Both fears may be true; may be not at all.

Russia is suspected to use the manouvre corridor for launching invasion to its neighbors.
10,000 Russian soldiers are reported to have taken part into the manouvre .
Otherwise reports claim 31,000 – the eyes of fear are big !
Poland claimed 40,000 soldiers as counter troops

Ukraine spokes persons declared as to the Russian provocation on Poland "NATO is crazy helpless". At the same time Russia decreased the credit rate down to 17% in order to boost economic growth. So who is really crazy ?? **Western media were as crazy as to accuse Putin as if he intends frantic war with Japan. As crazy as I find no words to comment.**

The Utah Governor accused Russia tries to encouraging violence in the USA after the assassination of Kirk ". This is quite possible : why not to use the flamboyant opportunity. The death of Charly Kirk generated a sheer waterfall, an avalanche of public grief about it. Obviously he was very close friend to President Trump.
Iran appealed for an Islamic NATO establishment. This the bitter fruit of the US-foreign policy. President Donald Trump attended a huge military royal parade at the Windsor Castle. Former U.S. President Barack O'bama commented viciously on this event "the assassination of Charlie Kirk threw the USA into a b tremendous political crises". The news as it is ….
 Garry O'Donehugh did not read his report, he talked to the cameras !
BBC News tumbled to praised Sir Keir Starmer & his policy
while the moderator mixed up U.S. politics and baby-boom in one pot only.
A sheer oil garbage of lies I kept to remain clean.

In demonstrations & meetings France denounced the 8 years old rule of Emanuel Macron.
A new choice is actually not available. Many French men demonstrated openly against massive French debts . France is once again deeply indebted.

Donald Trump's blitz visit ended with $300 billion U.S. investments into Great Britain.
Both sides could not reach any agreement both on Ukraine and Israel.
President Zelenskyy allowed young Ukrainian men to travel abroad with the clear aim to overwhelm the West with a new wave of Ukrainian refugees, expats and migrants to make the West bow to the failed Ukrainian cause. The number of the Ukrainian refugees in Germany surpassed the one million hallmark, reported the ZDF . And it will climbed up any further.

At U.S. President Donald Trump visited London for one day for talks with the royal family and

British Prime minister Sir Keir Starmer. He agreed to invest in Britain $300 billion and abolish the tax on British steel and aluminium . Keir Starmer – nick name the Yorkshire- got very pleased and satisfied. Slowly he gains altitude into the American relationship.
At the Windsor Castle military parade former U.S. president Barack Obama – Democrat commented viciously "Charlie Kirk death plunged the U.S.A. into a deep political crises". Obama was President 12 years earlier but continued to spat President Trump regularly – this the 3rd time in a year of malicious remarks against Donald Trump : something is brothing and roaring in the U.S.A.
The news as it is !

A massive Russian cybernetic attack destroyed three big European air ports schedule: London, Berlin & Brussels . with failed procedure of both check-in passengers and their baggage so that they had to manual check-in operations. They distincted clearly between hacker attacks and hack-in attacks and break-in attention.
 Moscow denied any responsibility as if in a schedule flights.

A raw broke out over Russian fighter jets disturbing Nato airspace over Estonia. EU-Vice President Kaja Kallas – who is native Estonian just like me – accused them of ringing the alarm. Kremlin refused any responsibility claiming the jets were on a regular mission just as many times as before. As a matter of fact Estonia scrambled 4 Italian fighter jets located there to respond to the Russian "attack". It became known in a core of truth that the Russian jets flew over the Bay of Finland thus not over Estonia. However Estonia demanded a special Nato meeting according to article 4 of the Nato statute. Allegedly the Russian fighter jets were said to have been flying at unbelievable 150 meter height.
Earlier Poland boasted to have downed an unprecedented number of Russian drones over its skies and insisted "the Russian planes should have been shot down" while Sweden distributed happening's videos. Yet again Polish government informed urgently Russia that "Every Russian equipment over Polish skies will be downed no matter of being there in a delusion, miscalculated or deliberately over supreme Polish sovereign .
Several British charities dropped off royal connections over the Epstein Royal (sexual) UK scandal. More to come in Part III of my book. Altogether the Brits dug in into a very deep long-rage scandal.
Russia attacked up new the Ukrainian city of Kharkiv close to the common border. 280,000 households remained again without gas & electricity shortly before winter step-in. In its part of of the happening Ukraine hit and destroyed a Russian fuel refinery depot deep inside Russia in the Saratow region.

Both Russia and the United States agreed to meet each other in 2-weeks time some place in Hungary to discuss the war and promote peace finally.

The Nato is vulnerable but n o t the Nato members, stated Nato Scry, Mark Rutte in an unevitable bad English. What I remember of him he liked to save his post as a Dutch Prime Minister even after 2 years after his resignation as a Dutch Prime Minister. Maybe the King helped him to ??
His native country of origin is The Kingdom of The Netherlands : an absolute monarchy
In many parts of the Dutch society deadly police shots appeared to the The Sun shines all over Holland - both North and South Holland. It's time for heaven, time for sin - let's start !! The clubs open already at 18:00 .

Germany rang its alarm bells after unidentified drones were spotted over both German and Polish skies. German defence minister Boris Pistorius – Boris just like the German tennis legend Boris Becker- declined to deal with the matter, because Germany is not at war yet.
He transferred the matter to the German police , but German interior minister Alexander Dobrindt

decline any comment.

Germany presented its new budget plan – 9 months after the year actually began.
It comprised 520 billion EUR 174 billions of which old debts as ZDF stated
For the year 2025 Germany was the venue of 200,000 bankruptcy – mostly small or middle enterprises.
With 3-4 workers it counts 800,000 new unemployed to the staggering XXXXXXXXXXXXX

All debts are very easy to plan but difficult to pay back.

No American leader said nothing about the latest Nato invasions by Russian drones & air planes.
German Defence Minister Boris Pistorius summoned to tranquility and Nato all in all
warned in for caution not escalation. In a rare speech Nato Secretary General Mark Rutte even
sounded not so very much enthusiastic. Danish prime minister Mette Fredericson condemned clearly
the Russian air forces intrusion into Denmark as a "provocation and intimidation". What else have
Denmark to serve back to the Russian intrusion ?? Otherwise many Western media pronounced
wrongfully the name of the big German city of Hamburg as "Hum Bugg". Could happen but why to us ?

U.S. President Donald Trump reversed yet again his Ukraine policy: in New York he urged Ukrainian
President Volodymyr Zelenskyy "he can received back his territorial already "and "Russia is a paper
tiger!" Kremlin spokesman Dmitryy Peskov countered "Russia is not a tiger but a bear". Followed
by lavish Dutch compliments : Mark Rutte looked all over his own pictures as nervous ?!
Volodymyr Zelenskyy replyed "Ukraine conspired peace and freedom all over Europe. "
Which might turn it free?! Rather free beyond 3.5 years of war with Russia which turned out a
spike all against Russia, nothing for Russia , despite U.S. demands to Russia. Could happen -
not rare into Russia in its recent history – Russia had had nothing else of all its invadors than
encounter them starting into The Great Nordic Russian invasion in the 1800ies.
Thus freedom of replica, freedom recess of all current History ?
Why not ?
White not at all??
Europe is rich – Europe can afford sniff a bad dog Russia ?? Why not ?? As long as Putin is in
we cannot expect anything progressive, no single deal into peace. Despite of all our short visioned
fouled down European politicians : without them we would have satisfied Europe without war?!
We failed.
All Europe failed and now Ukraine failed: Zelenskyy claimed his shadowed roll to please Europe :
and he failed to please Europe 3.5 years long of war against Russia:
The International Olympic Committee decided to lift its own decisions of ban imposed earlier on both
Russians and Belorussians sportsmen and sports women.
At the same time Ukrainian President Volodymyr Zelenskyy claimed reconnaisent drones
from Hungary flew in for several minutes into Ukrainian air space.

Police broke up ring trafficking Kenyans to fight for Russia in Ukraine. They were trafficking under
false job promises.
In the NRW German election lost the SPD to the CD for the first time in last 80 years.
NRW – Nord Rhein Westfallen – is the biggest German state with 18 million population -
thus more than the Netherlands .
Running afraid of all Russian (cyber) attacks Denmark and Scandinavia cut off all its commercial
flights in order to avoid any single Russian drones attacks adding additional havoc to the whole EU-
mess. Danish Prime Minister Mette Fredericson failed to comments on Danish (cyber) attacks

restrictions. Could happen !!

At Nato difference proximity in Warsaw 2,500 international visitors attended to denounce Russia:
Polish star chaser Donald Tusk attended limping on his own right knee. The European foreign
ministers came together in Copenhagen to form manifest their support to Ukraine.
If they fail the post-war aid to Ukraine will be suck in from the frozen Russian bank assets
equal to 200 billion euro. Meanwhile the Chief of the IAEA Raphael Grossi visited Ukraine and
expressed great concern about the state of the Russian nuclear power plant in Zaporzhizhia.
Ukrainian President Zelenskyy shuttles frantically to introduce insane crazy politics of the West
to benefit everything to Ukraine in terms of help to Ukraine where it does not remarks. More ??

Rather confess nor apologize for the current EU polish campaign . It will stop very soon
with all of our grievences.

Words 6,144 spilled on right now on Ukraine disaster. Even now 6,144 words had spent all the
West helps Ukraine – far less than current data . Ukraine is visible weak.
The German car producers' top with German Chancellor Friedrich Merz all clear and unclear tools
became introduced and glorified on the all over German glorification to spouse down the current
German unemployment The current German unemployment rate hit the 3,000,000 mark.

Poland refused to extradite to Germany the North Stream Pipe Line saboteur 2022 Volodymyr Zhuravlev "because
his deed was a military one and not a German one", so Poland which manufactured and glorified
all anti-Russian sabotages both home and abroad.
On his Washington talks with President Trump Zelenskyy failed to receive American Tomahawk missiles
by which he intended to hit targets deep inside Russia. The price of a single Tomahawk is $200 million and
their range is 2,500 km. Nevertheless Trump described the talks in Washington as "cardiac" and America needs the
Tomahawks too for its selfdefence". In fact Donald Trump demanded from Zelenskyy "All the parties
must get frozen their current frontiers, their boundaries". So President Zelenskyy had to fly back to his
native Ukraine empty handed : no destructive American made Tomahawk missiles were granted to Ukraine
in order not to escalate the war any further in the grave yard of Europe Zelenskyy push up to inseminate to
all of Europe".
President Trump has planned visits to Indonesia, Malaysia and Japan; so probably he will have no time
for the planned top with Vladimir Putin in Hungary this week. The planing collapsed and ended with
freezing of the U.S. assets of both major Russian oil suppliers Rosneft and Lukoil. U.S. President Donald
Trump literally said "we have to tighten the screws of the Russian economy" and "Putin has to come to the
tango". After his lavish luxusary and expensive visits to London, Paris and Brussels Ukrainian president
with an expired mandate Volodymyr Zelenskyy commented "Ukraine will cede no territory to Russia",
aiming the age of 73 years old ailing Russian President Vladimir Vladimirovich Putin.
Obviously the stakes are high of who will inherit him and his property estimated of $200 billion.
Donald Trump postponed his meeting with Putin for December 2025 : "Hopefully Putin will dance
to the tango", he said literary.
The EU failed to grant Ukraine 140 billion EUR state loan to combat the Russian aggression.
President Zelenskyy reckoned this not enough . Speaking at EU top in Brussels he demanded much more
from Russia whose assets are frozen in Belgian banks.
He stated, "This will help Ukraine produce weaponry faster and cheaper to defend
itself against the Russian aggression". In his speech Zelenskyy also criticized sharply China "because it has no interest
in the Ukrainian victory on Russia".

In the middle of his speech Zelenskyy lost the chain of his thoughts and started stuttering.
Finally he managed to uttered "Our plan does not begin with a cease fire but with our will to implement the the frozen Russian assets for production inside Ukraine of drones, missiles and electronic jamming gadgets which will be quicker, cheaper and faster".
The President of the European Commission Ursula von der Leyen dubbed this hypocritically "a reparation loan".
Afterwards Zelenskyy flew from Brussels to London for talks with both the British Prime Minister Sir
Keir Starmer
and the British King Charles III. All three decided to insist on more U.S. long-range U.S. missiles for Ukraine.
Now it became clear "Zelenskyy is gambling with World War Three" .
as President Donald Trump rebuked Zelensky already in February 2025 during his Washington visit.
However Zelensky was received by the Guard of Honour to display London support for Kiyv.

Parallel to Zelensky London visit German minister Reiche flew to Kyyv for talks with somebody who replaced him:
1st German Television ARD described Zelensky as "crippled,tired and warn off"
At a public rally Hungarian President Victor Orban denounced sharply the "Coalition of the Willings: they want to send people in the war, to let people die in the war and they called it poetically, inimitably and with elegance "Coalition of the Willing"", said Orban to a massive Budapest manifestation. He asked his supporters to choose between him and peace or choose his opposition rival ……………..
and war: we all are threatened and intimidated by war in the heart of Europe.

The Lithuanian President Gitanas Nauseda protested sharply – also in Brussels – against the violation by Russian air crafts of the Lithuanian airspace.
In the North Ukraine town of Ovruch a suicide bomber detonated his bomb at the local railway station killing himself and 3 Ukrainian policemen. The kamikaze bomber died later on in ambulance; his reasons and his motivation remained unknown, said Euronews used up as used as to use.
Reiche. And Reiche again: this is the name of the German female minister which repeatedly springs at the news.
German ZDF reporter in Kiiv is currently cut off. ZDF means Zweites Deutsches Fernsehen – Second German Television.

Joint training manoeuvres of the German police forces and German army – the Bundeswehr- ended with several wounded soldiers respectively policemen. German Chancellor Friedrich Merz took no stand on the victims and avoided all comments.
Finally the Russian position became known because it leaked, infiltrated through in the media:
Kremlin insists upon exit of the Baltic countries from both Nato and the European Union
and the exit of Poland from Nato.
It took three years of war until this position got known because it infiltrated to transparency
through in the media despite of both the muzzle and the sly censorship .
President Zelensky made several sebaceous trips both to Washington and other places of the world see-saw move but he kept hiding in swamps the Russian position which is crystal clear. It seems President Trump had right in saying "Zelensky gambles with world war three".

The commander of the sabotage team on the North Stream pipe line blowing was extradited to Germany, his name was said to be ……………..

Russia started bombing capital Kyiv with brand bombs, the city was engulfed by massive fires.
Russian oil giant Rosneft introduced new reorganisations in its structures and branches.
At Donald Trump Japan visit both the Emperor and the Prime Minister SanaeTakaichi
proposed him to be granted with the Nobel peace price

and presented Washington with 250 cherry trees.
Trump said "The new golden age of the bilateral relations is currently happening "
He granted $500 billion to boost the Japanese investment in the U.S.A.
He reduced also the U.S. tariffs on Japan down to 15%.
His next stop was South Korea which Trump visited a f t e r Japan.
There he met also the Chinese President Xi Jin Pin.
President Vladimir Putin advertised a new brand of nuclear powered cruise missiles which Russia had successfully tested . Donald Trump remained unimpressed by his intimidation. He advised Putin "to bring peace into Ukraine instead of testing new missiles". While making his statement Putin was dressed in a khaki coloured military fatigues.
In another interview Putin - dressed in different clothes – stated "Russia had tested successfully another nuclear powered torpedo "Posseidon "". It can not be intercepted and when it is close to the coast line it can provoke powerful radioactive tsunami. This was the second Russian nuclear test within a week.
As an aftermath of Putin's ample statement Donald Trump announced U.S.A. will renew its own nuclear tests the latest one of which was in 1992.
*

A LIST OF THE NAMES USED IN THIS BOOK

vassilev-missana number – U.S. AI judicial & court help
$15 billion – the price of any U.S.aircraft carrier
$3.00 - U.S. gas price for a gallon
96 hours – the detention limit in the French judicial system
1,832 euro – the monthly soldier's salary in the German Bundeswehr
1964 – gastarbeiter contract between Turkey and Belgium
1998 – Irish "goed fridayagreement"
10 billion euro The Netherlands pays annually to the EU
180,000 – the soldier number of the German Bundeswehr
2022-a failed Coup d'etat in Germany under Prince Roys leadership
210 – 210 billions euro amount of frozen Russian assets across all over Europe in a regional war
2,600 euro monthly –the German poverty line; Dutch – 1,250 euro
37,000 – the number of the U.S. rangers in Germany
396 billion euro = the EU trade deficit with China
@Golos.dagestana- Russian X-page with 1 million followers (Translation: The voice of Dagestan)
@CrimeanWind – Russian independent news web side
ABBA – Swedish music band established in 1974
ABC – Australian Broad cast Corporation
"Abram" – a brand of American tanks of disputed use by Ukraine
AFA- Anti Fascist Actie in The Netherlands and Vlanderen since 1992
AfD- Alternative for Deutschland, German far right party, engaged in spy scandals
Aggressor, The – mock name of Vladimir Putin coined originally in Hungary
AI – Artificial Intelligence
Allbright Stiftung – a German-Swedish foundation located in Berlin
Allbright Stiftung GmbH-Gormanstrasse 14, 10119 Berlin, kontakt @ allbright-stiftung de
Alexander Dobrindt-German CSU Parliamentary group leader (1970):against Ukrainian migrants
Alexander Graf von Lambsdorf-German Ambassador to Moscow
ALMA-Italian job, training and education program
Amanda Roberts – sister in law of Virginia Guiffre logically married to her Brother SKY in USA
Andrey Ostavsky- BBC Russian service to dub Putin "a dangerous man"
Andrey Belousov – the new Russian defense minister since May 2024
Andrei Kovalenko -head of anti-disinformation dpt. of the Ukrainian Defense Council
Andriy Yermak - head of the Ukrainian Presidential Office under Zelenskyy rule
Androdida – Greek air base in Pelopones
Anton Gerhard Hofreiter (Toni)– German MP Green politician,biologist, * 02-02-1970 in Munich
Antony Blinken-U.S. Secretary of State "to visit U.S.partner China"
Armin Coerper – ZDF Moscow correspondent

ATACMS-U.S. long-range missiles delivered to Ukraine to meet Zelenskyy thanks
Al Shiva-biggest Palestinian hospital in Gaza
Andrij Portnov – Ukrainian aid to the ex-pro-Russian president Victor Yanukovich. Assassinated in Madrid 2025
Anton Hofreiter-Head of the Europe Council of the German Bundestag, B-97 Greens
Antonio Salazar – Portugese dictator ,toppled down in 1974
Arohan Haliva – Head of Israeli secret service
ATACMS-U.S. missiles Ukraine used against Russia
Ausschwitz-Birkenau – a Polish foundation in Warsaw, founded in 2009
Bart de Waver – Belgian Prime Minister
Bauerntag- German farmer council
BBC-Technology – every Sunday at 13:30 GMT on BBC
Beate Bellman- advisor of the ex German Chancellor Angela Merkel: helped
with her Memoirs
Becky Anderson – CNN moderator to syllable her questions empty waiving hands
Bellmarsh - notorious London prison to keep computer lights such as Julian Assange
BKA – Bundes KriminalAmt – the German FBI
Benjamin Netanyahu – unpopular Israeli prime minister against Hamaz ,wanted by the ICC
Bitcom-German digital union
Brothers of Italy-ruling far right party in Italy founded by Mussolini's supporters in 1946
BKA – Bundeskriminalamt , the German FBI
Blair House – opposite to the White House in Washington, D.C.
Black Berry – the ruling political coalition of Germany
BMW-(Beyersche Motor Werke) – the cars of the Moscow Police
Boris Pistorius -German defense minister scandalized in Ukrainian phone calls leakage
Branstad- former U.S. Ambassador to China, "doubted on Donald Trump's fair trial"
BRICS-international club of Brazil, Russia,India,China, S. Africa with 35% of global economy
Brittany – U.S. female golf player
BSW-Bündnis Sarah Wagenknecht, left German party, against weapon exports to Ukraine.
Bucharest-9 – treaty of the new Nato- members in Eastern Europe
Buena Vista- Antifa Beach club in Scheveningen, The Netherlands
BCA – The_Bulgarian_Cyber_Army_Zone_H _a group of computer hackers difficult to detect
BSW- "Bündnis Sarah Wagenknecht" , left German opposition party
Bürgenstock-Swiss resort where the 90 countries peace conference took place
Bundestag- the German Parliament
Bundeswehr- the German defense
Carera- BBC correspondent in Kyiv
Carlo Masala – professor at the German Bundeswehr (Defense) University in Munich
CCC-Civilians Coordination Center
CDA- Dutch Christian Democratic Appeal in The Netherlands
CDU- German Democratic Union Party in Germany
China Gate – the Chinese spy scandal in Brussels
Chloropicrine – Russian chemical weapon used in Ukraine since February 2024 (NPO1)
Christian Amanpour – senior CNN correspondent with Iranian roots ,denied Gaza famine
Christopher Cavoli -futile NATO parrot general for Europe
CIA-Central Intelligence Agency, an American spy company
CNN- American Cable News Network, the biggest news provider world wide
Copernikus – EU climate office named after Nikolay Copernic- the creator of the current Calendar
 Council of Guardians – Iran body of government (CNN)

Cyril – Russian and Bulgarian orthodox Saint buried in Elwangen/ Germany
Cyril Ramaphosa – President of South African Republic
Czehia – the Czech Republic; in Dutch Tsjechië
Dan McEntyre -NBC – reporter who served me
Dan Rice – special U.S. advisor to the Ukrainian Army Commander
Daniël Medvedev – Russian tennis star ,nothing to do with former Russian President Medvedev
Daniela Klette- RAF terrorist arrested 2024 in Berlin, Germany
Darnetskyi- a suburb of the Ukrainian Capital Kyiv
David Lammy – British foreign minister with African roots
Davile Sakaliene – Lithuanian defense minister
dementia praecox – the mental disease of U.S. president Joe Biden with possession of the "red nuclear button"
Deutsches Orient Institute – German institution in Berlin, Beirut, Istanbul & Hamburg.
Didier Reynders – Euro Commissar of justice
DIW – Deutsches Institut für Wirtschaftsforschung for economic issues
Dmitrii Ivanov – Professor at the German Economy High school in Berlin
Dmitriy Kuleba- former Ukrainian replaced foreign minister
Dmitri Peskov- Kremlin spokesman
DOGE – The U.S. Department of Government Efficiency
Drug & Alcohol Charity – a British charity for the poor
Duma – the Russian Parliament
DUP- Democratic Unionist Party of Northern Ireland
Echo of Moskow.ru – Russian radio station in 30 languages 24/7
Eden Golan – Israeli singer singer expelled from the Malmö song festival in sign of protest
Edward Fishman – author and member of many U.S. delegations for Ukraine
EF-Education First, Swedish language private company University town of Lund
Emma de Ruiter – Euronews reporter in The Hague, The Netherlands
EN UMA- EU Military Assistance to Ukraine, a French organization & website
EPP-European People Party headed by Manfred Weber-Head of the European Parliament
Eric Adams – New York Mayor
EU-Commission – consistence of 11 men & 16 women
Euronews – NR.1 in Dutch advertising
EU – Trojka = Germany, France & Great Britain
Europaviertel– rich residential quarter in Frankfurt on Main, Germany
Favoritenstrasse – red light quarter of Vienna, Austria
FBI – Federal Bureau of Investigation
Faber – Dutch emigration minister
FDP-Free Democrats Party in Germany , liberals
Fidan, Hakhan – Turkish foreign minister
FIDESZ- Hungary ruling center-right party of prime minister Viktor Orban
Fiuggi – Italian city to host the G-7 meeting on 25-26.XI.2024
Frank Paaow – police chief of Amsterdam, Netherlands
Friedrich Merz-the new German Chancellor (CDU), furious critic of Chancellor Olaf Scholz
Forum Democratic Left- German SPD party left wing
Frankfurt am Main – German city neighboring the biggest European airport
FSB – the Russian Secrete Service
Fumio Kishida- Japanese prime-minister
Gabriel Attal -French acting prime minister insisting on sending French troops to Ukraine
Galina Polonskaya – Russian Euronews reporter off air for some time

GCSF – global Cyber Security Forum held for 2025 in Riyadh
Gallagher - U.S. ambassador to the U.N.
Gary Rose – BBC sport journalist
GDP – gross inland product
Geert Wilders – a far-right Dutch politician from the ruling PVV-party
Gelsenkirchen – Nato air forces military base in Germany
German Orient Institute – in Berlin, Beirut, Istanbul & Hamburg.
GMF – German Marshall Funds: 1744 R St NW, Washington D.C.,U.S.A.
Golden Dome – U.S. $175 billion strategic defense system plan in outer space
Grünheide- Tesla car factory in Germany
Gentleman–nickname of Russian dissident Alexey Navalny,died in Russian prison Feb. 2024
Gregor – Catholic Pope buried in Bologna, inventor of the current modern Calendar
Haag – also Haga – the Dutch name of The Hague, seat of the International Criminal Court (ICC)
Habarovsk – Russian atomic submarine
Hadush Kebatu - Somali prisoner managed to escape from Dutch prison
Hága- the Hungarian name of The Hague
Hunter Biden-Joe Biden's son; lied about his drug,alcohol addiction,age to buy weapons illegally
Hannah Miller – BBC NHS correspondent
Hendrick XIII Prinz Reuss – German business man who lead the failed coup d'etat in 2022
Hendrik Wüst-Minister-President of North-Rhein-Westfallen (NRW)
Hidankyu- Japanese peace Nobelist
Holger Münch – Chief of the German Criminal Department BKA (also BCA)
HQ – Head Quarter
Hybrid – a BBC coined term for alliance of army command and war industry
hypersonic- 5 times the speed of sound
I am truly sorry = I am very sorry
ICBM- Russian for Inter Continental Ballistic Missiles
ICC- international crime court in The Hague, The Netherlands
ICJ – International Court of Justice based in The Hague, The Netherlands
IG Metal – a big German Trade Union
IMF- International Monetary Funds
ISS – International Space Station
ISW – Institute for study of war in Washington, D.C. U.S.A.
ISW(2) - the Iranian division of the ISW
Horton impertinent arrogant BBC broadcaster
Jacques Baud- author of book "How West Lead Ukraine to Defeat "
Jean McCenzy- BBC Kiyv correspondent
James Moran – a coordinator at the Center for European Policies Studies in Brussels
James Schulz- Donald Trump's lawyer
John Kirby – WH security advisor , former Secretary of State
John Prescott–British dep. Prime minister died aged 86:"Very direct", Tony Blair said for him
John Reynolds – British Labor activist
Joos Klein – Dutch singer expelled from the Malmö song festival for his racist attitude
Jordan Bardella – French far right,against sending French troops but long range missiles to Ukraine
Joseph Borrel – Ukraine biased EU Foreign Affairs Chief
Julia Chatterley – sexy but withered British CNN moderator;for some time absent from air
Julian Assange – computer head kept in notorious London prison Bellmarsh; Nobelist
Kaja Kallas- EU foreign policy chief wanted by Russia per arrest warrant

Karl Neumann- Austrian minister-president
Karol Nawrocky – the new Polish Minister-President
Karsten Wildberger – German Digital Minister
Kash Patel – FBI – director
Katarzina Zysk- professor on the **Norwegian Defense Institute** with descent English
Kazan – Russian city which hosted the BRICS-top in 2024 despite the sanctions imposed on Russia
Kazan-Russian nuclear submarine sent in the Caribbean to demonstrate naval superiority to the U.S.A.
KNDR-Korean People's Democratic Republic , North Korea
Keir   Starmer – British Labor prime minister
Kim Jong Un – the leader of North Korea
Kursk – city & region across the Ukrainian border
Kursk – Russsian nuclear power plant near the disputed territories
 Lambsdorf- German Ambassador to Moscow
Landtag- German term for State Parliaments
Leerce – UN official, looks very much like German chancellor Olaf Scholz
Lenta.ru – Russian news webside
LNG - liquefied natural gas
Leonid Volkov-supporter and ally of the late Russian dissident Alexey Navalny
Louise Rodrigue – chief of EU Central Bank:"the EU may get as weak as its currency "
Lufthansa – German air flights company harmed severely by the sanctions against Russia
Lund – Swedish University town north of Malmö
MCC- Hungarian think tank
Malu Dreyer-German Minister-President of Rheinland-Pfalz resigned "because of exhaustion".
Marc Rouli- Head of Met police, London
Mark Rubio – U.S. Secretary of State
Mark Rutte-Dutch ex-prime minister , to replace J.Stoltenberg as Nato Scry general 2024-2028
Martin Jäger – the new BND President, former German Ambassador to Ukraine
Martina Rosenberg – Chief of German military secrete service
Mathias Marx – ARD Berlin correspondent
Matrëshka – a pro-Russian television campaign channel
Max Eder – German coup d'etat activist
Maxim Kuzminov- Russian army pilot defector, shot dead in Spain
Maximilian Krah – AfD; EP-member caught in a spy scandal,father of 8 children from 3 wives
Meanderfooler – the wrong BBC pronunciation of Neanderthaler
Meduza.io - Russian news webside
Medvedchuk- Russian Oligarch
Meloni , Giorga – Italian prime minister
MG 34 – a type of German sub-machine gun
MEP- Member of the European Parliament
Michael Cohen – lawyer of former U.S. President Donald Trump; replaced Rudolf Gulliany
MID- Russian ministry of foreign affairs
Mike Galsworthy-British Labor spokesman
Mike Pence- U.S. Vice President
Mike Johnson – spokesman of the U.S. House of the representatives
Minors –yet another EU program to limit teenager's rights
MEP-Member of European Parliament
MP-Member of Parliament
MRS- Multiple Rocket Launcher Systems : in all languages

MSS – Chinese secret service
Mützelich-German SPD member though critic on SPD Chancellor Olaf Scholz same party
Nataly Elphik- British MP to defect to Labor
Natasha Pirc Musar-President of Slovenia; former attorney
National Bolshevists- a new party in the German province of Thüringen
National Rally - far right party in France headed by Marine Le Pen
NATO-SEA– mock name of the Baltic sea
Nauseda, Gitanas - Lithuanian President & Banker since 2019
Navigate the world – an American peace movement
Martna Rosenberg – German Military Secrete Service activist, thus not the BND
Meadrefooler – the BBC mispronunciation of the name "Neanderthaler"
NHS-British National Health Service
Nigel Farage-British politician, UK-reform party leader
National Rally - far right party in France headed by Marine Le Pen
Norway- European country with no EU-membership
NRW-North-Rhein-Westfallen , a province in Germany
NRW – Nord Rhein Westfallen , the biggest German state with 18 mn inh-more than the Netherlands
NSU-National Socialist Underground , a German Nazi party
Odesa-also Odessa Ukrainian Black Sea port with soldiers' forcibly recruiting for the war :
It is not my war
Odyssey- U.S. AI administrative computer program & link
Oktyabrsk-Russian ammunition depot hit by Ukraine in September 2024
Oleg Kononenko,first man of 1,000 days off Earth,orbited it 16,000 times & flown 420 mn miles
Oreshnik – a brand of Russian medium range missiles to use against Ukraine
Ottawa Convention – U.N.1997 convention to ban anti-personnel mines Ukraine still use
Ovruch- an Ukrainian town where suicide bomber detonated his bomb killing himself & 3 policemen
Palos Verdes – Donald Trump's ranch in Florida, venue for the 2nd assassination attempt on him
Pam Bundi – female U.S. Justice Minister
Pat Ryder – Patrick S. Ryder, U.S. General-Major , Pentagon spokesman , 30 service years
Patriot-Surface- to-Air- missile , can destroy 5 flying objects simultaneously (ZDF)
Patriotic Union-German far right group led by Prinz von Reuss
Paul Adams – BBC Kyyv correspondent
Pavlo Palisa – deputy chief of the Ukrainian Presidential Bureau; colonel
Pedro Sanchez-Spanish prime minister whose wife was accused of corruption
Pete Hegseth – U.S. defence secretary , born 1980
Peter Tzolov – senior commentator of the Bulgarian National Radio in the 1970ies
Peter Velev – communist party secretary of the Bulgarian Medical Academy
PM-Prime Minister
plat- German word for bankruptcy
Puis Demont- Catalonia socialist party separatist leader in Spain
PvdA- Dutch workers' party central-left (Worker's Party)
Pyongyang- the Capital of North Korea
Radek Sikorsky – Polish defense minister
RAF – British Royal Air Forces with supreme commander Prince Harry Windsor
RAF – German Red Army Fraction: far left group
Rahm Emmanuel – U.S. Ambassador to Japan
Ralf Stegner – SPD-spokesman in the German Bundestag
Ramstein – U.S. air base in Germany 40 km from Frankfurt am Main

RBC – the Ukrainian military news broadcaster
Red Arrows – the British RAF
Red Storms Bravo – code name of German military manoevres near Baltic port Hamburg
Republic – a British anti-monarchy group
RFA- British Royal Force Artillery
Rhein-Metal- German metallurgic plant, produced artillery shells 8 billion euro worth
Riyadh- Saudi Arabia Capital
Robert Fico – President of Slovakia; criticized Western rocket delivery to Ukraine
Robert Habeck – German green economic minister,a candidate for German Chancellor
Roberta Metsola – speaker of the EU-Parliament in Strasbourg
Rostock- the new German marine command point
Rishi Sunak – British Prime minister with Indian roots and face, aged 44
Robert Habeck - German industry minister souring German relations to China
Roberta Metsola – speaker of the EU-Parliament in Strasbourg
Roskomnadzor – Russian media supervisor
RossAtom-Russian nuclear company with 300,000 employees.
Rouble ,also ruble - Russian national currency, 77 of which is equal to $1
Rouhani & Raisi – former Iranian hard-liner presidents died in 2024
RS-26 – brand of Russian ballistic missiles
RTV- rapid arrogant aggressive German news TV provider
RTVS- Slovakian wireless, cut off on 01.07.2024
Rudolf Gulliany- President Trump's lawyer, former New York Mayor
Sadiq Khan – Labor Mayor of London
Sarah Rainsford- BBC Eastern Europe correspondent
Sahra Wagenknecht-German politician against dislocation of U.S. missiles in Germany
Sanae Takaichi – Japanese prime minister
Scott Besent – U.S. finance minister
Sean Daley U.S. ambassador to London
Sergey Shoigu – former Russian defense minister, now Russian National Security Council secretary
Sophia Khatsenkova – Euronews reporter in Paris
Sophia Russenko – Euronews reporter
Sophia Starmer – spokes woman of British prime minister Keir Starmer (BBC)
Spacex – U.S. space ships provider
SPD – Socialist Party of Deutschland / Germany
Stahlenberg – prison in Germany
Starmer , Keir– British Labor leader
Stella Assange – wife of the computer whistle blower Julian Assange
Stephen Bates – The Guardian royal correspondent
Stephen Kornelius – speaker of the German government
Steuerschätzung – the planing of the German household budget one year ahead
Steve Rosenberg – BBC correspondent in Moscow
Six clerics – the Iranian revolutionary council
Storm Shadow – British air missiles used in Ukraine against Russia with 250 km scope
Stresener- district of the German city Dresden where politicians were recently beaten by far Rights
SU-34 - Russian jet bomber used frequently in Ukraine and elsewhere
Sumy- another Ukrainian nuclear reactor untouched by Russian fire
TASS-Telegrafna Agency Sovietskogo Soyuza – official and fair Russian state m edia
Ter Appel-a prison in The Netherlands near to Groningen-City

"The Troubles"- mock name of the Northern Ireland tumults
Timur Ivanov – deputy of Russian defense minister Sergey Shoigu, fired in corruption scandal

Tony Blair - former British PM to issue gratitude to me in written
Trade Republic – a German private bank
Tsarskoe selo – Lyceum in St. Petersburg
UAE-United Arab Emirates
UK – United Kingdom
Ukraine- a staunch trustful ally of the West (as a conclusion of mine)
Ukraine Council - the NATO council concerned of Ukraine
Ukraineenergo – the Ukrainian electricity provider
Ulf Kristerson – Swedish prime minister to support Ukraine militarily
UmV – UnMenned Vehicle
UNGA – United Nations General Assembly
UNO- United Nations Organization
Ursula von der Leyen- EU-Commission President, daughter of a Lower Saxony Minister-President
USPS-United States Postal Service
Valery Gerassimov – chief of staff in the Russian army
Wagner group – Russian private military company
vassilev-missana number – U.S. AI judicial & court help
Villa Borsik – The German Government residence near Berlin
Westfield-The Mall of The Netherlands
Wulf Schmiese – ZDF Washington correspondent with meager English
Victoria Vdovychenko – "Future for Ukraine " at the Cambridge University
Vitalii Shevchenko – BBC reporter, BBC Russian Department though his native Ukrainian name
Vodka Gorbatschov – German vodka brand est. 1928 in Berlin, Germany
Vodka Tsarskaya – a Chinese brand of vodka
Voice of Europe – pro-Russian media agency
Volodymyr Zelensky – Ukrainian president for many years
Vyacheslav Volodin – the speaker of the Russian **Duma** – the Russian Parliament
Warrior - German speculative private bank with Chancellor Olaf Scholz benevolence
Warburg- scandalous speculative private bank blessed by ex-Chancellor Scholz in fact furniture shop.
wash cam – car camera
Westfield – The Mall of The Netherlands
WH – the U.S. White House
What-a-Shot – CNN political moderation program
Wiesbaden-proposed German location for stationing the U.S. medium range missiles
Williams Windsor – British Prince of Wales, Crown prince, commander of the British RAF
Wirtz- German football player currently in FC Liverpool
Yvette Cooper – British foreign secretary
"X" – president Volodymyr Zelenskyy's official web site (former Twitter); private site ??
X-59 – highly sophisticated Russian missiles used widely in its war on Ukraine
ZDF – Zweites Deutsches Fernsehen – A German Television Channel
Zeleny, Jeff – CNN Moderator to enjoy my thanks
Zelenskyy-Ukrainian President born 1978, son of Ph.D.Alx.Zelenskyy for Cybernetics & Computing
Zelinskyy-Polish (non-political) football player to distinguish from President Zelenskyy
Ziggo Dome – a rock palace in The Netherlands
* * *